THE DIVING GUIDE

Cuba Scuba

By Amy Houghton

First Edition

D. Tipton

Published by

Cruising Guide Publications, Inc.
P.O. Box 1017, Dunedin, FL 34697-1017
(727) 733-5322 Fax (727) 734-8179
(800) 330-9542
info@cruisingguides.com
Website: www.diving-guides.com

Author: Amy Houghton
Website: www.cubascuba-thebook.com
Art Direction: Jessica Stevens, Affinity Design Group

Color Charts: Simon Charles and Amy Houghton

In this guide every effort has been made to describe conditions accurately, however, the publisher makes no warranty, expressed or implied, for any errors or for any omissions in this publication.

First Edition
Printed in China
ISBN 0-944428-65-7

Front Cover
Design: Michael O'Keene, Affinity Design Group
Photographer: Manuel Mola Pedraza
Model: Barbara Cornelli
Fish: Nassau Grouper
Place: Maria la Gorda, Cuba
Camera: Nikonos V, 15mm lens, f.5.6, Speed 1/60,
extachrom 100 ASA film, Nikonos Strobe sb105

www.diving-guides.com

Gearing up on the "China" Rocks for a shore dive.

W. Houghton

Table of Contents

E. Macao

M. Mola

Dedication

Dedicated to:
The wizard, the dream-maker, my father
WILLIAM HILARY HOUGHTON

Thank you for teaching me
the value of Persistence.
Our adventures will
live forever in my heart.
I love you.

Special Thanks to:
The Center for Marine Research, University of Havana;
My Cuban family that grows deeper with each visit;
My sisters, my mother and my beloved family;
and to Bellaire for solving my late night
computer emergencies.

Dear Fellow Divers:

The question I am asked most frequently is, "Where is the best diving in Cuba?" On such a large island, this is not an easy answer. I like pristine reefs and crystalline waters. I like plunging walls, sharks, and shipwrecks. In Cuba, I can satisfy my every underwater whim in tender climates of 75-83 degrees Fahrenheit all year.

Cuba is situated between the Caribbean Sea and the Atlantic Ocean. Winter months offer intense visibility and whale shark migrations all along the south side. Summer months boast more fish in the south, including Goliath Groupers of all sizes. Sea turtles nest along Maria la Gorda and swim along the Northern coast.

Yet if I had to choose my top five areas (in no particular order), they would be the following: To the extreme southwest, Maria la Gorda, Isla de Juventud, and Cayo Largo showcase spectacular walls with more than 200 species of sponges. This region is reminiscent of the Cayman Islands twenty years ago. Moving eastward to Las Jardines de la Reina, my imagination boggles to the max with abundant sharks, tarpon, grouper, gentle walls and thousands of secluded keys that only few privileged visitors have encountered. This is the world class diving of the Caribbean. But I keep coming back to the Northeast coast of Santa Lucia where ten-foot Bull sharks pump my adrenaline every time!

Wherever you choose to dive on this island, I wish you a fantastic and memorable trip to beautiful Cuba.
All the Best,

Amy Houghton

Background: W. Houghton, Top Left: D. Tipton, Bottom Left: W. Houghton, Right: M. Mola

Introduction

Why Cuba?

Minutes after the dive master bangs on his tank, 1,200-pound bull sharks are swimming circles around you, waiting to be hand fed. Nearby is the wreck of Mortera. You are in a channel near Santa Lucía. You are in a place that any adrenaline-loving diver would love to be.

You've been staying in a floating hotel. You're about to be a pioneer going out to look for the illusive whale shark.

Visibility: 100 feet. A deep blue abyss descends below a vertical wall of coral, with protruding sponges, timid lobsters, and schools of juvenile parrot fish are streaming by. You're not in Cozumel, you're not in the Caymans, you're not in the Red Sea. You're in Cuba.

Introduction

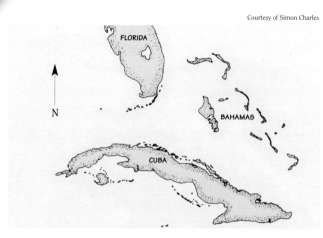

Courtesy of Simon Charles

Since the U.S. embargo against Cuba it seems as if time has stopped in the 1950s.

W. Houghton

You're drifting on the current, looking for ancient bottles in an old port frequented by Captain Morgan, the pirate, not the rum.

You're drift diving, floating around a Spanish galleon or a German World War II submarine, enjoying dives far from the tourist cattle boats and the flocks of rubber fins that might kick your mask off. You're in Cuba.

You're driving through lush patches of tobacco plants, past sheer cliffs that are the only Jurassic outcroppings in North America. You're on the way through Pinar del Rio, on your way to the diving camp at Maria de La Gorda. Ask any cigar aficionado. You're in Cuba.

Remember the Maine? You could see it on a one-day adventure from the Copacabana hotel in Havana, and be back in port in time to catch the plumed dancers on stage at the famed Tropicana. You're in Cuba.

On shore, Latin rhythms emanate from bars, cabs and family-run restaurants called *paladares*. People are genuinely warm and inviting. Stay at a *casa particular*, a bed and breakfast inn.

This is no "been-there-done-that" experience. This diver-to-diver guide is intended to help you plan your *first* trip.

When to Go

Go NOW! Go when you want sun and warmth. Go when it is convenient for you to travel. When the United States lifts its travel ban, curious Americans will flood across a 90-mile gap between Florida and Cuba. Overnight, Cuba could become the number one dive destination in the Caribbean. But right now, Cuba is unspoiled.

Cuba is in the same weather zone as the Cayman Islands, Cancun & Cozumel, and the Florida Keys. And the greatest diving perk is that Cuba has over 3,000 miles of coastline.

Cubans are experienced at dealing with wind and waves. When the Atlantic Ocean has high waves, they dive on the south side. On most Caribbean islands, to escape foul weather, you must fly home. In Cuba, just drive to the other side of the island or to a hidden inlet or key.

Insider's Tips

I have dived Cuba in the summer, fall, winter, and spring. Winter months bring opportunities to see whale sharks. Spring hosts more fish, but divers on the south side should be prepared for occasional Caribé, invisible jellyfish (see important chapter on this).

Travelling to Cuba

Getting to Cuba is as easy as surfing the web. Cuba's most profitable industry is tourism, which has been increasing by 18-20 percent annually since the 1990's. Although rules make it inconvenient for some Americans to visit Cuba, many are coming to experience the island. In 2001, according to Cuba's Ministry of Tourism, 80,000 Americans traveled to Cuba. Even more Americans are expected to come in the future. The great majority of visitors travel by air, although an increasing number come to Cuban marinas in private motor and sailing yachts. Currently the

See bright sponges that abound Isla de la Juventud.

M. Mola

national airline, Cubana de Aviación, brings about 20 per cent of visitors, while the rest come with one of more than 50 foreign airlines that land at Cuba's nine international airports.

Entering Cuba

All international flights to Havana bring visitors to José Martí Airport, where there are five small terminals. Most international flights arrive at Terminal Three (the new terminal). Direct flights from L.A., Miami and N.Y. arrive at Terminal Two. All passengers go through immigration before picking up luggage. You will need your visa and passport. Usually the Customs agent will ask, "Where are you staying?" It is very helpful to have the name of the hotel or *casa particular* with you. They will stamp your visa but NOT your passport. Once you collect your luggage, you should be able to pass right through customs. Sometimes passengers are randomly searched, especially if their bags or packages are unusually shaped. If visitors bring electronic devices that have a consumer value of more than $100, and do not intend to use them personally or as gifts, they will be charged a duty. Taxis are usually just outside the airport. For most areas of Havana the ride will be 15 to 30 minutes and should cost between $10 to $25 dollars.

Departing from Cuba

Check-in time is two hours before departure time. Cancun flights usually leave from Terminal Three and charters from Terminal Two. Travelers must pay a departure tax of $25. For overweight baggage (more than 44 lbs.) charges can usually be negotiated in the Havana airport.

Traveling Through a Third Country in Route to the U.S.

It is important to declare all products purchased in Cuba both on the declaration form and if asked by a customs official. In Mexico if you have more than one box of cigars, you will be asked to store them in their office until your flight departs. They will bring them to you at your gate. Sometimes they will try to charge a duty. Be sure to ask for receipts for everything. Remember that if an American travels to Cuba without a treasury license, he/she is not permitted to bring back any Cuban products.

Purchasing Tickets to Cuba from the United States

To reserve a roundtrip flight from Cancun to Havana, divers must call Mexicana airlines direct to Mexico City. The reservation agent will allow payment only with American Express cards. Any other credit card will be accepted only in person when picking up the ticket in Cancun. But, you can still make a reservation in advance. It is the responsibility of the passenger to present a reservation number at the Cancun Airport. At the Cancun Airport, if you give the flight number from your last flight and tell the ticket agent you are in transit to another country, you do not have to pay a $20 airport tax. Mexicana will typically hold the reservation until 2:00pm on the day of departure. If you arrive later than 2:00pm, it is your responsibility to ask for a later guarantee. The number to call:

011-52-555-448-0990

011 = International direct call; 52 = Mexico country code; 555 = Mexico City area code

Changing Ticket Dates While in Cuba

If you need to change your departure date and are traveling on Cubana or AeroCaribe airlines, try calling the Havanatur office at 203-9776. If you cannot change it over the phone, you will have to go in person to: Havanatur Office of Multidestionos, Calle 6 between 1st and 3rd, in Miramar. There is no charge unless you change your flight less than three days before your original departure date. In this case you may be charged $30. If you have been in Cuba for more than 30 days when you change your ticket, you will be charged an extra $80. To purchase a ticket to Santiago or other destination in Cuba, go to: Cubana Airlines, La Rampa, Calle 23 at

International Airlines Flight Schedule Information

INTERNATIONAL AIRLINES INFORMATION IN CUBA (Remember to dial first 011 from the United States).

Courtesy of Cayman Airways

Aerocaribbean
Terminal Aerocaribbean, Boyeros
Ph: 537-845-3013 / 537-833-5017

Aeroflot
Calle 23 No. 64, Vedado,
Plaza de la Rev.
Ph: 537-833-3200 / 537-833-3759

Aerogaviota
Ave. 47 No. 2814,
Reparto Kohly, Playa
Ph: 537-209-4990 / 537-833-2621

Air Jamaica
Hotel Habana Libre Tryp. Calle 23,
esquina L, Plaza de la Rev
Ph: 537-833-4011

ALM
Calle 23 No. 64 e/ Infanta y P,
Vedado, Plaza de la Rev.
Ph: 537-833-3730 / 537-833-3729

AOM
Calle 23 No. 64, interior,
Vedado, Plaza de la Rev.
Ph: 537-833-4098 / 537-833-3997

Avianca Sam
Hotel Nacional de Cuba, Mezzanine
Ph: 537-833-4700 / 537-833-4701

Copa
Calle 23 No. 64, interior, esq. Infanta,
Vedado, Plaza de la Rev.
Ph: 537-833-1758 / 537-833-3657

Iberia
Calle 23 No. 74 esq. P, Vedado
Ph: 537-833-5041 / 537-833-5042

Lacsa Tikal Tours
Calle L e/ 23 y 25, Vedado,
Plaza de la Rev.
Ph: 537-833-3114 / 537-833-3187

LTU
Calle 23 No. 64 esq. Infanta,
Vedado, Plaza de la Rev.
Ph: 537-833-3549 / 537-833-3590

Martinair Holland
Calle 23 esq. P, Vedado,
Plaza de la Rev.
Ph: 537-833-4364 / 537-833-3730

Mexicana
Calle 23 esq. P, Vedado,
Plaza de la Rev.
Ph: 537-833-3531 / 537-833-5532

TAAG
Calle 23 No. 64 esq. Infanta,
Vedado, Plaza de la Rev
Ph: 537-833-3597 / 537-833-3049

Viasa
La Habana
Ph: 537-833-5068

Cubana
Calle 23 No. 64 esq. Infanta,
Vedado, Plaza de la Rev.
Ph: 537-833-3911 / 537-833-3323

Airports
José Martí Airport
Ave. Hguyen Van Troi,
Boyeros, La Habana
Ph: 537-833-5177 / 537-833-5178

Juan G. Gómez
Playa Varadero, Matanzas
Ph: 534-836-3018 / 534-836-2010

Máximo Gómez
Provincia de Ciego de Avila
533-833-2525 / 533-834-3695

Ignacio Agramonte
Provincia de Camagüey
Ph: 533-226-1000

Antonio Maceo
Provincia de Santiago de Cuba
Ph: 532-269-1014

the Malecón. It is best to go early in the morning.

Although flight schedules often can change, the following information gives divers an idea of which airlines fly to Cuba.

From Grand Cayman

Now you can dive the Cayman Islands and Cuba on the same trip.

Effective December 6th, 2002, Cayman Airways launched weekly, non-stop jet service to Cuba. The fare is a very competitive $179 round trip plus tax (approximately US$36.25). The standard fare will be $209 roundtrip. Passengers are allowed two bags, EACH with a maximum total weight of 70 pounds. An excess surcharge for over-weight bags is a flat rate of US $35. Flights are every Friday and Sunday from Owen-Roberts Grand Cayman Airport to Jose Martí International Airport in Havana. The flight schedule is as follows:

Fridays	
Depart Grand Cayman	4:30pm
Arrive Havana	5:20pm
Depart Havana	6:20pm
Arrive Grand Cayman	7:10pm
Sundays	
Depart Grand Cayman	8:35pm
Arrive Havana	9:25pm
Depart Havana	10:25pm
Arrive Grand Cayman	11:15pm
To make a reservation, clients may call:	
1-800-CAYMAN or 345-949-2311	

From Mexico

The cost of flying on Mexicana Airlines varies, but is usually about $250 from Cancun each way. To book a flight from the United States, you must call Aero Caribbean in Mexico City. You can pay by American Express over the phone or you can make a reservation and pay at the ticket counter in Cancun. Cuba Travel Service has prices for about $180 roundtrip on Cubana Airlines. Taxes can be up to $60. To contact Cuba Travel, email: null@cuba-travel.com.mx. Travel packages with air only or with several nights' accommodation are readily available on short notice from many travel agents around Cancun. There is a 30 day limit on tickets. Examples of flight schedules are the following: *(Times and prices are subject to change)*

Daily: Cancun-Havana on AeroCaribe	
Flight # MX 7902	7:40pm
Daily: Cancun-Havana on AeroCaribe	
Flight # MX 7538	12:15am
Daily: Cancun-Havana on Cubana	
Flight # CU-153	12:00m
Daily: Havana-Cancun on AeroCaribe	
Flight # MX 7901	7:10am
Daily: Havana-Cancun on AeroCaribe	
Flight # MX 7539	3:00pm
Daily: Havana-Cancun on Cubana	
Flight # CU-152	10:40am

Flight time is one hour between Cancun and Havana. Havana is one hour later than Cancun on the time schedule. For more information or to book a ticket, contact:

Roberto Paneque Fonseca
Tele: 52-98-80-8160

Cuba Travel Service Cancun
Fax: 98-48-0175
Ave. Xpuhil, 3-A Suite 277 SM 27
Cancun Centro, 77502 Quintana Roo, Mexico

From Miami

Direct flights from Miami are authorized only for travelers with U.S. Treasury/

OFAC license. Tickets are non-refundable and start at $299 roundtrip plus $20-50 in taxes. Tickets have a 30-day limit. Example flight schedules are on the following page.

Tue.: Miami-Havana on Mexicana	
Flight # 2336	2:00pm
Wed.: Miami-Havana on FalconAir	
Flight # 717	8:00am
Thu.: Miami-Havana on United	
Flight #9023	8:00am
Fri.: Miami-Havana on FalconAir	
Flight # 717	8:00am
Sat.: Miami-Havana on United	
Flight # 9021	8:00am
Sat.: Miami-Havana on Mexicana	
Flight # 2336	2:00pm
Sun.: Miami-Havana on United	
Flight # 9023	8:00am
Tue.: Havana-Miami on Mexicana	
Flight # 2337	3:55pm
Wed.: Havana-Miami on FalconAir	
Flight # 718	10:00am
Thu.:Havana-Miami on United	
Flight # 9024	11:00am
Fri.: Havana-Miami on FalconAir	
Flight # 718	10:00am
Sat.: Havana-Miami on United	
Flight # 9022	11:00am
Sat.: Havana-Miami on Mexicana	
Flight # 2337	3:55pm
Sun.: Havana-Miami on United	
Flight # 9024	11:00am

All air travel is comfortable in United Airlines wide body Boeing 767's, Mexicana's modern Boeing 727, or FalconAir Express modern Boeing 727. Flight time between Miami and Havana is approximately one hour.

From Los Angeles

Cuba Travel Services offers weekly non-stop service from Los Angeles to Cuba. Flights depart from and return to Los Angeles every Friday. For reservations, contact Paulina at (800)963-2822.

From New York

Marazul Charters offers trips from New York, Miami, Cancun, and Nassau to Cuba. Many of their trips are cultural exchanges. They specialize in group travel. For more information or to book a reservation, ontact Karim Lopez at klopez@ marazulcharters.com or call 800-223-5334.

From Tampa

According to the St. Petersburg Times, Nov. 25th, 2002, Robert Curtis of Air MarBrisa plans to launch a new charter airline with service from St. Petersburg-Clearwater International Airport to Havana. Flights must stop in Miami for about 45 minutes to clear customs before continuing to Cuba. The estimated round-trip costs will start at $400. This route could be an excellent way to travel to Havana in the future.

M,T,W,Th, F: Nassau-Havana	
Flight # CU 9251	3:45pm
Sat.: Nassau-Havana	
Flight # CU 9251	11:05pm
Sun.: Nassau-Havana	
Flight # CU 9251	5:30pm
M,T,W,Th,F: Havana-Nassau	
Flight # CU 9250	1:15pm
Sat.:Havana-Nassau	
Flight # CU 9250	8:30am
Sun.: Havana-Nassau	
Flight # CU 9250	3:15pm

From Nassau

Tickets from Nassau, Bahamas to Havana, Cuba are approximately $215 roundtrip plus $15-20 in taxes. One way tickets are priced at $165. There is a $15 departure tax and a 30-day limit on the tickets. Only cash is accepted.

From Jamaica

Flights run from Montego Bay to Havana or from Kingston to Havana. Prices range from $350 to 400 round trip.

From Tijuana

Taino Tours charters Aero Mexico for a once a week flight for $530 roundtrip. It leaves on Saturday at 6:00pm PST, stops in Monterrey, and arrives in Havana at 3:30am EST. For more information, call: (66) 84-70-01.

From Canada

Toronto is the most common Canadian point of exit to enter Cuba. Try watching the major Canadian newspapers for tour companies offering last-minute air fares for low prices. Vancouver to Varadero round-trip tickets have been seen for as low as $199. One of the best ways to find out fares from Cuba is to contact a Canadian Travel Agency. Some excellent Canadian tour package companies provide roundtrip and direct flights from Canadian gateway cities to various international airports in Cuba. In addition to airfare, some packages will include resorts and all inclusive pricing for the following companies:

Sunquest   Signature Vacations
Hola Sun   World of Vacations
Air Transat

An excellent resource in bookstores is "The Canadian Travel Press" from Baxter Publications. Baxter has a free web site for travel information at:

http://www.travelpress.com/ctp

Those who are interested can order direct travel programs by email from Baxter at: sales@baxter.net

Another source for Canadian/Cuban travel packages is:

http://www.travelbestbuys.com

From Holland

Martinair offers low fares and flies from Amsterdam to Holguin and Varadero and back each Sunday.

From France

AOM flies Monday and Friday from Paris to Havana.

From Spain

Iberia Airlines flies daily from Madrid to Havana. Watch out for delays.

From Belgium

City Bird flies weekly from Brussels to Cuba alternating between Varadero and Camaguey for about $550. Cubana flies from Brussels to Havana every week for about $590.

From Denmark

Cubana flies from Copenhagen to Havana via Manchester.

From Austria, Czech Republic, Slovakia, Switzerland, and Ireland

Aeroflot flies via Moscow and Shannon, Ireland to Havana for $630. From Switzerland, Czech Republic, or Slovakia to Havana is about $560. Jets are comfortable and the luggage compartments are large.

From Central America

Third hand reports say that inexpensive packages such as $350 roundtrip from Costa Rica to Havana including a week in a hotel can be available.

Tickets within Cuba

Havana-Santiago-Havana:	
$170 roundtrip	$90 one way
Havana-Isla de Juventud-Havana	
$54 roundtrip	$32 one way
Havana-Holguin-Havana	
$158 roundtrip	$84 one way
Havana-Camaguey-Havana	
$130 roundtrip	$70 one way
Havana-Guardalavaca-Havana	
$170 roundtrip	$90 one way
Havana-Ciego de Avila-Havana	
$110 roundtrip	$60 one way
Havana-Manzanillo-Havana	
$142 roundtrip	$76 one way
Havana-Tunas-Havana	
$142 roundtrip	$76 one way
Havana-Moa-Havana	
$170 roundtrip	$90 one way
Havana-Baracoa-Havana	
$170 roundtrip	$90 one way
Havana-Varadero-Havana	
$54 roundtrip	$32 one way
Havana-Bayamo-Havana	
$142 roundtrip	$76 one way
Havana-Cayo Largo-Havana	
$110 roundtrip	$60 one way
Havana-Cayo Coco-Havana	
$110 roundtrip	$60 one way

Airport Transfers

Jose Martí Airport (Havana)-Havana Hotels	
$18 roundtrip	$10 one way
Jose Martí Airport (Havana)-Varadero	
$60 roundtrip	$35 one way
Jose Martí Airport (Havana)-Santa Maria Beach	
$25 roundtrip	$15 one way
Jose Martí Airport (Havana)- Pinar del Rio	
$60 roundtrip	$35 one way
Jose Martí Airport (Havana)-Cienfuegos	
$90 roundtrip	$50 one way

Travelers' checks are accepted in some cases as long as they are not drawn from American banks or companies.

Credit cards such as MasterCard, Visa International, JCB, Access, Banamex, Bancomer, Carnet, and Diners Club International are acceptable as long as they were not issued by an American bank or company. It would be useful (especially for Americans) to obtain a credit card from Canada. The Visa Card application takes about three weeks to process. You can contact several banks in Canada.

Bank of Nova Scotia
Ph: 1-519-973-5300
388 Ouelette Avenue
Fax: 1-519-973-5398
Windsor, Canada N8S1T6
Branch 71852

Main Office: 1-800-472-6842, then menu option (3), then menu option (2), then menu option (1), then menu option (2) for a customer service representative. Ask to be transferred to branch 71852.

The Bank of Nova Scotia requires that the account be opened in person. When driving through the tunnel from Detroit to Windsor, Canada, you will see the Bank of

Cuban Currency

The Cuban Peso is worth 100 cents (centavos). There are also coins valued in 1, 2, 5, 20, and 40 cents (centavos). Only Cubans are permitted to use this money. It is forbidden to import or export this currency from Cuba.

U.S. dollars are accepted everywhere on the island. Because local prices have been fixed in U.S. dollars, all business transactions are made in U.S. currency. According to USA Today published on December 6th, 1999, U.S. dollars are preferred since they became legal tender in 1993.

Nova Scotia sign above the main office as you exit the tunnel.

Canadian Imperial Bank
of Commerce
Ph: 1-800-465-2422
100 Ouellette Avenue
P.O. Box 180
Windsor, Canada N9A6K5
Branch 00182

See an amazing array of bright sponges. A. Nachoum

Royal Bank of Canada
Ph: (416) 974-3940
200 Bay Street
Toronto, Canada M5J2J5
Toll Free (in some areas)
1-800-387-3023

Non-resident accounts may be opened by mail. For more details, call the toll free line and ask for new accounts, and then ask for non-resident.

Weight Limitations

From Mexico via Mexicana or Cubana airlines, 44 pounds of baggage per person is allowed without extra charge. Anything over this weight limit could cost up to $2.50 per pound up to a maximum total of 66 pounds. Cubana Airlines allows 20 kilograms (44 pounds) of baggage per person in the coach class. This does not include your carry-on. Usually your carry-on limit is 5 kilograms (10 pounds). It can be useful to put the heaviest items, such as regulators, in the carry-on. First Class allows 30 kilograms (66 pounds) of baggage per person. During the holidays from October 15 to December 15, the allowance is 70 pounds for checked bags and 22 pounds for a carry-on. Overweight charges are $2 per kilogram.

When flying through Nassau, Bahamas, passengers may bring up to 20 pounds of humanitarian donations free of charge. Sixty-eight pounds of total baggage weight is free. Anything over 68 pounds costs $2.00 per pound.

Insider's tip

When flying on Mexicana Airlines, sometimes a little "tip" at the ticketing/check-in counter can be cheaper than paying excess baggage.

Cuban Phone Numbers

Cuba Scuba has gone to great lengths to ensure the validity of phone numbers listed in this guide. However, as Cuba advances to the digital age, many changes often occur. Therefore, if some numbers appear to have changed, you may try the following options recommended by the Canadian Embassy in Havana:

Items You'll Be Thankful You Brought

Bug bombs	Aloe	Alarm lock
Paper and pencil	Dramamine	Band-Aids
Extra Batteries	Wash Cloth	Spanish-English
Tampons	Soap	Dictionary
Insect repellent	Calamine Lotion	Personal ID
Laundry detergent	Anti-itch cream	Passport & copy
Extra rolls of film	(Lanocaine)	of passport
Sun glasses	Shampoo & conditioner	*Cuba Handbook* by
Toilet paper	Aspirin	Christopher P. Baker
Sun block	Anti-inflammatory pills	*Cuba Scuba* by Amy
Extra razor blades	(Benadryl)	Houghton
Toiletries	Plastic dirty laundry bag	$2 bills are useful
Snacks	Tissues	for tipping

All numbers starting with 60, 61, 62, 63, 67, 70, 73, 74, 77, 78, 79, 80, 81, 82, 84, 85, 30, 31 and 32, you have to add 8 at the beginning to show: 860, 861, 862, 863, 867, 870, 873, 874, 877, 878, 879, 880, 881, 882, 884, 885, 830, 831 and 832 and the last four digits do not change. Ex.: the number 60 3333 will now be 860-3333.

All numbers that contains only five digits (ex.: 3-3552), you have to add 83 to get for example: 833-3552.

All numbers starting with 22, 23, 24, 25, 28, 29, you have to add a 0 after the number 2 (ex.: 202 or 203, 204, etc.).

The number starting with 21, you have to add 7 after the number 2, (ex.: 271).

Americans in Cuba
Safety

Contrary to what some propaganda may imply, it is very safe for tourists to visit Cuba. In fact, tourism is Cuba's number one source of income. Cuban laws are very protective of its visitors. Tourists are free to experience almost any part of Cuba they wish. There are few restrictions for visitors.

Cuba has many historic shipwrecks.

A. Nachoum

Introduction

Suggested Humanitarian Donations

Paper/ pens	Athletic jerseys	American music tapes
Perfume	Camera & film	All types of medicine
Chocolate	Soaps	Lotion
Razors & shaving cream	Bug bombs	Spanish-English
Sanitary napkins	Vitamins	Dictionary
Magazines	Baseball hats	Tampons
Baseballs	Batteries	Bibles in Spanish
Sheets	Computer items	Eye Drops
Warm weather clothes	Deodorant	
Envelopes	Candy & gum	

It is jokingly said that the main purpose for the police is the safety of tourists. Still, one should use respectful etiquette and conduct when visiting a foreign country.

The Cuban people treat Americans with respect and dignity. They are impressed that an American would take the trouble to visit their country. Many like to share stories about having relatives who live in the United States. Some may even ask that you mail a letter for them when you return to the U.S. Cubans are some of the most highly educated people in the world. They want to learn about the U.S. first-hand. Although they are all too familiar with the U.S. government and the embargo, Cubans seem to distinguish the difference between Yankee government and its citizens. Cubans believe the American people are generally good, genuine people. After all, many Cubans are related to an American family in some way.

Returning home to Uncle Sam

Traveling to and within Cuba is virtually hassle-free. The toughest part for Americans is returning to the United States. Laws and relations between the U.S. and Cuba are in a constant state of flux. American travelers are well-advised to do research on the current status of the politics before making a decision to travel to Cuba.

Many Americans who return to the United States after visiting Cuba for the first time do not know what to expect from U.S. custom agents. Whether you are armed with a treasury license, some fully hosted documents, or nothing at all, before you cross that yellow line, this section is worth reading.

Americans who travel to Cuba illegally can be subject to penalties as high as a $250,000 fine, up to 10 years in jail, and loss of passport for 10 years. U.S. law places such a potentially high penalty on illegal travel on the basis that you have spent money in Cuba and thereby have broken the Trading with the Enemy Act.

Most U.S. Treasury Department procedures make many stipulations in which Americans must have documents proving that they did not spend money in Cuba. Thus, Americans should consider applying for a treasury license to travel to Cuba, or have fully hosted documents. Chances are

The Diving Guide to Cuba Scuba

that the customs department has bigger issues to deal with such as drug lords, smugglers, and illegal aliens, than to press charges in court against an American tourist who spent some money in Cuba while scuba diving for a week or two. In fact, according to sources on the Internet, travel writers uniformly contend that they have not heard of the government prosecuting any ordinary Americans for making an innocent excursion to Cuba.

Does this mean that no one could ever be prosecuted in the future? "Of course not", says Joseph R. Perez, the former airport chief of Tampa, Florida and current Port Director of St. Petersburg, Florida. If a customs inspector finds evidence that an American has spent money in Cuba, he has the authority to issue a variety of punishments. However, customs inspectors are more likely just to issue verbal warnings, a small fine, or simply seize any cigars or goods the American is trying to be bring back. The punishment is all in the luck of the customs line you pick. There is always an element of risk for punishment if one has traveled to Cuba without a treasury license or fully hosted documents.

Interestingly, congress recently passed a law that prohibits the US government to spend money to enforce the Trading with Enemy act against Cuba. However, some travelers have received letters in the mail with the choice of a $2,500 fine or the option of going to court to contest. For those travelers who chose the second option, all charges were dropped and the government has never prosecuted.

The Declaration Form

Many Americans wonder whether they should declare their trip to Cuba on their customs declaration card. On the front side of the card, question number eight asks to list "Countries visited on this trip prior to U.S. arrival." Some people choose to leave Cuba off the list here.

According to Joseph Perez, if an American has visited Cuba and does not put it down on his/her customs form, they have NOT violated the law. He says, "Passengers read the customs declaration form so quickly and erroneously that customs agents give them a chance to amend their statement". However, if the passengers verbally lie to a customs agent, then they

Cuban flag   D. Tipton

would be in violation and subject to a possible punishment.

It is your choice whether or not to declare that you have been to Cuba on your declaration form. If you do declare Cuba, it is likely that your bags will be subject to a search and you will face more questions about your visit to Cuba. If you do not declare Cuba on your form, and the customs inspector does not ask you if you've been to any other countries such as Cuba, you could possibly sail right through the line.

Also notable is that U.S. customs agents may only detain Americans for up to one hour. When the hour is up, customs must make a decision to either issue a punishment or let the traveler go on. Usually, if the traveler does not incriminate himself, it is difficult for the customs agent to issue punishment.

DEPARTMENT OF THE TREASURY
UNITED STATES CUSTOMS SERVICE

FORM APPROVED
OMB NO. 1515-0041

Customs Declaration
19 CFR 122.27, 148.12, 148.13, 148.110,148.111, 1498; 31 CFR 5316
Each arriving traveler or responsible family member must provide the following information (only ONE written declaration per family is required):

1. Family Name   Middle
   First *(Given)*
2. **Birth date**   Day   Month   Year
3. Number of **Family** members traveling with you
4. (a) U.S. Street **Address** (hotel name/destination)

   (b) City   (c) State
5. **Passport issued by** (country)
6. **Passport number**
7. Country of **Residence**
8. **Countries visited** on this
   trip prior to U.S. arrival
9. Airline/Flight No. or **Vessel Name**
10. The primary purpose of this trip is **business**:   Yes   No
11. I am (We are) bringing
    (a) fruits, plants, food, insects: Yes   No
    (b) meats, animals, animal/wildlife products: Yes   No
    (c) disease agents, cell cultures, snails: Yes   No
    (d) soil or have been on a farm/ranch/pasture: Yes   No
12. I have (We have) been in close proximity of
    (such as touching or handling) livestock: Yes   No

Are Some Passengers More Likely to be Searched?

Many travelers often wonder why inspectors search certain people and not others. Inspectors have an idea about which passenger they might search before a passenger even walks off the plane. This idea comes from a computer database of passenger profiles. According to Perez, here is how it works: The airline gives a list of all the passengers on the flight. The names are entered into the database, which then prints out characteristics, history of travel, and other information for each passenger.

A customs inspector uses this information along with the appearance and behav-

ior of a passenger to determine any further questions or searches. Of course there are still random searches too. First impressions are important. If a passenger declares Kahlua or Tequila, it is obvious that those purchases were probably made in Mexico. Sometimes it is useful to declare items purchased in the country from which you are arriving. For example, if you arrive with a group of passengers from the Bahamas, a straw, hand-woven bag from the straw market would be a nice item to declare. Some travelers try to plant an impression in the mind of the custom agent, so that if he does ask you questions, it will be more likely that he will ask about the country from which you are arriving instead of Cuba.

Recent Experiences of Other Americans

My own experience of traveling to Cuba with a treasury license was virtually hassle-free. After returning to the United States, I declared Cuba on my customs declaration form. I also declared four boxes of authentic Cuban cigars and two bottles of Cuban

Carnival occurs in July   W. Houghton

"El Capitolio" W. Houghton

rum. The total did not exceed $100. I handed the form to the Customs agent who then asked to see my treasury license. He glanced through my license papers, smiled and sent me on my way.

U.S. citizens returning from fully-hosted trips to Cuba, may have documents proving that they were fully-hosted. Please remember when traveling on a fully-hosted trip it is prohibited to bring back any souvenirs from Cuba. In order to bring back $100 worth of Cuban goods, you must obtain a U.S. treasury license.

I have also traveled as a fully-hosted guest in Cuba. I arrived to Houston, Texas from Cancun, Mexico. When I returned to the U.S., even though I possessed legitimate, fully hosted documents, I forgot to declare that I had been to Cuba. The customs officials in Texas did not ask about Cuba, so I did not need to show my fully-hosted documents. The experience was hassle-free. I simply walked through the inspection line like any other tourist returning from Cancun. Had the officials asked me if I had traveled to Cuba, I would have said yes, and immediately shown my

documents. However, as it was, I did not break any laws by simply forgetting to list Cuba on my declaration form.

I interviewed an American with multiple experiences in traveling to Cuba. His experience upon returning home with fully-hosted documents from Cuba was: "When I listed Cuba as one of the countries that I had been to before returning to the United States, a customs agent who was screening declaration forms, circled the word Cuba in red ink and directed me to a special line of passengers. Upon entering this line, I was sniffed by a ferocious-looking German Shepherd, which was trained to detect drugs. Even though I was fully-hosted, when the dog was directed to put his nose in the crack of my pants, I was intimidated. The agent asked me questions about my documents. He seemed almost displeased with me that I was able to produce all of the fully-hosted documents. After satisfying himself with the competency of my papers and my knowledge of my right to travel to Cuba, he grudgingly dismissed me without searching through my luggage. He recognized that I was intelligent enough not to smuggle prohibited items into the United States. As I toted my bags away from the counter, I vowed never again to intentionally inflict special attention from U.S. customs by declaring Cuba on my Customs form, even when traveling with legal documents."

Customs Inspectors
Are Not the Bad Guys

U.S. customs agents and inspectors have a very tough job to protect our nation's borders. They must uphold the law and keep illegal persons and items from coming in or going out of the country.

Therefore, they must use every resource available to them. They understand and respect that most passengers are legitimate, law-abiding citizens. It is the small percentage of people who break the law with whom inspectors must deal. So be courteous and cooperative with your custom agents because they are just doing their job.

Something to Consider

El Caribé

Most foreigners are not familiar with the term "El Caribé", which translates to "The Caribbean." According to Dr. Manolo Ortiz of Havana's Center for Marine Research, Cubans use this word to lump together several species of stinging coelenterates, or what we divers commonly refer to as jellyfish. These particular jellyfish visit the Caribbean every year, usually dur-

ing late April until the end of May. Cozumel and other areas in the Caribbean, which have a consistent current do not experience the invasion of these tiny creatures. They are only found in parts of the Caribbean where waters are calm and stagnate. Therefore the southern coast of Cuba is a great host to the little varmints. There is just one more thing: these jellyfish are invisible to the naked eye. You cannot see them, but you can sure feel them!

The effects of a sting can last anywhere from five to fourteen days. The first stage is a burning sensation and a swelling red rash in every spot where one of those tiny creatures bumped into your skin. Headaches and tiredness sometimes occur. The second and third days are the worst: the skin becomes overwhelmed with uncontrollable itching. With each scratch, the welts become larger, redder, and filled with watery, clear puss. Some people are more

Goliath Groupers of all sizes can be seen off the coasts of Cuba. M. Mola

These divers aren't taking any chances with "El Caribé", and wear full wetsuits.   A. Houghton

susceptible to the effects of Caribé than others. Nevertheless, according to Dr. Ortiz the effects are cumulative, so several bouts with Caribé could produce more severe consequences.

Precautionary Measures

If you plan to dive in Cuba during these months, try to dive mainly on the north coast. There are usually no problems with Caribé on the Atlantic side. Also, if you do plan to dive on the southern coast ALWAYS wear a full wetsuit, regardless of the water temperature. The Caribé cannot sting through a wetsuit. Yet, keep in mind, that any part of the body not covered by a wetsuit is considered fair game for those annoying jellies. The face, neck, hair-line, and hands commonly fall prey to the Caribé. Some suggest that applying sunscreen will deter the Caribé. Another helpful tip when entering the water is to descend immediately to the bottom and reunite with the group there. The least amount of time spent on the surface reduces Caribé time! Additionally when concluding the dive, hover at a depth between twelve and fifteen feet until you are absolutely sure it is your turn to get into the boat. Then, just before you ascend to Caribé level, take your spare regulator, turn it upside down and purge it a few times. Give the bubbles two or three seconds to begin rising, then let yourself ascend under them. The bubbles act as a momentary shield, pushing the invisible Caribé aside and creating a clear path. Some dive masters may promise there will not be any Caribé. I warn you not to take a chance.

Easing the Pain

If you know that you were stung, immediately pour vinegar on your skin. If you develop symptoms from Caribé, try covering the affected areas with a cold compress.

Never take hot showers because the heat will only aggravate the predicament. Take antihistamine pills such as Benedryl. Use Tylenol for headaches. It is recommended to drink a lot of water in order to increase excretion. Stay away from alcoholic beverages for a few days. The best lotion to put on the burning and itching is Calamine lotion. Lotions containing zinc or zinc silicate are also soothing. There is a lotion available in the U.S. called "Sting-Kill", which can be purchased from a drugstore. The active ingredients are 20% benzocaine and 1% menthol. It is advisable to bring your own Sting-Kill, Calamine lotion, Tylenol and antihistamines as these products are often difficult to locate in Cuba. For severe burns from Caribé, Dr. Manolo Ortiz suggests that an injection of a thiosulfate solution may be necessary.

Purge your regulator to deter Caribes. M. Mola

W. Houghton

PADI in Cuba

According to Ted Mortera, Manager of PADI International Business, to the best of his knowledge there are no PADI instructors in Cuba. If PADI instructors have been encountered in Cuba, it is likely that a PADI staff from a different country such as England, Canada, Australia, or Europe has trained them.

Roger Josselyn of PADI headquarters in Rancho Santa Margarita, California says, "The only persons in Cuba that PADI certifies are Americans on Guantanamo Navy Base, because the United States leases this property".

Sharon McFaddin of PADI-Canada says that there are PADI instructors in Cuba. The paperwork for PADI certifications in Cuba are sent first to a PADI office in Europe or Canada, depending on which country the Cuban PADI instructor was certified. The paperwork is then mailed to PADI headquarters in Rancho Santa Margarita, California. The paperwork must go through a third country because it cannot have a Cuban return address. Next, PADI headquarters mails the C-card back to the third country, which then mails the card back to the new diver. The PADI C-card will still say that the diver was certified in Cuba. The process is a bit lengthy due to all the countries involved, but it does happen.

It is possible to find some dive shops with PADI operations, although it is not common. All the dive shops in Cuba are of high standards using the European equivalent to PADI.

Puertosol and Cubanacan Nautica (Scuba Cuba)

Cuba has many dive centers most of which are operated by Puertosol or Cubanacan Nautica. Puertosol is the chief managing company of many nautical ports and marinas in Cuba. They specialize in providing first class scuba diving. They also offer sea safaris and other boating services. The management is friendly and knowledgeable and can customize nearly any kind of dive trip.

Cubanacan Nautica, also known as "Scuba Cuba" (formerly called Marlin), specializes in resorts that also offer diving. Cubanacan manages many dive centers located in or near their resorts. Because

Cubanacan is Cuba's largest tour operator, divers can arrange nearly any type of vacation they desire. Cubanacan Nautica is a customer friendly organization.

Both agencies are an excellent resource for planning your ultimate dive trip. For further inquiries, divers can contact either agency at:

Puertosol
Calle 1 ra No. 3001 a 30
Miramar, Playa,
Ciudad de la Habana
Ph: 537-204-8563
Fax: 537-204-5928
Email: explotac@psol.mit.tur.cu
Website: www.puertosol.net

Cubanacan Nautica
Calle 184. No. 123 Rpto
Flores, Playa, Habana, Cuba
Ph: 537-833-6675 / 537-833-7969
Fax: 537-833-7020
Email:
commercial@marlin.cha.cyt.cu
Website: www.cubanacan.cu

Other scuba diving entities in Cuba include:

Ecotur S.A.
Calle 158 y 31
Hotel Bello Caribe
Miramar, Playa, Habana, Cuba
Ph: 537-833-0061 / 537-833-0430
Fax: 537-833-0062
Email: ecotur@teleda.get.tur.cu

Cubamar Travel Agency
Calle Paseo. No. 306 e/ 13 y 15
Vedado Habana, Cuba
Ph: 537-866-2523 / 537-866-2524
Fax: 537-833-3111
Email: cubamar@
cubamar.mit.cma.net

Puertosol boats make diving easy.   W. Houghton

Cubanacan Nautica's dive boats accommodate up to 8 people.   W. Houghton

Gaviota Group
Edificio la Marina,
Ave. del Puerto No. 102
Habana Vieja, Cuba
Ph: 537-833-9780 / 537-860-2971
Fax: 537-833-2780
Email: gaviota@nwgaviot.cma.net
Website: www.gaviota.cu

Club Habana
 5ta Ave. e/ 188 y 192 Rpto. Flores
Playa, Habana, Cuba
Ph: 537-204-5700

Fax: 537-204-5705
Email: clubhaba@ceniai.inf.cu

Horizontes Hotels
Calle 23, No. 156 e/ N y O
Vedado, Habana, Cuba
Ph: 537-833-4090
Fax: 537-833-3722
Email: crh@horizontes.hor.tur.cu

Diving Safety in Cuba

Over the years, Cuba has developed many safety standards to ensure an excellent dive experience. In addition to a well-trained staff, and efficient dive centers, Cuba offers insurance and numerous hyperbaric chambers to support the industry.

Although DAN (Diver's Alert Network) does not operate in Cuba, divers have the option of an alternative insurance plan through Aseguradora La Isla, a company that works closely with the Ministry of Tourism. Aseguradora has a special policy for American citizens of $5 per day that will cover up to $25,000 in medical expenses and $7,000 in repatriation in case of an emergency to fly out of Cuba. This insurance policy can be purchased from any Cuban travel agency that sells tourist packages to clients.

In the case of a diving accident, all dive centers have an emergency plan to reach the nearest hyperbaric chamber. Cuba has hyperbaric chambers in various locations around the island. Most of the chambers hold up to eight people with the exception of Gerona chamber, which only holds four people. The approximated time for evacuation from a diving accident depends on where it occurs.

Location of Accident	Nearest Hyperbaric Chanbers	Est. Time of Travel
Maria la Gorda	Ciudad de la Habana	4 hrs 10 min (helicopter)
Cayo Levisa	Ciudad de la Habana	4 hrs 20 mins (helicopter)
Punta Frances	Colony	1 hr (boat)
Punta Frances	Gerona	2 hrs (boat & ambulance)
Punta Frances	Ciudad de la Habana	2 hrs 25 mins (helicopter)
Cayo Largo	Ciudad de la Habana	2 hrs 20 mins (helicopter)
Playa Giron (Bay of Pigs)	Ciudad de la Habana	2 hrs 20 mins (helicopter)
Cienfuegos	Ciudad de la Habana	5 hrs (helicopter & ambulance)
Jardines de la Reina	Ciudad de la Habana	4 hrs 48 mins (helicopter)
Marea del Portillo	Santiago de Cuba	2 hrs 26 mins (helicopter)
Sierramar	Santiago de Cuba	1 hr (ambulance)
Sigua & Bucanero	Santiago de Cuba	1 hr (ambulance)
Holguin	Santiago de Cuba	1 hr 23 mins (helicopter)
Santa Lucia	Santiago de Cuba	2 hrs 23 mins (helicopter)
Cayo Coco	Ciudad de la Habana	4 hrs 40 mins (helicopter)
Cayo Guillermo	Ciudad de la Habana	4 hrs 40 mins (helicopter)
Varadero	Cardena	25 mins (ambulance)
Varadero	Ciudad de la Habana	1hr 50 mins (helicopter)
Marina Tarara	Ciudad de la Habana	20 mins (ambulance)
Copacabana Hotel	Ciudad de la Habana	25 mins (ambulance)
Marina hemingway	Ciudad de la Habana	35 mins (ambulance)
El Salado	Ciudad de la Habana	1 hr (ambulance)

Cubans are skilled fisherman.   W. Houghton

Protected Areas for Fish

Underwater, the life in Cuba seems to be an advertisement for fish. There is abundant, healthy coral, nice formations, walls, tunnels, caves, sea fans, soft coral, shipwrecks, vibrant colors, good visibility, and comfortable temperatures. It is an aquatic scene, simply begging for fish.

The Center for Marine Research of the University of Havana has been monitoring fish life. During the mid 1990's, over-fishing by commercial fisherman began to take a toll in surrounding waters. With the U.S. embargo restricting many food items and other goods, Cuba has compensated with available resources. Most of the fish are used for food consumption or exported for hard currency.

The Center for Marine Research devotes most of its energy to the protection of marine life. Yet, this is not a simple task. Compromises must be made with other governmental agencies such as the Ministry of Fisheries, the Ministry of Agriculture, the Ministry of Science, and the Ministry of Tourism.

The compromise between all these agencies was a Protected Area (P.A.'s). A Protected Area is not equivalent to a marine preserve. A Protected Area is an economic agreement mainly between the Ministry of Fisheries and the Ministry of Tourism where fishing is approved in the area during certain times of the year.

However, the Center for Marine Research obtained permission for a grant to implement an Integrated Coastal Management project. This plan's goal was to declare some Protected Areas as National Marine Parks. As a result of joint efforts among several government agencies, Punta Frances of Isla de la Juventud, Maria la Gorda, and Los Jardines de la Reina have become National Marine Parks. Future plans will include reviewing the current fishery regulations, producing a diving code to be used by tourists, and enacting a set of rules to control the use of these areas.

While the debate continues over Protected Areas and National Marine Parks, fishing continues. Regulation of fishing is extremely difficult. However, Cubans are working diligently to find solutions to this long-standing problem so that divers may continue to enjoy the pristine ecosystems.

D. Tipton

Driving in Cuba

Driving around Cuba can be a breathtaking adventure and an economic way to travel. The countrysides and scenic landscapes create vivid portraits of lush colors. But, if you have a choice, do not drive at night. Unmarked potholes on some roads can be devastating to tires. Reflective painted lines are rare. Furthermore, side markings do not exist on highways. Add in dark clothed pedestrians, incognito bicycles, ox carts, pigs, chickens, cows, and horses and you'll feel like you are inside a driving video game with only one chance left! If you must drive at night, try to follow at a safe distance behind a local car. When it swerves to avoid something, slow down and be prepared for obstacles.

Road maps do not always closely resemble the true path. For this reason, we often have offered rides to Cuban hitchhikers, also known as "botellas" in Spanish. Hitchhikers are in groups everywhere and are like living road maps. Even if divers do not speak Spanish, simply roll down the window and say the name of your destination. Usually several hands will raise. Let the Cubans sort out who gets to ride with you. Although there is always a little risk, Cuba is so well controlled that it can be quite safe. Policemen even hitch rides to and from work. My father and I always felt safer riding with "officials" in the backseat to help us find our way since road signs are a luxury not always found in Cuba.

A LIVE-ABOARD LEGALLY TAILORED TO AMERICANS

Americans now have a way to dive the waters of Cuba legally and in most cases, a tax write-off on their trip expenses may be forthcoming! Aboard the m/v Oceanus with comfortable accommodations of seven double bunk beds, divers can experience some of the most attractive areas of the island: Maria la Gorda, Isla de la Juventud, and Cayo Largo. What makes this nine-day trip possible is a partnership between a non-profit foundation, the University of Havana and an American travel company.

Salty Dog Adventures (SDA) is an educational research & adventure travel company, which has complied with all the criteria set forth by the Office of Foreign Assets Control (OFAC) of the U.S. Treasury Department. Divers who participate in this research program will receive documentation from SDA explaining the expedition parameters to present to U.S. customs. Since they are traveling to Cuba under the auspices of the OFAC, divers are allowed to spend up to $180 per day and bring back $100 in souvenirs, including cigars.

Salty Dog Adventures works in conjunction with the Reef Environment Education Foundation (REEF), a public charity under Section 501 c(3) 509 a(1) and 170 b(1)(A)(vi) of the Internal Revenue Code. The Reef Foundation utilizes volunteer research divers to collect data. The data is then entered into a publicly accessible database on the website: www.reef.org. No experience is necessary to volunteer. A reef fish I.D. seminar will be given the first night so divers will know exactly how to use the scan forms to collect data. Snorkelers can also participate in the research.

The science and technology department as well as the Center for Marine Research of the University of Havana are optimistic about the research on their reefs. Cuba also has a current program with sea turtles, which they foresee as another opportunity for synergy with the American research volunteers.

"This is an important area to REEF, due to its location", says Capt. Rib Bolton, President of Salty Dog Adventures. "There are currents traveling from west to east on the north of Cuba and east to west on the south. You're going to have 'larval drift' from everywhere and it is vital to know what is going on there (which also impacts Florida's coastal waters)." Bolton has a Bachelor of Science in Biology with a minor in Chemistry from Southeast Missouri State University and some graduate work in marine biology from Florida Institute of Technology. He is also working with the Philip Cousteau Foundation to establish a marine education program for middle and high school students in the St. Louis metropolitan area.

This program allows divers the opportunity to participate in preserving the reefs, dive excellent areas in Cuba, bring back souvenirs legally, write-off expenses to their taxes, and the entire cost is a great value. The Oceanus has two packages. A six-day package that includes all meals, roundtrip flight from Cancun to Havana, all transfers, diving, and a city tour and night in Havana for only $1,250 per person. A longer package of nine days is only $1,800 per person. For more information or to book reservations, contact:

> Capt. Rib Bolton
> Email: Capt.Rib@sdadive.com
> Ph: (636) 677-7504
> Fax: (636) 677-1875
> Web: http://www.sdadive.com

W. Houghton

The Diving Guide to Cuba Scuba

Cuba's mangroves are great for snorkeling.

D. Tipton

U.S. Department of State
Bureau of Consular Affairs
Washington, DC 20520

Consular Information Sheet

September 12, 2002

COUNTRY DESCRIPTION: Cuba is a developing country with a totalitarian, communist government. The United States has no direct diplomatic relations with Cuba, but provides consular and other services through the U.S. Interests Section in Havana. The U.S. Interests Section operates under the legal protection of the Swiss government, but it is not co-located at the Swiss Embassy.

ENTRY REQUIREMENTS/TRAVEL TRANSACTION LIMITATIONS: The Cuban Assets Control Regulations of the U.S. Treasury Department require that persons subject to U.S. jurisdiction be licensed to engage in any transaction related to travel to, from and within Cuba. Transactions related to tourist travel are not licensable. This restriction includes tourist travel to Cuba from or through a third country such as Mexico or Canada.

The following categories of travelers are permitted to spend money for Cuban travel and to engage in other transactions directly incident to the purpose of their travel under a general license, without the need to obtain special permission from the U.S. Treasury Department:

- U.S. and foreign government officials traveling on official business, including representatives of international organizations of which the U.S. is a member;
- Journalists and supporting broadcasting or technical personnel regularly employed by a news reporting organization;
- Persons making a once-a-year visit to close family relatives in circumstances of humanitarian need;
- Full-time professionals whose travel transactions are directly related to professional research in their professional areas, provided that their research : (1) is of a noncommercial academic nature; (2) comprises a full work schedule in Cuba, and (3) has a substantial likelihood of public dissemination;
- Full-time professionals whose travel transactions are directly related to attendance at professional meetings or conferences in Cuba organized by an international professional organization, institution, or association that regularly sponsors such meetings or conferences in other countries;
- Amateur or semi-professional athletes or teams traveling to Cuba to participate in an athletic competition held under the auspices of the relevant international sports federation.

The Department of the Treasury may issue licenses on a case-by-case basis authorizing Cuba travel-related transactions directly incident to marketing, sales negotiation, accompanied delivery, and servicing of exports and reexports that appear consistent with the licensing policy of the Department of Commerce. The sectors in which U.S. citizens may sell and service products to Cuba include agricultural commodities, telecommunications activities, medicine, and medical devices. The Treasury Department will also consider requests for specific licenses for humanitarian travel not covered by the general license, educational exchanges, and religious activities by individuals or groups affiliated with a religious organization.
Unless otherwise exempted or authorized, any person subject to U.S. jurisdiction who engages in any travel-related transaction in Cuba violates the regulations. Persons not licensed to engage in travel-related transactions may travel to Cuba without violating the regulations only if a person not subject to U.S. jurisdiction covers all Cuba-related expenses and provided that the traveler does not provide any service to Cuba or a Cuban national. Such travel is called "fully-hosted" travel. Such travel may not by made on a Cuban carrier or aboard a direct flight between the United States and Cuba.
Failure to comply with Department of Treasury regulations may result in civil penalties and criminal prosecution upon return to the United States.
Additional information may be obtained by contacting the Licensing Division, Office of Foreign Assets Control, U.S. Department of the Treasury, 1500 Pennsylvania Avenue NW, Treasury Annex, Washington, DC 20220, telephone (202) 622-2480; fax (202) 622-1657. Internet users can log on to the web site through http://www.treas.gov/ofac/.

Overview of Cuba

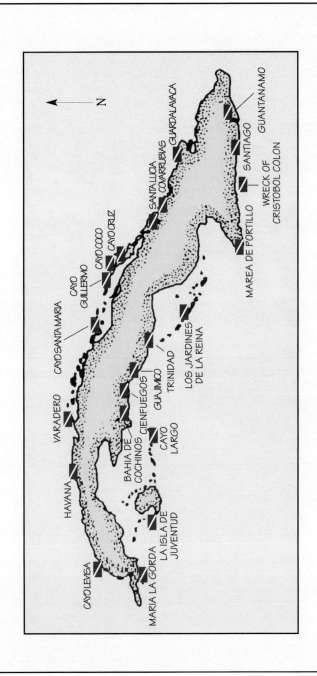

Western Cuba

Havana Province

Where else could one find the heart of Cuba, but in its capital? Wherever I travel in Cuba, I always like to stop in Havana for a couple days. Everyone should take a gander at Castro's neighborhood. Full of adventure, life, friendship and history, this city is an explorer's treasure. Havana has excellent restaurants where you can dine like locals, warm Bed & Breakfasts with friendly service, and discos where you can try to dance like Cubans. The Cuban people give this monumental city its real beauty.

Havana has a large venue of hotels from which to choose, such as the five-star Melia Cohiba. The most nos-

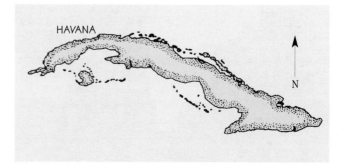

talgic hotel is the famous Copacabana. It is extremely convenient for divers to take a plunge right off the back yard. Divers can refer to the resort appendix for more accommodations. If you're looking for the soul of Cuban culture, then *casa particulares* (private bed and breakfasts) are the way to go. These accommodations have great service, comfortable rooms, and friendly hosts. The price is right too. Most homes cost between $25.00 and $40.00 per night. For more inside tips on *casa particulares*, see the Private Bed & Breakfasts of Havana section.

Dive Sites

The dive zone is nearly 65 miles in its entirety, and covers the whole coastline of Havana. There are five dive centers located in Havana's province, all of which have access to Havana's hyperbaric chamber. Each has its own unique characteristics. On the western part of the coastline, Blue Reef Diving Center is located in the Villa Cocomar hotel. La Aguja Diving Center is located in Marina Hemingway. The Copacabana dive center is located in this famous hotel. Blue Scuba Dive Club is situated in downtown Havana. Toward the east, Puerto Escondido and Marina Tarará each have dive centers.

Enjoy a smooth rum at Hemmingway's favorite pub.

Blue Reef Diving Center

About 13 miles west of downtown Havana, established in 1998, this dive center is located on Playa El Salado. The center is owned by Cubanacan Nautica and is part of Villa Cocomar. The village is quaint with a restaurant, large pool, ponds, and small air-conditioned bungalows. Rooms run between $36.00 and $47.00 per night. The dive center is situated on the beach. Two instructors work at Blue Reef. Both speak English and are ACUC certified. The center has one Bauer compressor, which fills its 25 steel tanks. There are 15 sets of Cressi-sub rental equipment. It is best to bring your own gear because the cost to rent an entire set for the day is $20.00. The diving capacity is 18 divers per day. However, there are usually no more than four or five divers. Diving usually takes place from a 23-foot, 10-passenger motorboat. It has two 60-horse power engines. The diving schedule is flexible. Usually two dives are scheduled. The first one begins at 10:00am. The second dive is made about one hour after the completion of the first one. The boat visits 20 dive sites, all within 10-30 minutes from the Center. Selected dive sites follow (See dive map on pg. 64):

Guajaibon Smiles

About five miles from shore, Guajaibon Smiles lies in 45 feet (15 meters) of water. Here, divers may see a coral wall with tunnels and sandy bottom patches. The site marks where the river joins the sea. Lobsters and eels sometimes hide in crevices of the wall. Maximum bottom time depends on consumption of air.

Playa Banes

The maximum depth at this site is 120 feet (40 meters). Divers will encounter a coral wall followed by a drop-off. Caves and tunnels are abundant in this area. Fish life includes groupers, tarpon, amber jacks, barracuda, and snapper. Black coral and colorful sponges can also be seen in this region.

Playa el Salado Diving Center

W. Houghton

Los Paraguas de Baracoa

This site is characterized by flat coral formations. When seen from the surface, the coral resemble large umbrellas, hence its name. Divers may see schools of adult fish and large sponges, together with colonies of black coral.

El Muerto

The tip of a coral mountain begins at 75 feet (25 meters) and descends past 120 feet (40 meters). This mountain consists of many types of hard and soft coral. Hidden in the crevices of the mountain are lobsters and moray eels. Occasional barracudas cruise by.

Blue Reef Diving Center Dive Prices	
Average price for one dive	$25.00
Average price for two dives	$40.00
Average price for night dive	$30.00
Average price for package of dives	negotiable
Average price for a resort course	$60.00
Average price for open water course	$300.00
(ACUC certification)	

For more information or to book a reservation, contact:

Blue Reef Scuba Cuba
Ph: 537-680-8290 ext. 72
Fax: 537-204-6848
Carretera Pan Americana Km 23½
Caimito, Havana Province, Cuba

La Aguja Diving Center

This dive center, owned by Cubanacan Nautica, is located in Marina Hemingway. There are three instructors employed here. All of them speak English and are CMAS or

Dive boats don't drop anchors. D. Tipton

ACUC certified. There are two Bauer compressors, which fill the center's 50 steel tanks.

There are 30 sets of Technomar rental equipment. Divers can use the gear free of charge at the dive center. The total diving capacity for the center is 30 divers per day. La Aguja has one dive boat. Diving usually takes place at 10:00am and 2:00pm.

The diving area runs parallel to the coast and sites are at depths between 15 and 130 feet (5 – 43 meters). They comprise sandy prairies carpeted by corals, gorgonians and sponges with schools of tiny fish swimming among them. Small caves and shipwrecks display curious histories. (See dive map on pg. 65)

Coral Island

This dive site hosts a merchant shipwreck in about 75 feet (25 meters) of water. The ship caught fire before it sank. It is divided into three sections. The stern section has the most fish life. The frame of the ship is ideal for corals, sponges, bivalves, hydrozoa and algae. Maximum depth is about 105 feet.

Comodoro

The Comodoro is the name of a fishing boat. It was intentionally sunk in order to make an artificial reef. Extremely well preserved, this boat is a playground for small coral fish.

Canto de Viriato

Staggered coral formations resemble small hills that drop to a depth of 60-90 feet (20-30 meters). Adult and juvenile fish and several lobster may also be found here.

Cabezo de las Chopas

The main feature of this site is a vertical coral wall that begins at about 45 feet (15 meters) and continues to descend. Nearby, there are large outcrops of coral that dot the sandy bottom, followed by a cave, which houses several types of fish. There are also pillar corals, blue sponges, and Venus Basket sponges. Schools of chubs also sometimes swim through this area.

Canto de Hollywood

Maximum depth at this site is about 45 feet. Walls with caves, a small tunnel, abundant corals, sponges and gorgonians may be seen here. Coral reef fish also inhabit this area.

Sanchez Barcastegui

This dive site is a host to an old armored Spanish vessel that failed after colliding with another ship while maneuvering to enter Havana Harbor in 1895. Among the remnants of the man-o-war are tarpon, snook, and grouper.

"Remember the Maine"

The 1898 controversial exploding and sinking of the U.S. Battleship Maine led to its present resting site directly in front of the Hotel Nacional. Randolph Hearst newspapers and his biased articles promoted the theory that Spanish terrorists bombed the steel hulled ship. Hatred for Spain was fed

Poolside refreshments draw a crowd.

W. Houghton

41

Monument with canons from the battleship, Maine. The eagle "cap" was removed in 1960.

by newspaper writers and grew with the declaration of the Spanish American War and the formations of Teddy Roosevelt and his famed rough riders. The end of the war gave way to the U.S. Navy sinking several Spanish ships, including the battleship Cristobal Colón along the eastern coast of the Granma Province.

After the war ended, the American public demanded the truth about the cause of the sinking of the Maine. Millions of dollars were spent to pump seawater out of the wreck. The Maine was completely exposed and examined. Pieces of the wreck were removed and placed in monuments across the United States. Two cannons were placed on a Cuban monument that can be seen while driving west on the Malecón from Old Havana. Historians say that evidence points to the probability that the Maine exploded from within its own coal-fired boilers rather than from terrorists.

Not much remains of the wreck. Divers can find steel plates scattered in layers that provide habitat for lobsters and juvenile reef fish. The closest dive shop to do this dive is located in Copacabana Hotel.

La Aguja Diving Center Dive Prices	
Average price for one dive	$25.00
Average price for two dives	$40.00
Average price for six dives	$157.00 total
Average price for ten dives	$240.00 total
Average price for twenty dives	$440.00 total
Average price for a resort course	$66.00
Average price for open water course	$400.00

Marina Hemingway offers every kind of water sport. For more information or to book a reservation, contact:

Marina Hemingway
Calle 248 y 5th Ave. Intercanal B.
Santa Fe, Havana City, Cuba
Ph: 537-204-1150 / 537-204-6848

Copacabana Dive Prices (Including Rental Equipment)	
Average price for one dive	$25
Average price for two dives	$40
Average price for package of three	$65
Average price for package of five	$120
Average price for a night dive	$35

Blub Scuba Club Dive Prices	
Average price for one dive	$25.00
Average price for two dives	$40.00
(it is $70 if you want lunch included)	
Average price for a night dive	$35.00
Average price for ten dives	$220.00
Average price for twenty dives	$350.00
Average price for a resort dive	$40.00
Average price for open water course	$350.00
Average price for advanced course	$280.00

Copacabana Dive Center

Owned by the Spanish Gran Caribé hotel chain, this four-star hotel is an icon in Havana. Copacabana offers kayaking, catamarans, wind-surfing, water tricycles, snorkeling, and scuba diving. It's dive center has great facilities, including a fresh water pool and also a natural saltwater pool fenced off from the ocean. Open water certifications are $300 and open water referrals are $150. They also offer special packages to dive the Bay of Pigs.

For more information or to book a reservation, contact:

Cobacabana Hotel
Playa, La Habana, Cuba
Calle 1ra No. 4404 e/ 44 y 46
Ph: 537-204-1037
Fax: 537-204-2846
Email:
commercial@copa.gca.tur.cu

Blue Scuba Club

The Blue Scuba Club is a privately owned center. It does not have insurance. It is similar to a *particular* dive center. The center pays a fee to the government in order to obtain a license to operate its club. The center employs two dive instructors. Both speak English and are ACUC certified. The center has one compressor that fills its 45 steel tanks. There are 15 sets of rental equipment, of which most brands are Cressi Sub (Italian), Scuba Pro (American), and Spiro (Italian). The cost to rent an entire set of rental gear is $15.00 per day. The diving capacity is about 35 divers per day. The center does not own boats, therefore all dives are beach dives and usually done near the center. Sometimes a bus takes divers to the Bay of Pigs to dive. Dives are normally done at 10:00am and 2:00pm.

For more information or to book a reservation, contact:

Blue Scuba Dive Club
Ave. 1st no. 2401 e/ 24 y 26
Miramar, Playa, Havana City, Cuba
Ph: 537-209-3660

Tarará Diving Center

It is a good idea to bring your passport to dive here. In order to enter the Tarará Marina, sometimes one must show identification. The dive center, owned by Puertosol, is located 15 minutes east of downtown Havana. There are four instructors employed at the center, of which three speak English and are CMAS certified. There are two Bauer compressors, which fill its 40 steel tanks. The rental equipment consists of 18 full sets of Mares (Italian) gear. The total cost for usage of rental equipment is $10.00 per day. The center has a capacity for 40 divers per day, but there are usually no more than 14 divers during the high season. There are six dive boats ranging in size from 29 feet to 42 feet long. Most boats have toilets and bottled water ($1.00) available on board. The diving schedule is flexible, but usually there is a dive at 9:00am and at 1:30pm. The center visits 16 dive sites, all of which are accessible by no more than 20 minutes by boat. Popular dive sites are as follows (See dive map on pg. 66):

La Canal

Only a three-minute boat ride from the center, this dive site lies in 60 feet (18 meters) of water. There are two walls made up of large heads of coral. Between the two walls is a large canal. Divers can see good coral life and small tropical fish. Sometimes barracuda enjoy this area. Maximum bottom time is about 45 minutes.

Justiz

Similar to La Canal, this site is characterized by its large coral head formations located in approximately 90 feet (30 meters) of water. In addition to soft and hard coral, bright sponges are also quite decorative along the walls. The boat ride is about 20-25 minutes. Total bottom time is 35 minutes.

La Chalupa

Seven minutes from the dive center, La Chalupa is in 75 feet (25 meters) of water. La Chalupa is the name of a sunken, iron ship. Colorful sponges, coral, and algae cover this ship. Moray eels sometimes swim in its portholes.

Tarará Diving Center Dive Prices	
Average price for one dive	$30.00
Average price for two dives	$50.00
Average price for only a boat ride	$15.00
Average price for a resort dive	$40.00
Average price for open water course	$300.00

For more information or to book a reservation, contact:

Marina Tarará
Villa Blanca km 18
Playa Tarará, Habana del Este
Ciudad de la Habana, Cuba
Ph: 537-897-1462
Fax: 537-897-1333
Email:
commercial@tarara.mit.tur.cu

Puerto Escondido (Hidden Port)

About 35-40 miles east of Havana is Puerto Escondido, owned by Cubamar. This gorgeous port rests between two small mountains. Protected by rocky cliffs, it cannot be easily seen from the ocean. In 1980 Fidel Castro dived this area and discovered the reefs. Liking it so much, he ordered a nautical base to be put in the region. In 1983 three underwater cameras were dedicated to the study and documentation of its coral reef. Now there are two instructors employed at Puerto Escondido. Both speak English and are CMAS certified. The center has two German compressors that fill its 15 tanks. There are five sets of Mares (Italian) rental equipment. There is no charge for usage of the rental equipment. The diving capacity is for 15 divers. Usually there are only 5-6 divers during the weekends. There is one 10-passenger dive boat that is 32 feet long. Toilets and bottled water ($ .70) are available on board. The diving schedule is flexible, but two dives are usually made per day. The first dive begins at 9:00am and the second at 1:00pm. The dive zone consists of four large reefs and one smaller reef, which vary in depth from 45 feet to 105 feet (15-35M).

Puerto Escondido Dive Prices	
Average price for one dive	$25.00
Average price for two dives	$40.00
Average price for a package of dives	negotiable
Average price for open water course	$350.00

For more information or to book a reservation, contact:

Centro de Buceo Puerto Escondido
Via Blanca, La Habana, Cuba
Phone number: 537-866-2524
or 537-866-2523, 537-66-2523

Insider's Tips

Almost all of the marinas in Cuba have "Guarda Frontera", which is similar to a Coast Guard. For security reasons most people boarding a dive boat are required to show their passports. So, just to be safe, carry your passport in addition to your C-card.

Above the water

Havana has so much to offer. There are museums, historical sites, markets, palaces, discos and nightclubs. For more details, see the *Cuba Handbook*, by Christopher P. Baker.

Getting There

Travelers are likely to strike a better deal on taxi costs if they convince the driver to take them from Havana to Puerto Escondido "off the meter". For a reasonable price, between $40-50 U.S. dollars, a cab will usually escort up to three divers, all their gear, and even wait for them after their dives are completed. The drive lasts about one hour each way along the scenic coastal highway.

The Havana Taxi Companies are Panataxi Ph: 855-5555 and Havanautos Ph: 832-3232 (both inexpensive); TurisTaxi Ph: 833-6666 and OK Taxi Ph: 204-0000 (both most expensive).

Author and father are ready for another beautiful dive.   M. Mola

Private Restaurants of Havana

Every dive vacation includes time to dissipate the nitrogen from your blood and Havana is one of the greatest places on the planet to spend your surface interval! Try a seven-year old Havana Club rum straight (the Cuban way), while the vintage cars roll by with salsa tunes filling the air. Take your choice of a myriad of fine cigars, and belly-up to the table for some good old-fashioned Cuban cuisine. Our recommendations will help divers explore the path less traveled on the top-side of their vacation. We scouted out the private restaurants, bed & breakfasts, and party places that may otherwise be obscure to the average tourist or typical guidebook. Divers can eat well and save money in Havana.

W. Houghton

The food quality in Cuba began to improve in 1994, when the government loosened its stance on private enterprise and allowed opportunities for a small percentage of the population to open private restaurants in their homes. These private restaurants are called *"paladares."* The name is derived from a popular Brazilian television series in which Cubans identified with a suffering heroine who overcame her struggle for survival by opening a small restaurant called 'Le Paladar'. *Paladares* are by far the best way to enjoy the dining experience Cuba has to offer. In general the service, ambience, and fare of a private restaurant is superior to that of a state-owned restaurant.

Paladares pay heavy license fees to the government, exist under stringent regulations, and are subject to regular and sometimes irregular inspections. Even though *paladares* compete with state-owned restaurants, they are not allowed to serve lobster or beef (the most profitable entrées). They also operate with very little marketing opportunities and depend heavily on word-of-mouth publicity. Furthermore, they are only permitted to serve 12 patrons at a time and credit cards are not accepted. *Paladares* have labor restrictions that only allow owners and extended families as employees. This restriction seems to precipitate pride and commitment that resonates in better customer service. Even with such limitations, these private entrepreneurs are finding creative ways to be successful.

We have evaluated these successful *paladares* on a five-star rating. Yet, please note that due to their limitations, a five-star rating for a *paladar* does not necessarily translate to world-class gastronomic standards of which some may be accustomed. *Cuba Scuba* has uncovered more than 50 *paladares* in greater Havana (Habana Vieja, Vedado, and Miramar). Of these, we have selected the top ten to help divers determine where to go to satisfy their taste buds. Restaurants with stars have been reviewed with the purchase of at least two meals on different occasions and many were reviewed as many as five times. Kitchens, bathrooms, and dining facilities were inspected for cleanliness. Hours of operation and reservation information were checked where possible. Recommendations by local and foreign reviewers were considered and sometimes noted as well. For divers who only have a few days in Havana, the first four suggestions are definite winners. Divers are encouraged to send their restaurant reviews and opinions to www.cubascuba-thebook.com .

★★★★★
La Fontana
Calle 3ra A esq. 46, No 305
Miramar, Ciudad de la Habana, Cuba
Ph: 537-202-8337
Cell: 537-880-1352
Hours: Noon to Midnight daily
Owner:
Horacio Reyes Novio Bauta

Horacio has an excellent paladar! Favorably reviewed by **Saveur Magazine**, La Fontana is located in a trendy section of Miramar within the afternoon shadow of the Russian Embassy. A guard will direct guests to park nearby, as varnished wooden gates between stonewalls welcome visitors to one of Havana's premier restaurants. Diners have the option to experience the outdoor vine covered courtyard by the flowing fountain, relax inside in the air conditioning, or step down into the thatched bar area to sample the Spanish wine collection in the cave-like cellar. The Madrid-educated sommelier can also offer wines from Portugal, Germany, France, Italy, and yes California.

If diners are torn between choosing from the vast authentic menu items, they can walk over to the outdoor grill. Visitors may influence their decision by smelling delightful aromas from fresh seafood and meats cooking in the open air or sneaking a peak at classic Cuban creole hors d'oeuvres being delivered from the modern, spotless kitchen.

W. Houghton

Reasonably priced, immaculate cleanliness, inventive and extensive selections, great presentation, attentive service and warm ambience with live music in the evenings make La Fontana an excellent dining experience. This is my favorite restaurant in Havana!

★★★★★

La Cocina de Lilliam
Calle 48 #1311 e/ 13 y 15, Playa
Ciudad de la Habana, Cuba
Ph: 537-209-6514
Hours: Noon to 3pm, 7pm-10pm,
Closed on Saturdays
Owners: Lilliam and Luis

Dine like the heads of state at this neatly decorated, peaceful *paladar*. Featured twice in the "New York Times", and also in the prestigious "Cigar Aficionado" magazine, patrons can order the same sumptuous dinner as former U.S. president Jimmy Carter did during his visit in May 2002.

Beautiful settings give diners the choice of inside dining with air conditioning or outside with romantic candlelight and relaxing sounds of dripping fountains, which encompass the patio. The ingredients of otherwise standard Cuban fare, is consistently concocted with a creative gourmet flare. The fish is excellent.

Furthermore, some of the wines and liquors offered at this *paladar* cannot be experienced anywhere else in Cuba.

Privacy is masterfully supported through the unique use of tiny bells located on each of the tables, which are tastefully tucked between potted trees and plants. Waiters and waitresses are out of sight, but readily appear at your every whim with a slight shake of the bell.

A. Houghton

The ever popular Casa de Lilliam's hours of operation are strict here, allowing time between lunch and dinner to restock and prepare fresh ingredients for the evening diners. And prices are still reasonable even though many have discovered this exquisitely quaint restaurant. Thus, reservations are a must even during the low season.

The owners acquired the house in 1987 and extensively re-modeled the 1937 property for two years. Lilliam was a former dress designer who has since embraced her perfectionist passion for the culinary arts, which was sparked from her childhood. Her husband, Luis, a chemical engineer is a perfect project manager and teammate. Together this duo has created a winning recipe for success that few others can match. This is the favorite restaurant of *Cuba Scuba* photographer (and father), William Houghton.

★★★★★

La Guarida
Concordia 418 e/Gervasio y
Escobar
Centro Habana, Cuba
Ph: 537-762-4940
Hours: 7pm – Midnight daily
Email: enriqueyode@hotmail.com

La Guarida is a fanciful retreat into history as visitors step through the antique door from an old narrow street of Havana. The crumbling, but beautiful building has three floors connected by six curved and worn marble stairs. These guide the visitor to three main diving rooms with high ceilings where tables are nestled around a gleaming petite kitchen. Movie props from the famous award-winning film "Strawberry & Chocolate" decorate the rooms. Locals simply refer to the restaurant by the film's Spanish name: "Fresa y Chocolate". Many families now live in the huge mansion that formally was home to just a single family of four. Much of the restaurant is kept original, with antique furniture and décor of picture collages of famous Cubans and icons- everyone from Fidel Castro and Ernest Hemmingway to an old legendary Cuban whose only claim to fame was that he actually died from laughing.

The food is excellent. Everything on the menu is tasty and of voluptuous portions. The side dishes are authentic. Appetizers are fun to share. This is a great place to take out-of-town guests for an original taste of Havana. Reservations occasionally must be made a week in advance and then re-confirmed by 4pm on the day of arrival. To be sure, guests can email ahead. The dining choice of the Queen of Spain, some suggest that this is arguably the best restaurant in Cuba.

Homemade ice cream on the street corner is a refreshing and cheap treat!

D. Tipton

★★★★★

La Esperanza
Calle 16 #105 e/ 1ra y 3ra
Miramar, Ciudad de la Habana,
Cuba
Ph: 537-202-4361
Hours: 7pm-11:30pm,
Closed Sundays

Located on the other side of the street from the Icimar hotel is a well-manicured entrance of La Esperanza. Guests arriving at night should note there is no lighted sign. Visitors are encouraged to ring the doorbell to begin their culinary experience. Once inside, echoes of vintage Benny Moore melodically set the tone as diners can have a cocktail and relax on a sofa surrounded by eclectic knick-knacks and books of Cuban art and architecture. Hungry visitors can focus directly on dinner by sitting outside under the vine-covered patio with romantic candlelight or inside in the charming dining area. It is not uncommon to encounter diplomats and

W. Houghton

Cuban celebrities dining at the next table.

Entice your appetites with the waiter's painstaking descriptions of chef Manolo's inventive recipes of house delicacies. Unique sauces will tantalize the taste buds. An especially enjoyable entrée is the house chicken, slowly cooked with red tomato, onion, garlic, rosemary, red wine and sprinkles of red chili peppers. The appetizers are original. Desserts are classic. And after dinner, the aged rum is complimentary. The anticipatory service and hospitality are genuine.

★★★★

La Casa
Calle 30 No 865 e/ 26 y 41
Nuevo Vedado
Ciudad de la Habana, Cuba
Ph: 537-881-7000

We couldn't agree more with Dining Out Guide to Havana: "A friendly, homey restaurant that has earned rave reviews in several international travel magazines, La Casa offers good food in a beautiful leafy indoor-outdoor patio. The lush atmosphere is enhanced with live turtles and alligators." Three fuchsia bougainvillea bushes and a lighted sign frame the entrance to La Casa. Once inside, prepare to be greeted by friendly Cuban smiles, spotless terrazzo floors, and Panasonic speakers that often whisper classical piano background music. The walls display photographs of famous 'gringos', including some members of the Kennedy family who dined here in the summer of 2001.

An excellent entrée is the tender roasted lamb, presented as a stew in wine sauce with mushrooms and green olives. The lamb is as tender and flakey as French Beef Burgandy. Portions are very healthy and

W. Houghton

may be enough to split with your dive buddy.

Lunch requires no reservations. However, for dinner, visitors would be advised to make reservations. Figoberto Ruiz Garcia and family have transformed their lovely home into a "must visit soon" *paladar*.

★★★★
Gringo Viejo
Calle 21 No. 454 e/ E y F
Vedado, Ciudad de la Habana, Cuba
Ph: 537-831-1946
Hours: Noon-11pm, Daily

This unmarked *paladar* is a local's delight! It is a unique window to genuine native culture. The only clue a tourist has of this restaurant is the polite doorman next to the polished wooden gate who greets visitors and guards their cars. After ringing the doorbell, the locked gates open, inviting diners downstairs to the quaintly lit dining room. Walls are adorned with pictures of the owner and famous Cubans. The center of the main dining room features a movie poster from an American film (Old

Gringo) starring Gregory Peck who holds a striking resemblance to the bearded owner, Omar.

The food is quite tasty with the authentic Cuban "corillo" flare. In English or Spanish, waitresses will happily give an account of the fresh concoctions of the day. Patrons rave over the "pollo a la cazuela", a popular chicken dish of the house. We especially enjoyed the red snapper, which was cooked to perfection with light seasonings.

Complete dinners are a bargain, ranging from five to eight dollars per plate. Gringo Viejo is a wonderful, air-conditioned, cozy *paladar* for mingling with indigenous traditions and for soaking up genuine Cuban energy!

★★★★
Vistamar
Avenida 1ra e/ 22 y 24, No. 2206
Miramar, Ciudad de la Habana, Cuba
Ph: 537-203-8328
Hours: Noon-Midnight, Daily

Located only two blocks west of the expensive state restaurant "Don Congrejo", Vistamar has better food, attentive service, and the same magnificent ocean view, but at half the price. This *paladar* was nearly destroyed by a hurricane and has been completely remodeled with stone tiled floors, fine porcelain vases, Cuban sculptures, and fertile potted plants. The artful paintings are of Cadaques, Spain where Salvador Dali liked to paint as a young boy. The second story balcony beckons diners to sit and enjoy the view of rolling waves where snorkelers like to swim. Even on hot days there is usually a cool ocean breeze with a refreshing mist.

Entrees are fulfilling. The seafood is fresh and deliciously prepared. The friendly staff speaks English well and is so considerate that smokers can barely pull out a cigar without waiters quickly offering to light it.

★★★★

Huron Azul
Humbolt No. 153 esq. P
Vedado, Ciudad de la Habana,
Cuba
Ph: 537-879-1691
Hours: Noon-Midnight, Daily

Huron Azul is the name of a Cuban television show about art and culture. The show and this *paladar* both derived their title from the name of the home of a famous Cuban artist, Carlos Enrique, who lived in the mountains. Carlos Enrique threw many parties with elegant feasts and wine that were attended by numerous literary geniuses and artists. The fantastic stories from Huron Azul are depicted in the paintings that cover the walls and corridors of the *paladar*. Part of the enjoyment of this restaurant is to have Juan Carlos, the owner, bring the legends to life through his anecdotes about the artwork.

The fresh fruit appetizers are sweetly ripened and tastefully arranged. Most everything on the menu is flavorsome. The 'puerco grunon' (pork) and the 'pescado pepperone' fish are wonderful choices. A full dinner with cocktails, appetizers, entrees with side dishes, desserts, wine, and coffee only totaled $16 per person. Furthermore, the restaurant even passes around complimentary cigars or lemon triple sec after dinner.

Huron Azul is also a nice place to go just for desserts and coffee. The presentation is marvelous and the portions are size-

W. Houghton

able. This *paladar* is also a pleasant spot for wine tasting of Spanish reds and whites, French champagne, Italian, Chilean, Australian, Portuguese, Cuban, and even Californian wines. The ambience is entertaining. The cool air conditioning is refreshing. However, ladies may want to bring a sweater just in case.

★★★★

La Chansonnier
Calle J #257 e/ 15 y Linea
Vedado, Ciudad de la Habana,
Cuba
Ph: 537-832-1576
Hours: Noon-Midnight, Daily

With an excellent word of mouth reputation, this obscure *paladar* is always busy. La Chansonnier is a favorite with many Havana restaurant reviewers. Since the place is also a *Casa Particular* (Private Bed & Breakfast), it is a very convenient location. Miriam Marques of the Chicago Tribune likes to stay here and take her meals whenever she writes stories about Cuba.

The old mansion is adorned with hand carved doors that invite patrons to come inside to enjoy the antique collection of clocks and furniture. As diners walk from the rouge living area trimmed in white fresco to the blue air-conditioned dining room, their senses are relaxed by fresh cut flowers that soak in crystal vases in every room.

The owner's son, Hector Martinez, recently studied in Paris where he perfected his skills of preparing French sauces. He imports mushrooms directly from France for his recipes. With substantial portions, deliciously fresh ingredients, good service and a clean home, this *paladar* is a great choice for authentic Cuban food with a French twist.

Calle Diez

Calle 10 No. 314, 3ra y 5ta Avenida
Miramar, Ciudad de la Habana
Ph: 537-209-6702
Hours: 11am-Midnight, Daily

Calle Diez's unassuming entrance is well-lit and easy to find. The thatched, open-air restaurant is located around the right side of the house. The bamboo and soft lighting create a pleasurable Caribbean atmosphere. Live music is an added touch in the evenings.

The aroma from meats grilling on an open pit is an appetizer in itself. The barbequed baby back ribs are the absolute best in Havana. The service is good and prices are reasonable. Frequent diners can sometimes receive a 20% discount.

State-Owned Restaurants

Joint venture restaurants or state owned restauarants that are interesting choices other than *paladares*:

El Aljibe

7ma. Avenida e/24 y 26, Miramar,
Ciudad de La Habana
Ph: 537-204-1583

El Aljibe is a very popular restaurant specializing in "all you can eat" roasted chicken and typical Cuban *Criolla* food.

Floridita

Calle Monserrate No. 557,
La Habana Vieja.
Ph: 537-833-8856

Floridita is the restaurant/bar made famous as Ernest Hemingway's favorite "watering hole."

Roof Garden

Hotel Sevilla, Calle Trocadero #55,
esq. Prado, Habana Vieja
Ph: 537-860-8560

Roof Garden had a very romantic view and features international food.

Jazz Café

Galerias Paseo
1 y Malecon, Vedado
Ph: 537-855-3170 ext. 121

Jazz Café has reasonable international fare served up with nice music and a good second floor view of the Malecon.

Getting There

This section offers divers business cards from the previously mentioned *paladares*. These cards, located on page 232, can be torn out and shown to taxi drivers to conveniently take guests directly to the restaurant. Independent and extremely adventurous visitors may also use the cards as a back up if they need to ask for directions when driving or walking to the *paladar*.

Insider's Tips

Taxi drivers and "street hustlers" often take a client directly to a restaurant of their own choice so that they can collect a 'finder's fee' from the restaurant. Some restaurants pay up to $5 per entrée or 20% of the meal price to the person who delivers clients. Unscrupulous guides may try to convince visitors not to follow our advice: "the restaurant is closed", "that *paladar* is too expensive", "it is too far away", etc. Nonsense! Most of our top-rated *paladares* pay no "commission" and rely solely on their reputation for great food at a good price to be successful.

For more dining choices, see the Appendix for Private Restaurants of Havana.

Five Star Hotels

The following 5 star hotels have good restaurants with decent service and good travel agents who can book diving and transportation anywhere on the island:

Melia Cohiba
(Cubanacan)
Avenida Paseo E/l.ra y 3 era,
Vedado
Ph: 537-833-3636

Lobsters are not available at "Paladares."

W. Houghton

Private homes downtown near elegant hotels.

D. Tipton

Melia Habana
(Cubanacan)
Ave. 3 E/76 y 80, Miramar
Ph: 537-204-8500

Nacional de Cuba
(Gran Caribé)
Calle O esq. 21, Vedado
Ph: 537-833-3564

Parque Central Habana
(Golden Tulip/Cubanacan)
Neptuno E/Pardo y Zulueta
Habana Vieja
Ph: 537-860-6627

Riviera
(Gran Caribé)
Ave. Malecon esq. 21
Vedado
Ph: 537-833-3733

Private Bed & Breakfasts of Havana

While all-inclusive hotels can be comfortable and convenient, they can sometimes be isolating from Cuban culture. There are many hotel chains in Cuba of various standards of luxury, depending on one's budget and lifestyle. Although some of the prices are reasonable, the attractively presented food can be quite mediocre in taste. In remote dive regions such as Isla de Juventud, Maria la Gorda, and other pristine cays, lodging alternatives can be limited. Yet, in Havana, visitors have a smorgasbord of choices.

Havana offers a multitude of delightful bed and breakfasts where guests can stay for about $30 per night and wake up to a homemade Cuban meal. These down to earth accommodations give guests the opportunity to experience the roots of Cuba and mingle with pleasant people in a safe environment. Do not miss this chance to establish life-long friendships! Furthermore, visitors can save tremendous money when they realize they do not have to spend: up to $250 per night plus $15 per breakfast at a hotel.

Cuba Scuba offers a selection of valued *casa particulars* based on cleanliness, location, air conditioning, spaciousness, privacy, protected parking, helpful service, and security. Most of these recommendations also offer divers the convenience of online reservations. Additional options are also listed in the appendix of Official Private Bed & Breakfasts of Havana (although not reviewed by *Cuba Scuba*). All display the blue and white triangle symbol that indicates they have been inspected by the government and pay the "room rental tax".

Divers can also visit www.cubascuba-the-book.com for more details or to post comments about their experiences.

Casa Blanca   D. Tipton

Casa Blanca
Calle 13 No. 917 e/
(between) 6 & 8, Vedado
Habana, Cuba
Ph: 537-833-5697
Email: CBL917@HOTMAIL.COM
http://WWW.CASPAR.NET/CASA/
Owner: Jorge Luis Duany,
Years in business: 7

This is where Amy (author) and her father stay whenever in Havana. Centrally located in a tree lined quiet neighborhood, Casa Blanca is only a few blocks from the 5-star hotels: Melia Cohiba and The Riviera and only one block from "John Lennon" park. Jorge and his mother, Mercedes, a former art professor, have decorated this quaint former 1920 city mansion with original Cuban art, incredible fake impressionist paintings, and colonial antique furniture. We jokingly refer to it as "Musee Duany." A half dozen excellent *paladares*, several night clubs, museums, theatre, cinemas, shopping center, and historical edifices are within walking distance. Casa

Blanca has been written up in nearly every Havana guidebook, as well as "Lonely Planet", "Insight", "Moon Travel" "Routard", "Le Petit Fute", "Panorama Travel" (an Italian magazine). There is always someone home to lend a helping hand. And no matter what time visitors arrive, the light is always on outside. For fenced off-street parking, clients are given a set of keys to the parking gate, the front door, the room door and room safe. There are two queen beds and a spotless bathroom, which are cleaned daily. Amenities include TV, VCR, CD player, air conditioning or ceiling fan. Nearly anything is possible here- all you have to do is ask. The customer service is first class because of Jorge's genuine "amistad" (friendship). This is the best value in Havana at only $30 per night and negotiable for extended stays. This very popular accomodation should be booked well in advance. If space is not available, Jorge, who is fluent in English and Spanish, can also make good arrangements at nearby *casa particulars*. This is a

W. Houghton

This symbol identifies the official "Casa Particulars" of Cuba.

great place to make lasting memories! Distance from Jose Martí airport is about 17 kilometers (30 minutes) and costs about $15 by taxi.

Aurora & Nelson Benitez
Calle 15 No. 962, Apt. 5,
entre 8 y 10, Vedado
Ph: 537-833-8659
Email: neymo@yahoo.com
http//www.geocities.com/
auroraynelson/
Years in business: 7

Ten blocks South of the Melia Cohiba, as the street rises to meet the monument of Jose Marti, is a modern building with a stone circular stair case entrance. At the crest of the hill on the third floor, the Benitez apartment commands a good view of central Vedado. Clients are greeted with a presence of musical instruments (piano and guitar) resting on stone terrazzo floors. Local original paintings decorate the interior walls. Nelson speaks English and is on the premises around the clock. Guests will be given a key to the home that will be shared with the Benitez family (including two children ages nine and sixteen). Listed in Italian Travel magazines, the apartment is in the middle of the historical district. Within a short walking distance are monuments, parks, night life, museums, and even a cigar emporium. Amenities include TV, VCR; receive only fax, air-conditioning, private bath, and private off-street protected parking.

Private Apartment
Owners: Sonia & Raisa
Linea & 4, No 812
(3rd floor), Vedado
Ph: 537-833-4434
Years in business: 5

This apartment is conveniently located near the Riviera and Cohiba Hotel. After climbing three winding stairways guests enter a spacious living room surrounded by

Cooling off in the Havana Harbor W. Houghton

enter a spacious living room surrounded by antique furniture from the Colonial period. This place offers an air-conditioned bedroom with a queen size bed and private bathroom/shower. The rooms are immaculately clean. This accommodation is a good value for $25 per night and includes amenities of TV, VCR, phone, CD and cassette player. The price is negotiable depending on length of stay. In addition to a private key, someone is always home. This place is a twenty-five minute taxi ride from the Jose Martí airport. Restaurants, bars, and a taxi stand are accessible by walking.

Colonial period antique furniture. The entrance to the apartment is through the owner's kitchen. This separate private apartment has a small, fully equipped, kitchenette/ bar, and dining room before entering the air-conditioned bedroom with king size bed and private bathroom/shower. The rooms are immaculately clean. This accommodation is a good value for $25 per night and includes amenities of TV, VCR, phone, ceiling fan, CD and cassette player. The price is negotiable depending on length of stay. In addition to a private key, someone is always home. This place is a twenty-five minute taxi ride from Jose Martí airport. Restaurants, bars, and a taxi stand are accessible by walking.

Private Apartment
Owners: Zoe y Rogelio
Linea & 4, No 812
(2do floor), Vedado
Ph: 537-833-4819
Years in business: 3

This apartment is conveniently located near the Riviera and Cohiba Hotel. After climbing two winding stairways, guests

Norma Labrada Diaz
Calle L # 314, 2nd floor,
between 19 & 21, Vedado
Ph: 537-832-9672
Years in service: 5

Only 11 blocks from the Malecon ocean drive, L Street rises to a small hill where this private room and bath are located. The

The famous "Hotel Inglatera" W. Houghton

Havana skyline   W. Houghton

room does not always need the air-conditioner due to the ocean breeze. Arriving for the first time creates a "fortress" effect. After ringing the bell near a huge wooden door, Norma (she speaks broken English, so try to practice your Spanish here) opens the second floor window to lower a basket on a rope to deliver the key. The entrance at the top of the spiral marble stairs welcomes guests to a clean, spacious, and well-ventilated apartment with a great view of the city. The exquisite porcelain tiled fireplace is surrounded by antique furniture and a porcelain elephant collection. Despite being located directly next to Coppelia Ice Cream park, and not far from the Habana Libre Hotel, this B&B offers a good night's sleep. The bedroom has two single beds. It is simple, comfortable, and clean, but the single bathroom is shared with Norma. The amenities are few (TV, a radio, no protected parking). Pets are welcome! The rate is $25 per night without breakfast.

For up to six divers
Martha Vitorte
Avenida de los Presidente, no. 301, esq 13 apto 14, Vedado
Ph: 537-832-6475
Martavitorte@hotmail.com
Years in business: 8

Three blocks south from the Hotel Presidente, an American construction company completed this modern high-rise apartment building in 1959. Martha, who retired from civil service after working in Havana's International Press Center, is well traveled throughout Cuba and is a wealth of information about Havana. Her apartment occupies the entire 14th floor and offers a 360 degree-panorama view of the entire downtown (including beautiful ocean vistas from the glass balcony/porch). Even though her apartment is popular with Americans (Martha is fluent with English), this B & B offers an interesting cosmopolitan mix of nationalities. This place would be an excellent accommodation for a group of up to six divers. Each bedroom has a private bathroom with tub/shower.

Laundry service is available. Secure parking is located below. Amenities include TV, VCR, Fax, answering machine, and air-conditioning. The bus stop is two blocks away. The taxi stand is within three blocks. Close by are major hotels, bars, nightclubs, dancing, historical buildings, paladares, and three museums. Rates are $35 per night per bedroom. The distance from Jose Martí airport is about 16k (about 25 minutes) and will cost approximately $15 for 3 people in a Panataxi. We have not stayed here, but a visual inspection and interview displayed a very clean and modern apartment with incomparable views. Martha's rooms have been mentioned as favorites in several guidebooks and international magazines.

A trusted Cuban friend of *Cuba Scuba* manages an Italian web site that arranges *casa particulares*. He personally inspects each *casa particular*, takes pictures with a digital camera, and posts them on a web site in which a diver can book a bed & breakfast, a bedroom, an apartment, or even an entire house! His best recommendations in Havana are as follows:

For two or four divers
Habana Vieja (Old Havana)
Apartment Name:
Suites Penthouse Manolo
Ph: 537-830-0208

It is rare to find decent rooms in the crumbling original old district of the city. On the 9th floor, with a view of the bay and El Morro fort preceded by the famous Malecon are two bedrooms (each with private bathrooms, air conditioning, and hot water) and a private entry. This is a private apartment of a Cuban family who will be happy to provide breakfast each day for $5.00 per person.

Each room costs $35 per night, but is negotiable for longer stays.

By night one can see the famous lighthouse across the bay at El Morro. Guests are within a few blocks from the Cristóbal Cathedral and 100 meters from el Paseo del Prado, one of the loveliest streets in Old Havana. One of the best *paladares* in Old Havana is La Guarida, however there are

Traditional cannons are fired once every night at the fort.   D. Tipton

not many other private restaurants nearby. The rest are "touristy" state run restaurants.

Amenities include two large terraces (each with a view of the bay), TV & VCR. There is no protected parking. The distance from the airport is about 20 kilometers (about $20 taxi ride).

This is a deluxe option for a pair of divers.
Ph: 537-830-0208
Miramar

This one room with a private entrance is only 50 meters from the ocean. The location is near two nice *paladares*: Vistamar and La Esperanza. It is also near the aquarium and the foreign embassies of Miramar. Amenities include a king size bed, air conditioning, private bathroom, pantry, and dining room. The owners will prepare breakfast for guests who also have the option to dine outdoors by the swimming pool. The cost is $40 per night, but for only $10 extra per night, the pool can be exclusive to guests for washing dive gear, enjoying a midnight skinny dip, or just sitting out and working on a sun tan! The ocean view is free. When the sea is calm, it is a very popular area for locals to snorkel. Breakfast is extra charge.

For a group of up to ten divers
Ph: 537-830-0208
House name: Casa Olga

Enjoy your own private seaside two-story home with 5 bedrooms for only $125 per night! Located 50 meters from the beach and just 300 meters from a shopping center, this completely furnished home is perfect for a dive group that wants to kick back and relax away from the crowds. West

Vistamar is located near a nice B & B. W. Houghton

day (approximately $50) and utilize the protected parking that is available. The two upper bedrooms have 2 French beds and share one bathroom with shower. The three ground floor bedrooms each has king size beds. The master bedroom has a master bathroom, but the other two lower bedrooms share a bathroom. The kitchen is fully equipped, and some guests arrange for a chef to prepare meals. Amenities include beach chairs, TV, phone and all rooms are air-conditioned.

of Havana by 25 kilometers this taxi ride requires $20 whenever divers wish to go to town. The best option is to rent a car by the

Sunset view from Havana's Malecon D. Tipton

Havana Salsa Clubs

No matter what day of the week, there is always a disco palpitating with hot Latin rhythms. I have never seen anything in the world like the nightclubs in Cuba. The dances in every club resemble choreography from the wildest Hollywood movies! Divers truly do not want to miss this experience. Most people go to the discos around 11pm. Although many discos rise and fall like the ebb and flow of the tides, some have flourished over the years. *Cuba Scuba* recommends a few clubs that will put a smile on your face and make you scratch your head in amazement at the way those Cubans can bend and twist every vertebrae in their trim bodies!

> La Tropicana
> Pizarra- 72
> No. 4504, Mnao
> Habana, Cuba
> Ph: 537-267-1717

The oldest outdoor nightclub in the world has beautiful dancers in elegant costume that perform a famous cabaret show. Tickets are expensive (around $60 per person), but it is a one-time experience in Havana.

> **La Casa de la Musica, Havana Vieja**
> Galimo between Concordia
> and Neptuno
> Habana Vieja, Cuba
> Ph: 537-862-4165

Recently opened in July of 2002, this is my all-time favorite disco club! A renovated old movie theatre has an elevated stage where famous, top-notch salsa bands play nightly in the heart of old Havana. Bands like Van Van and also Pupi y el Son Son have played here many times. The D.J. is the most famous D.J. on the island. The cover charge depends on who is playing and normally ranges between $10-$25 per person after 10pm. The band usually starts

La Casa de la Musica

W. Houghton

The Diving Guide to Cuba Scuba

around midnight. Often there is a pre-show with dancers or singers. Happy hour is from 4pm-8pm with a $5 cover charge.

La Casa de la Musica, Miramar
20 No. 3308
Miramar, Habana, Cuba
Ph: 537-204-0447
or 537-204-9898

This is a fun disco with good salsa bands and mirrors its namesake in old Havana.

El Café Cantante, Mi Habana
Paseo y Vedado
Habana, Cuba
Ph: 537-873-5713
or 537-879-0710

This is a quaint salsa club down in the basement of a building with bright disco lights. The cover is reasonable for groovin' live music. If this salsa club is too crowded, sometimes the lounge upstairs has live music as well. The setting is more intimate with plush couches and waiters who bring drinks to you.

Ma Cumba
Calle 222, esq. 37
La Coronela, La Lisa
Habana, Cuba
Ph: 537-833-0569
or 537-833-0568
Email:
gerencia@giralda.cha.cyt.cu

This club is about a 20-minute taxi ride outside of Havana. The setting is outdoors allowing for the soft breeze. The stage hosts good salsa bands. Many of the patrons here are tourists, but you can still catch a local flavor.

Salsa bands groove with Latin beat.   W. Houghton

La Casa de la Amistad
Pizarra- Paseo 406
Vedado, Habana, Cuba

This club has great live salsa music. There are plenty of tables and chairs to share a bottle of rum with friends. When the music moves you (and it will sooner or later), there is room to dance near the stage.

Las Zorra y el Cuevo
23 No. 155 Vedado
Habana, Cuba
Ph: 537-866-2402

This is a popular club, recommended by a Cuban friend of *Cuba Scuba*.

Habana Café
Cohiba Hotel
Habana, Cuba
Ph: 537-833-3636

Tourists enjoy the live music and atmosphere at this club.

HAVANA
El Salado, Blue Reef Dive Center

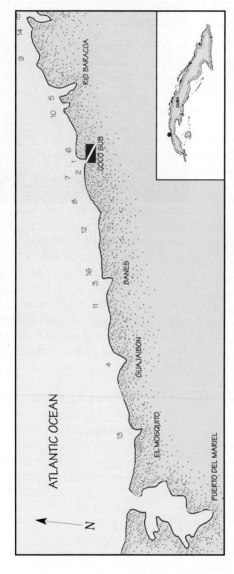

Dive Site		Depth
1.	Canal de la Chopa	15-50ft (5-17m)
2.	Canal de Viera	15-50ft (5-17m)
3.	Canal de Banes	20-70ft (7-23m)
4.	Canal de Guajaibon	20-70ft (7-23m)
5.	Baracoa	20-70ft (7-23m)
6.	Cabeza de La Cherna	100ft (33m)
7.	Pista de Ski	100ft (33m)
8.	Balcón	80ft (27m)

Dive Site		Depth
9.	Paraiso	100ft (33m)
10.	La Pared	Wall
11.	Orejones	80ft (27m)
12.	Cabeza de los Cajies	60ft (20m)
13.	Canal del Mosquito	15-50ft (5-17m)
14.	Entrada de la Bahía	80ft (27m)
15.	Cabeza de Santa Ana	50ft (17m)
16.	Los Tarugos	100ft (33m)

HAVANA
Marina Hemingway, La Aguja Dive Center

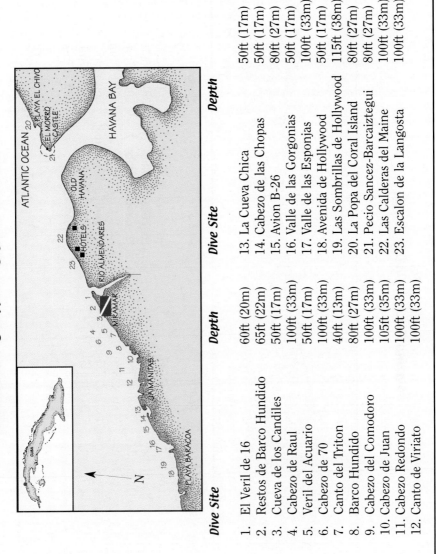

Dive Site — **Depth**

1. El Veril de 16 — 60ft (20m)
2. Restos de Barco Hundido — 65ft (22m)
3. Cueva de los Candiles — 50ft (17m)
4. Cabezo de Raul — 100ft (33m)
5. Veril del Acuario — 50ft (17m)
6. Cabezo de 70 — 100ft (33m)
7. Canto del Triton — 40ft (13m)
8. Barco Hundido — 80ft (27m)
9. Cabezo del Comodoro — 100ft (33m)
10. Cabezo de Juan — 105ft (35m)
11. Cabezo Redondo — 100ft (33m)
12. Canto de Viriato — 100ft (33m)

Dive Site — **Depth**

13. La Cueva Chica — 50ft (17m)
14. Cabezo de las Chopas — 50ft (17m)
15. Avion B-26 — 80ft (27m)
16. Valle de las Gorgonias — 50ft (17m)
17. Valle de las Esponjas — 100ft (33m)
18. Avenida de Hollywood — 50ft (17m)
19. Las Sombrillas de Hollywood — 115ft (38m)
20. La Popa del Coral Island — 80ft (27m)
21. Pecio Sancez-Barcaiztegui — 80ft (27m)
22. Las Calderas del Maine — 100ft (33m)
23. Escalon de la Langosta — 100ft (33m)

HAVANA
Marina Tarará, Diving Center

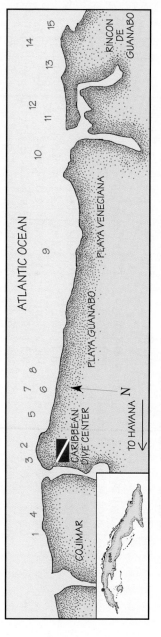

Dive Site — **Depth**

1. Punta Judio — 45ft (15m)
2. Canal Bacuranao — 30ft (10m)
3. Piedra Quebrada — 80ft (27m)
4. Cabezo del Medio — 115 (38m)
5. Campismo Celimarina — 100ft (33m)
6. Canal de Tarara — 20-60ft (7-20m)
7. Chalupa — 115ft (38m)
8. El Botiquin — 100ft (33m)

Dive Site — **Depth**

9. Canto Marazul — 100ft (33m)
10. Poza de Militar — 30-100ft 10-(33m)
11. Canto de Itabo — 50ft (17m)
12. Justiz — 100ft (33m)
13. Codillo de la Canal — 60ft (20m)
14. Herradura — 50ft (17m)
15. La Campana — 50ft (17m)

HAVANA
Puerto Escondido, Puerto Escondido Dive Center

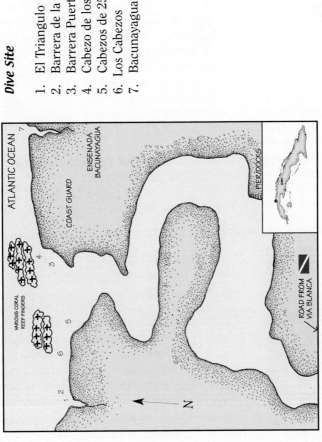

Dive Site

1. El Triangulo
2. Barrera de la Caleta
3. Barrera Puerto Escondido
4. Cabezo de los Perros
5. Cabezos de 25 meters
6. Los Cabezos
7. Bacunayagua

Depth

60ft (20m)
60ft (20m)
50ft (17m)
70ft (24m)
80ft (27m)
85ft (29m)
Wall

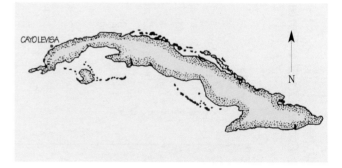

Pinar Del Rio Province

Cayo Levisa

Located in the Archipelago de los Colorados about 95 miles from Havana, Cayo Levisa's island stretches for two miles. Formed on a coral reef, Cayo Levisa has its own beautiful beach, and is the only key in this archipelago that has hotel accommodations. It is just 25 minutes by ferry boat from mainland.

The village hotel, Horizontes Cayo Levisa, is made up of 22 simple bungalows ranging from $55.00 to $81.00 per night. These bungalows were built with local material and have private bathrooms, satellite TV, and air conditioning. Each room is located on a ribbon of sand that overlooks the ocean. The restaurant is centrally located and mainly serves Cuban dishes. However, clients can order lobsters whenever they wish on the dive boat. Mojitos and other drinks are offered at the hotel bar. During surface intervals, divers can rent kayaks and explore unspoiled shorelines.

This nearly deserted key is like having your own semi-private island. Because divers share this *cayo* with only a handful of locals, the underwater landscape and coral reef

Wet your whistle at this cavern bar and disco near La Cueva del Indio.

W. Houghton

Cayo Levisa Dive Prices

Average price for one dive	$25.00
Average price for two dives	$45.00
Average price for a night dive	$35.00
Package of ten dives	$210.00

(No certification courses are offered here)

Cayo Levisa Rental Equipment Prices

Average price for an entire set	$20.00
Average price for only a BC jacket	$8.00
Average price for only a regulator	$8.00
Average price for mask/fins/snorkel	$5.00
Average price for a wetsuit	$8.00
Average price for a dive light	$5.00

There are 16 sets of rental equipment, which is of the Italian brand, Mares. The dive center also has two Bauer compressors, which fill their 50 tanks (both aluminum and steel).

are quite pristine, with soft corals and interesting seabeds. The dive center has been in operation for twelve years.

Dive Sites

Giant sponges, sea fans, black coral, walls, and platforms characterize the waters of Cayo Levisa. There are 23 dive sites ranging in depths from 24 feet (8 meters) to 105 feet (35 meters). On shallower dives, explorers can expect to see massive formations of brain coral and star coral, sea fans, sponges, surgeonfish, snappers, parrotfish, grunts, grouper, moray eels, and lobsters.

Deeper dives have large coral walls and platforms inhabited by various kinds of tropical fish, including queen angelfish, gray angelfish, grouper, barracuda, snappers, stingrays, eagle rays, and manta rays. (See dive map on pg. 75)

La Corona de San Carlos

Considered to be one of the more popular dive sites, this area is a long ridge with coral and sandy belts. Canyons, caves and holes are common to this region. There are opportunities to see families of stingrays and eagle rays at this site. Also, during the breeding season, divers can discover schools of various types of snapper. Grouper also seem to covet this site. This dive is for experienced divers.

Spiny lobster   W. Houghton

La Cueva de Lorenco

This dive site requires a 45-minute boat ride to reach the area. The depth begins at 60 feet (20 meters) and continues to 120 feet (40 meters). Divers can expect to see black coral, colorful red coral, grouper, snapper, lobsters, and sometimes little sharks and eagle rays. The average bottom time is 40 minutes plus a five-minute safety stop.

La Pequeña Groutta

A twenty-minute boat ride from shore, this site is named for its small cave. Two people can fit inside. It is well illuminated and does not require a dive light. The maximum depth is 75 feet (25 meters). Divers can expect to see brain coral, barracuda, moray eels, and many other fish.

Other sites local dive masters enjoy are: *La Espada del Pirata, El Infierno, and La Cadena Misteriosa*.

For more information on diving or to book a reservation contact:

> **Diving World**
> Ph: 537-866-6075
> Cayo Levisa, La Palma
> Fax: 537-833-1164
> Pinar del Rio, Cuba

Divers can also book with the concierge at any Horizontes hotel:
Hotel Capri: 537-833-3747
Panamericano Resort: 537-895-1010
Hotel Horizontes Vedado:
  537-833-4072
Hotel Deauville: 537-833-8812
Horizontes headquarters:
  23, No. 156 e/NYO
  Vedado, Cuba
  Ph: 537-833-4042

Insider's Tips

Three CMAS certified instructors work at the Village's Diving World center. There are two available dive boats for a total capacity of 28 divers. One boat is 45 feet long with two toilets. The other is 33 feet long. A full day of diving includes lunch and bottled water or soda. Dives are usually scheduled for 9:00am and 2:00pm. The nearest hyperbaric chamber is at Havana Naval Hospital. Water sports are available, including: sea kayaking, windsurfing, catamaran boating, and waterskiing.

Some people venture to the island for a day trip, but it is possible to stay overnight. Be sure to make advanced reservations because the "resort" has only 22 individual bungalows and is usually completely booked even in the low season. If you plan to dive Cayo Levisa, be sure to stay overnight because the day-trip ferry that leaves at 11:30am guarantees you will miss the morning dive. Furthermore, it is difficult (but not impossible) to reserve a space for diving in Cayo Levisa until you arrive on the island.

Butterfly fish often swim in pairs.   M. Mola

More than 200 species of coral can be found.   M. Mola

Closer to Cayo Levisa, Vinales (Pinar del Rio) is a good place to stay. A recommended *casa particular* is Mariana Grajales, 1 e/ Salvador Cisneros y Rafael Trejo. Email: CBL917@hotmail.com for assistance with reservations.

Getting There

A ferry boat runs from 10:00am to 5:00pm everyday. The Horizontes travel agency in Havana offers several options for travel to Cayo Levisa. Prices may vary. First option is a day trip to Cayo Levisa for $65.00/person. Everyday except for Monday, this trip begins at 8:00am. The price includes round-trip bus transportation from Havana to Palma Rubia, round-trip ferry transportation from Pinar del Rio to Cayo Levisa, a welcome cocktail, sailor's lunch and drink, snorkeling, free time on the beach, and a tour guide.

The second option at $129.00 per person, divers can take a helicopter day trip to Cayo Levisa. On Wednesdays and Saturdays, this trip begins at 7:30am and terminates at 5:00pm. The price includes round-trip transportation from Havana to Playa Baracoa airport, a round-trip helicopter ride from Havana to Cayo Levisa, 35 minute aerial tour of the mountains and valleys of Pinar del Rio, a welcome cocktail, snorkeling, sailor's lunch and drink, and free time at the beach. A 30% discount is given to children between the ages of 2 and 12.

For more information or to book a reservation to Cayo Levisa, divers can contact the Cayo Levisa Hotel at:

537-833-4238 or 537-866-6075

Divers can also contact the Horizontes agency at:

Trumpet fish

E. Macao

Agencia de Viajes Horizontes
Calle 23 # 156 E/N y O
Vedado, Cuba
Ph: 537-833-4042
537-833-4090
Fax: 537-833-3722
or 537-833-4361
E-mail:
silva@horizontes.hor.cma.net
or crh@horizontes.hor.tur.cu
Web site: www.horizontes.cu

For booking, divers also can go to Puertosol:

Puertosol, Casa Matriz
Calle 1 era #3001 a 30
Miramar, Playa,
Ciudad de La Habana, Cuba
Ph: 537-204-8563
Fax: 537-204-5928
Email: psolgen@psol.mit.tur.cu
Website: www.puertosol.net

Divers may want to rent a car or hire a private taxi to drive to Cayo Levisa. From Havana, divers should travel westward along the mountains on the north shore to the small island. The narrow road is filled with potholes and weaves through small mountain villages. It is about a two-hour drive to the ferryboat, which departs at 11:30am to Cayo Levisa. The ferry returns to the mainland every day at 5:00pm.

While driving back from Cayo Levisa, there are charming areas such as La Cueva del Indio (Indians' Cave), which has an underground river where visitors can take boat rides. Lunch with traditional music is available. Hours are from 11am to 5pm. The location is on km 38 highway to Puerto Esperanza, Vinales.

Also very interesting is the disco in a cave, called Las Cuevas de Jose Miguel. After driving through the countryside, visitors can take a rest and enjoy a Coke. Or, a little later in the evening you can dance at the disco.

Incognito stingray

M. Mola

Crystaline seas in Cuba offer good visibility.

D. Tipton

CAYO LEVISA
Diving World Dive Center

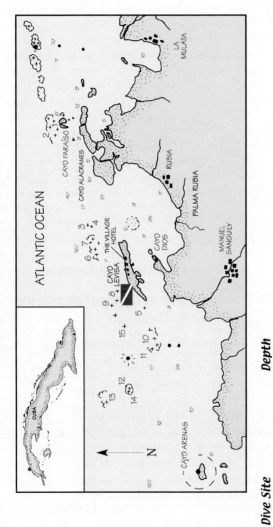

Dive Site   ### Depth

1. La Cadena Misteriosa   40ft (13m)
2. La Espada del Pirata   60ft (20m)
3. El 7-15   50ft (17m)
4. La Pequeña Groutta   80ft (27m)
5. La Boya Roja   40-130ft (13-43m)
6. La Canal   40-130ft (13-43m)
7. El Arco de Ludovico   40-130ft (13-43m)
8. El Milagro   40-130ft (13-43m)
9. Las Uvas   25-80ft (9-27m)
10. Los Cuernos del Alce   Wall
11. El Hueco de Lorenzo   Wall
12. El Infierno   Wall
13. Los Mogotes de Viñales   40-130ft (13-43m)
14. Los Gangilones   20-65ft (7-22m)
15. La Corona de San Carlos   40-130ft (13-43m)

Maria la Gorda

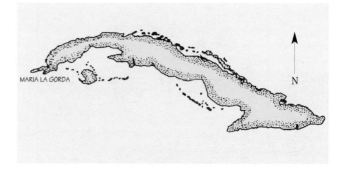

Pinar Del Rio Province

Maria la Gorda (Fat Mary)

Known for its spectacular wall diving, this region is claimed to be named after a young woman captured by pirates and abandoned at Bahía de Corrientes. Apparently the emotional trauma of being kidnapped and discarded led to Miss Mary's plumpness.

This is Fidel Castro's favorite getaway.

W. Houghton

Maria la Gorda's International Diving Center is located in Corrientes Cape in the westernmost province of Cuba known as Pinar del Rio. This diver's retreat is one of Fidel Castro's favorite underwater playgrounds. Understandably so, as the remote, pristine coral gardens are fantastic. The area was declared a world reserve of the biosphere and rivals the diving in the Cayman Islands.

After a $3^{1}/_{2}$ to $4^{1}/_{2}$ hour drive, 190 miles from Havana on mostly gravel roads, divers arrive at the area's only hotel, Villa Maria la Gorda. This hotel is more like a quaint diver's village. The hotel rooms are similar to individual apartments. There are 55 rooms at the villa owned by Puertosol. There have been recent renovations to include 20 new bungalows. These comfortable rooms include a TV, safety deposit box, mini-bar, private bathroom, and air conditioning. Incidentally, you will grow to love your air conditioning and your bug-bomb when thousands of mosquitos come stalking after sunset.

The food is served buffet-style. Be prepared to shell-out $10.00 for breakfast and $15.00 for dinner, unless you buy an American package (AP) from a travel agency in Havana. The AP is much less expensive than the "à la carte" meals. The food is average. There is a bar near the front desk that serves sandwiches for lunch. You may want to bring some snacks and drinks along.

The bar sometimes doubles as a night-club. Most of the workers and divemasters frequent this bar in the evenings. There is salsa music and a small outside dance floor to practice your moves. Be sure to lather on the insect repellent if you plan on going.

The beach at Maria la Gorda is exquisitely quiet and uninhabited. Its peacefulness is magnified by vacant hammocks, which bridge many palm trees together. Looking at this picturesque scene beckons divers to leave their busy work life to come here and relax.

Maria la Gorda's underwater world is characterized by an abundance of coveted black coral, antique anchors and cannons, extensive walls, spotted with sponges and bright corals. Fish life here is full of barracuda, snapper, and tropical reef fish. Larger creatures such as eels, rays, turtles and whale sharks also inhabit this great diving treasure.

Diving begins at 9:00 in the morning. Just after breakfast, divers begin taking their gear to the 55-foot dive boat at the end of the pier complete with an in-house doctor who monitors clients' blood pressure. After the first dive, the boat makes a return to the village for lunch. The second dive begins at 3:00 in the afternoon. If you plan to dive more than one day, you can leave your gear on the boat. There is an

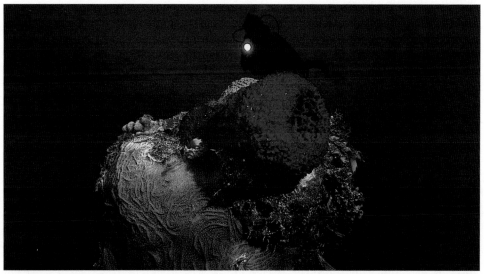

M. Mola

Maria la Gorda

M. Mola

Lobster migration

additional 41-foot boat that serves as both a dive boat and a fishing boat depending on the desires of the clientele.

The diving center has two Bauer compressors, which fill approximately 40 aluminum tanks and 48 steel tanks.

Dive Sites

There are over 50 dive sites, many of which are a two to five-minute boat ride from the beach. All sites are less than one hour's travel by boat, and located within the limits of a marine preserve known as the Peninsula de Guanahacabibes. Maximum depths for these dives range from 15 feet (5 meters) to 99 feet (33 meters). Water temperature runs from 78 degrees Fahrenheit to 82 degrees Fahrenheit. Visibility is excellent all year round, averaging 80-feet of clarity. There is great diving here.

Divers can expect to experience caves, large canyons, tunnels, and of course walls. There is also the opportunity to visit a sunken Spanish galleon. Marine inhabi-

Maria la Gorda Dive Prices

Average price for one dive	$30.00
Average price for two dives	$57.00
Average price for a night dive	$35.00
Average price for a wreck dive	$35.00
Average price for a resort course	$20.00
Average price for open water course	$300.00
Average price for a package of dives	$200.00
(Includes 10 dives)	
Average price for snorkeling	$5.00
(Includes boat ride to the reef)	

Rental Equipment Prices

Average price for entire set per day	$15.00
Average price for only a BCD jacket	$5.00
Average price for only a regulator	$5.00
Average price for masks/fins/snorkel	$5.00
Average price for only a dive light	$5.00
Average price for only a wetsuit	$5.00

The brands of rental equipment are Spirotechnique and Technisub. There are about 15 full sets of rental equipment.

tants include snappers, schoolmasters, bar-racuda, lobsters, morays, crabs, jacks, stingrays, eagle rays, and manta rays. (See dive map on pg. 83):

Ancla del Pirata

This dive site was named after an an-chor from the eighteenth century. It was found here, weighing over two tons. The anchor lies in 33 feet (11 meters) of water and about 30 minutes by boat away from the village. This antique anchor is covered with coral life and small tropical fish. Beautiful sponges also accompany this site. On occasion, divers can see roaming fish such as angelfish, snappers, squirrelfish, and barracuda.

M. Mola

Paraiso "Perdito"

This site's average depth is 66 feet (22 meters), although divers can go as deep as 100 feet (33 meters). The top of the reef begins at 66 feet (22m) but slowly slopes into a drop-off. A wild bouquet of corals, with tube and basket sponges, are all color-fully intertwined on this wall. Lobsters and crabs find crevices and intricate holes in this flavorful scene. Other neighbors include snappers, surgeons, black durgons, small groupers, and many types of angelfish.

Yemayá

Named after the Cuban Santería Saint Yemayá, Goddess and Protector of the Sea, this site is enchanting. Divers enter through a porthole of a cave in 96-feet (32-meter) of water. It is seemingly guarded by tarpon. Divers ascend through this cave to about 48 feet (16 meters). Be sure you have a flashlight for the dive.

El Almirante

Dive masters attest to having seen a whale shark in this area. The wall begins at 78 feet (26 meters), continuing to drop into the cobalt blue. Black coral and brilliant sponges shoot up from everywhere along the wall. Small tropical fish can be found closely hovering above the coral. Angelfish, tarpon, and grouper inhabit the outer waters.

Las Tetas de Maria

The name "Mary's Breasts" commonly refers to the two rock developments on the cliffs that jut out into the ocean. If you look from the beach at Maria la Gorda you can see these cliffs off of Punta Caiman. This dive site sports many coral fingers with sandy channels in between coral heads. Divers can reach these corals in 66 feet (22 meters) of water. Many species of both hard and soft corals are located at this site, providing good opportunities for photographs. Small tropical fish include yellowtail snappers, angelfish, parrotfish, and sea bass.

El Faraon

"The Pharaoh" refers to a mammoth coffee colored barrel sponge. Standing nearly 6 feet high, this sponge appears as the mother to many smaller basket sponges, which are huddled around her. Divers can see this "Pharaoh" at about 66 feet (22 meters). Amberjacks, small grouper, and other fish may also be seen here.

El Salon de Maria

El Salon, or "the hall" is a cave characterized by its sponges and coral formations beginning at 60 feet. It is located 10 minutes away from Maria la Gorda by boat. Divers may enter it from one of three entrances. The bright purple, pink, blue and green coral decorations greet divers. The cave is home to a number of tropical fish as well as many corals and sponges.

For more information on diving or to book a reservation contact:

Diving Center of Maria la Gorda
Cabo Corrientes, Sandino,
Pinar del Rio, Cuba
Ph: 538-277-1306
Fax: 538-277-8077
Email: mlagorda@ip.etecsa.cu

Insider's Tips

Whale shark season is during the latter part of summer and early autumn. With considerable luck, divers can spot these beautiful creatures in the waters off the coast of Maria la Gorda. Schools of dolphins and tuna occasionally swim through this same area.

Snorkelers can enjoy the coastline of Maria la Gorda's beach for free. Divers may also enjoy this opportunity for snorkeling during the afternoons between dive excursions, but are not permitted to make unaccompanied beach dives.

The diving center employs six instructors, who are all CMAS, and ACUC, certified. The center has a diving capacity for up to 100 divers per day, but usually there are never more than 35 at a time.

The nearest hyperbaric chamber is in Havana and for this a helicopter service is provided. The chamber can be reached by helicopter in one hour.

Above the Water

Besides scuba diving, the only other activity Maria la Gorda offers is sport fishing. For more details, see the *Cuba Handbook*, by Christopher P. Baker.

Getting There

Divers can book a package trip to Maria la Gorda through any Puertosol agencies or travel agencies located in a few major hotels around the island. If you plan to be in Havana, the Hotel Nacional and Havana Libre are two hotels that book trips to Maria la Gorda.

"Lola" enjoys visiting with divers.

M. Mola

For direct booking, divers can go to Puertosol. The address is:

> Calle 1 era #3001 a 30
> Miramar, Playa,
> Ciudad de La Habana, Cuba
> Ph: 537-204-5923
> Fax: 537-204-5924
> Email: comerc@psol.mit.tur.cu
> Website:
> www.Puertosol.cubaweb.cu

Or divers can contact the concierge at the five-star **Melia Cohiba Hotel** at:

> Ph: 537-833-3636
> Fax: 537-833-4555
> Email: jef_rec_mic.cohiba1
> @solmelia.cma.net

Maria La Gorda is a breeding ground for sea turtles.

M. Mola

MARIA LA GORDA
Maria La Gorda Dive Center

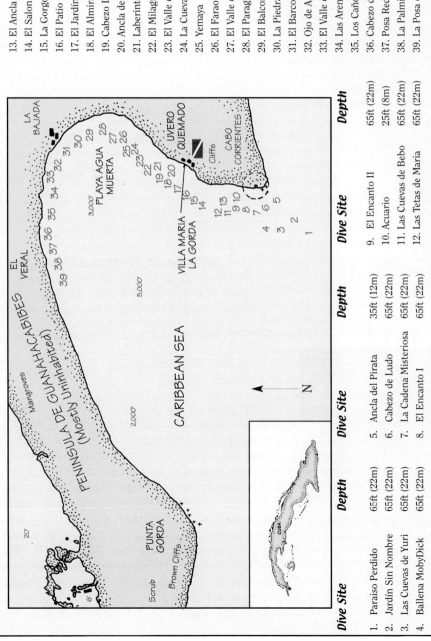

Dive Site		Depth
13.	El Ancla de Francois	45ft (15m)
14.	El Salon de Maria	100ft (33m)
15.	La Gorgonia	45ft (15m)
16.	El Patio de Vanessa	45ft (15m)
17.	El Jardin de la Gorgonia	50ft (17m)
18.	El Almirante	100ft (33m)
19.	Cabezo De Marcel	100ft (33m)
20.	Ancla de Masaya	15ft (5m)
21.	Laberinto	65ft (22m)
22.	El Milagro	70ft (24m)
23.	El Valle de Coral	70ft (24m)
24.	La Cueva Misteriosa 40-140ft (14-47m)	
25.	Yemaya	50ft (17m)
26.	El Faraon	50ft (17m)
27.	El Valle de las Esponjas	50ft (17m)
28.	El Paragua de Maria	50ft (17m)
29.	El Balcon del Caribé	50ft (17m)
30.	La Piedra Blanca	50ft (17m)
31.	El Barco Hundido	20ft (20m)
32.	Ojo de Agua de Juan Carlos	50ft (17m)
33.	El Valle de las Viñales	50ft (17m)
34.	Las Arenas Tenebrosas	50ft (17m)
35.	Los Cañones Silenciosos	50ft (17m)
36.	Cabezo de Rosendo	50ft (17m)
37.	Posa Redonda	50ft (17m)
38.	La Palmita	50ft (17m)
39.	La Posa de los Negritos	50ft (17m)

Dive Site		Depth
1.	Paraiso Perdido	65ft (22m)
2.	Jardín Sin Nombre	65ft (22m)
3.	Las Cuevas de Yuri	65ft (22m)
4.	Ballena MobyDick	65ft (22m)

Dive Site		Depth
5.	Ancla del Pirata	35ft (12m)
6.	Cabezo de Ludo	65ft (22m)
7.	La Cadena Misteriosa	65ft (22m)
8.	El Encanto I	65ft (22m)

Dive Site		Depth
9.	El Encanto II	65ft (22m)
10.	Acuario	25ft (8m)
11.	Las Cuevas de Bebo	65ft (22m)
12.	Las Tetas de Maria	65ft (22m)

La Isla de la Juventud

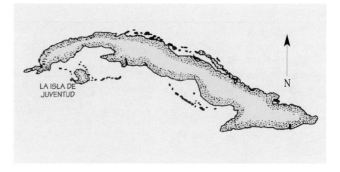

LA ISLA DE JUVENTUD

N

Isla De La Juventud Province

This small island located off the Southwest of Cuba's mainland has had many names, including The Isle of Parrots, The Isle of Treasure, The Isle of Pines, and of course, The Isle of Youth. The island itself consists of about 3,050 square kilometers and is home to a mere 70,000 people, most of whom live in Nuevo Gerona, the only consequential town located on the northeastern side.

Forty-five minutes away from little Nuevo Gerona lies an untarnished, divers' colony. In fact, the hotel is named "Hotel Colony". Established in the 1950's just 23 days before the defeated Fulgencio Batista fled the country, this hotel has been transformed into a diver's hideaway. The diving is some of Cuba's finest and has been a site for several international underwater photography competitions.

Climbing for coconuts

W. Houghton

It is important to keep in mind that the scuba diving is the main attraction of Hotel Colony. While some books have boasted about the facility, this two-story hotel is really nothing special. There are 77 air-conditioned rooms with color-television hosting American stations, telephone, refrigerator, radio, and private bathrooms. There is a saltwater pool, but sometimes it is drained. There is no elevator, so you may want to consider either asking for a room on the first floor or leaving a small tip at the front desk for assistance to take luggage up to the second floor. The good news is that heavy renovations are scheduled soon. During the low season, usually summertime, a double room with breakfast costs approximately $38.00, with lunch $72.00, and with dinner $86.00. In the high season, one should figure about $20.00 more for each price. (Non-divers can stay at the hotel for about ½ the cost.) The food is mediocre, consisting of three options: Creole beef (an over-glorified name for noodles with a spaghetti meat sauce), fish (that tastes very fishy), or pork. Side dishes are included which usually are: black beans and rice, boiled potatoes and salad (which is really fresh-chopped tomatoes and cucumbers). Dessert is a small sliver of flan and a cookie. If you would like to finish your meal with coffee, be prepared to pay extra. The entire meal costs between $12-$16 on the à la carte plan.

At the end of a 700 foot-long pier, The Mojito Bar offers MUCH better food for a little cheaper price. When the bar is open, menu options consist of grilled lobster for $20, roasted chicken for $10, ham and cheese sandwich for $3.00, or a chicken sandwich for $3.50. Daiquiris and frozen drinks go for about $2.50 and Cuban beer or rum is about $1.50. Soft drinks are $1.

If you plan to stay more than a couple of days, it is a good idea to bring your own snack foods, drinks, or liquor because there are no convenience stores anywhere. Likewise, transportation to Nuevo Gerona is rare and expensive. Due to the seclusion of the Colony, clients are subject to inflated prices on food and beverage. Also, renting dive equipment can be very expensive. If you do not have your own gear, it

Punta Francis is a marine protected area.

M. Mola

is advisable to rent equipment before arriving at Hotel Colony. It is cheaper to stop in Nuevo Gerona to pick up these amenities prior to making the journey to the Colony.

Diving begins in the morning. Divers are asked to meet in the hotel lobby at 8:30 am to fill out release forms. Be sure to have your c-card and your dive gear with you. When the registration process is finished, a 20-passenger bus transports divers to the marina. More than 20 people are allowed to squeeze onto the bus, so it could be cramped quarters. The Siguanea Marina, owned by Puertosol, is about 2 minutes from the hotel.

Once at the marina, divers will be assigned to a boat and asked to assemble their weight belts. It may be a good idea to keep one extra weight in case you dive with an aluminum tank rather than a steel tank (the latter of which most divers use in Cuba). There are 13 dive boats operating with a maximum capacity of 12 persons each. There is also one 65-foot live-aboard with a maximum capacity of 8 people, which travels beyond the wall. It is equipped with a compressor, 2 electricity generators for 220 or 110 voltage, air conditioning, TV, and music. The price for the live-aboard depends on the amount of fuel used and the number of days on the boat. Divers interested in booking a trip on this live-aboard should fax the Hotel Colony at 53-619-8420 to obtain prices and information.

All boat dives are made at Punta Frances, a protected marine area. Depending on which dive boat the diver is assigned, he/she will arrive to the Punta Frances dock in about 1 hour and 1½ hours. Snorkelers disembark here. Then, the boat travels to the dive sites, which are

M. Mola

all located five minutes from the dock at Punta Frances. The first dive begins around 10:15, and serves as a checkout dive. The divemaster will assess each diver to determine his/her level of experience. Later the boat returns to the dock for lunch at the Ranchon restaurant, which sits on the end of the dock. Lunch is buffet style and costs between $10-$12. If the diver is doing a wreck dive, usually lunch is served on the boat because wreck sites take a little longer to reach. During summer months there are opportunities to see an occasional whale shark in this area.

After your stomach is full and your blood is free from nitrogen, the second dive begins around 2:00 o'clock. The boat then returns to the dock one last time to pick up snorkelers and shoves off for the harbor. Divers can expect to arrive back at the harbor around 4:45. If you plan to dive several days, there is a room in which to leave your dive gear at the harbor.

Usually you will see military officers at the harbor. They are responsible for tracking the number of persons on each boat.

The same number of persons that go out of the harbor, must come back. These officers are stationed at all harbors and check all boats.

La Isla de la Juventud
Dive Prices

Average price for one dive	$30.00
Average price for two dives	$50.00
Average price for night dive	$45.00
(Includes dive light)	
Average price for wreck dive	$40.00
(Plan on 2 hours in the boat to get to the wreck)	
Average price for snorkeling	$8.00
(For boat ride to snorkel off of Punta Frances)	

Rental Equipment Prices

Average price for entire set of equipment per day	$15.00
Average price for only a BCD jacket per day	$10.00
Average price for only a regulator per day	$10.00
Average price for only a wetsuit per day	$10.00
Average price for mask, fins, and snorkel per day	$6.00

The brands of rental equipment are: Cressi-Sub (Italian) and Spiro-Sub (French). There are 20 full sets of rental equipment.

There are two Bauer compressors and one Canadian compressor at the marina. They can fill 100 tanks in an hour. There are also 362 tanks, of which 50 are American aluminum tanks received in 1999.

Dive Sites

There are 55 dive sites located off of Punta Frances, which was declared a Protected Area (P.A.) in 1996. However, if fish life seems a little sparse, it may be because local licensed fisherman are allowed to fish the preserve during the months of April and May. Buoys 1-34 are deep dives with bottom time not to exceed 45 minutes, and the maximum depth must not exceed 120 feet. Bottom time at these buoys is normally one hour. Wind is almost always from the west, which allows for about 305 good days for diving per year. Year-round visibility runs between 150ft-225ft (50m-75m). Water temperature ranges from 75 degrees Fahrenheit in the winter to 82 degrees Fahrenheit in the summer. All of the dive sites should have buoys. Yet, during the past two years, less than half of the buoys have remained intact.

Divers can expect to see a wide range of notable underwater landscapes, including tunnels, valleys, drop-offs, canyons, caves and grottoes. The corals and sponges are exquisitely shaped, healthy, and colorful. The interspersed marine animals consist of stingrays, eagle rays, manta rays, sea turtles, barracuda, lobsters, shrimp, crabs, grouper, snapper, grunts, spadefish, jacks, schoolmasters, hogfish, angelfish, snooks, parrotfish, tarpon, glassfish, and other small tropical fish species. Occasional nurse and reef sharks can be seen. Dive masters attest to also having seen lemon, bull, hammerhead, and whale sharks. If you fancy sunken ships, there are about seven buoyed wreck sites. (See dive map on pg. 93):

Cueva Azul

This dive is usually the first dive of the day due to its maximum depth of 126 feet (42 meters). There is little or no current. Divers can see three types of bottom here: reef, sand, and open sea. The site has two caves usually occupied by tarpon fish. Divers usually enter the cave through what appears to be a hole in the coral rock. Once inside, you are greeted by tarpon. Divers exit the tunnel to an outer wall. Other marine residents include glassfish, barracuda, morays, lobster and black coral. Total dive time is estimated as 45 minutes. This is one of, *Cuba Scuba* photographer, Manuel Mola's favorite dives in Cuba.

Reino Magico

The reef begins at 30 feet (10 meters) and then continually drops to 6,000 feet (2,000 meters) or more into the blue abyss. Divers descend to 99 feet (33 meters) to find three caves. Divers enter the first cave and swim through a connecting tunnel to a second cave in 114 feet (38 meters) of water. Upon exiting the second cave divers may swim to the last cave and then begin their ascent. Total dive time is about 45 minutes.

Pasaje Escondido

Divemasters will bring only experienced divers here after they have had the opportunity to dive with them for two or three days. This dive is a multi-level dive.

Divers drop into the water to 99 feet (33 meters) and navigate around a large coral rock formation before swimming into a tunnel. After exiting this tunnel, divers swim over another large coral formation to enter a second tunnel at 118 feet (36 meters). Divers ascend to make a safety stop. Maximum bottom time is about 40 minutes.

La Pared de Coral Negro

The name of this dive site is derived from the plentiful growth of black coral. The wall's beloved black coral can be found in 105 feet (35 meters) of water. There are about twenty black coral plants in all. Green, blue, red, purple, and yellow tube sponges also inhabit the wall. There are many gray sponges in the form of cups. The trained eye of a diver can see covert morays. There are some opportunities to see parrotfish, yellow-tailed snappers and other small tropical fish. On average, the duration of the dive lasts 45 minutes.

Red lipped bat fish

M. Mola

El Valle de las Rubias

This site is referred to as the Valley of the Blondes. No, there are no beautiful blonde women down there, but there are thin sandy channels on the sea bottom accompanied by coral formations. This is a shallow dive with a maximum depth range of about 36 feet (12 meters). Small groupers and sea bass can be detected as they dart in and out of coral fingers. Dive masters may warn you of poisonous scorpionfish, which are often difficult to spot because they camouflage themselves. Average bottom time is about an hour.

El Sitio de Todos

This dive site is a shallow dive with a maximum depth of 45 feet (15 meters). The site is often visited on the second dive after Cueva Azul because of the closeness in proximity. This area has a little bit of everything; hence the name. Divers can expect to see sea fans, bright sponges, all types of coral, small crabs, and many different small tropical fish species. Average bottom time is an hour.

Esparta / Jibacoa

These two wrecks are located in the most northern part of the Punta Frances Marine Preserve near the Los Indios dive site. It will take the boat about one hour to reach this site from the dock at Punta Frances. In order to save time, divers usually dive this area, eat lunch on-board, and then do a second dive in the vicinity. The Esparta was a military ship and the Jibacoa a cargo ship. They were scuttled in 1963 for practice by the military. Both wrecks rest in about 24 feet (8 meters) of water. You can see part of the Jibacoa jutting up through

Tarpon   M. Mola

the surface of the ocean. While the large ships tower over little tropical fish, brightly colored corals and sponges form a blanket over the dilapidated frames of these vessels. The average bottom time is about one hour.

El Cabezo de las Isabelitas

This site is recommended as a good opportunity for photographers. Descending from the buoy, divers reach a large number of coral outcroppings surrounded by sand. Tropical fish swim around star, lettuce leaf, and brain coral heads. As divers approach the wall, the topography of the underwater terrain becomes more rugged with a greater density of marine life such as snappers, goatfish, parrotfish, hamlets, angelfish and trumpet-fish. The colorful green-tip anemones share the coral heads with tube and vase sponges.

La Cueva de Leclere

Snorkelers, this is for you! Named after the French pirate Francois Leclere, this cave is accessible by snorkeling into an opening in the rocks just down the beach at Punta Frances. Legend describes Leclere as a pirate with a wooden leg who used to hide in this cave to surprise unsuspecting passing ships. It is said that he buried his treasure here. Upon entering the cave, one can crawl onto the sand and view an ancient drawing carved into the ceiling. Most recently the cave has been named "La Cueva del los Alemanes" (Cave of the Germans) because, besides local Cubans who have visited this cave, the only other foreigner to see it was a German man... until now. For more information, or to book a reservation contact **Celino Rives Amador**, manager of Agronomy, Ecology, and Botany of Punta Frances at:

> Calle 4 No 3125 % E Y D
> Rpto. Micro- 70
> Nueva Gerona, Isla de la Juventud
> Ph: 537-832-2129
> Email: cmictij@ceniai.inf.cu
> (Make sure you address it to
> Celino Rives)

Insider's Tips

A hyperbaric chamber is located in the Siguanea harbor. It has two compartments and holds up to four people simultaneously. It can simulate up to 300 feet (100 meters). One doctor and a technician are always on call to operate the chamber.

November, December, January, June, July, and August are usually the busy diving

Marine Iguanas inhabit Isla de la Juventud and Cayo Largo.

D. Tipton

seasons for Hotel Colony. During these months there are 50 divers per day on average. In past years, the month of October has had hurricanes. May is usually the rainy season.

A CMAS open-water course (the French organization equivalent to PADI) is offered, which mandates one day of instruction in a pool and two days of open water instruction. Seventy-five percent of the instructors speak English.

Deep-sea fishing and water safaris are also offered through Puertosol's Marina. For more information on fishing and diving or to book a reservation contact:

> **El Colony**
> Parque Nacional Marino
> Punta Frances
> Carretera Siguanea, Km 42
> Isla de la Juventud, Cuba
> Ph: 536-19-8181
> Fax: 536-19-8420
> Email:
> gergomcerc@colony.gerona.inf.cu

For information and reservations, divers can also contact Puertosol Headquarters in Havana at:

Puertosol
Calle 1ra No. 3001 Esquina a 30
Miramar, Cuba
Ph: 537-204-5923
Fax: 537-204-5928
Email: comerc@psol.mit.ter.cu
Website:
www.puertosol.cubaweb.cu

Above the Water

Special attractions on land in Nuevo Gerona include: The Model Prison Museum, where Fidel Castro was imprisoned; El Abra, the house of José Martí; Villa Gaviota, which has the best Cuban disco on the island; and Playa Bibijagua, a black sand beach frequented by many locals. Horse and buggy is the cheapest and most fun way to travel around this town. For more details see the *Cuba Handbook* by Christopher P. Baker.

Getting There

Divers can book through any Puertosol agency located in prominent hotels of Havana. Airplane tickets must be purchased from Cubana Airlines on Rampas St. The tickets cost about $22.00 each way. Prices can vary.

Rooms and meal packages can be purchased at any Cubatur agency in major hotels. Havanatur can also book the hotel packages and even confirm the airline ticket on Cubana Airlines. However, divers are still required to pay for and pick up the airplane ticket at Cubana on Rampas Street.

There is also an airline called Aero Taxi, which books flights for about $50.00 each way from Havana to Gerona, Isla de Juventud. Flights depart daily at 11:15am. Children under 12 can fly for $37.50 each way. Reservations can be made at:

Aero Taxi (Inter/Lacsa office)
Lobby Hotel Habana Libre
Ph: 537-866-2703/537-866-2728
Fax: 537-833-3728/537-833-7996

Reservations also can be booked directly through the airport at :
Ph: 537-845-1024

Nassau grouper peeks at divers along the wall. M. Mola

Isla de Juventud has a myriad of vivid sponges.

M. Mola

ISLA DE LA JUVENTUD
El Colony Dive Center

Dive Site	Depth
1. Pared de Coral Negro	50ft (17m)
2. Valle de los Guacamayos	50ft (17m)
3. El Hueco	50ft (17m)
4. Tunel del Amor	50ft (17m)
5. Paraiso de las Esponjas	40ft (14m)
6. El Mirador	50ft (17m)
7. Cueva Azul	40ft (14m)
8. Salon Maravillosos	45ft (15m)
9. El Escondito del Buzo	40ft (14m)
10. Cueva del Misterio	40ft (14m)
11. Cueva del Ensueño	40ft (14m)
12. Reino Mágico	40ft (14m)
13. El Crater	50ft (17m)
14. El Pasaje Escondido	50ft (17m)
15. Cueva del Sabalo	40ft (14m)
16. Cueva Profunda	50ft (17m)
17. La Cueva de la Bruja	45ft (15m)
18. El Centro de las Gorgonias	65ft (22m)
19. La Gruta Negra	40ft (14m)
20. Cañon Negro	50ft (17m)
21. La Cascada	45ft (15m)
22. Piedra de Coral	55ft (18m)
23. Pisa a las Profundidades	50ft (17m)

Dive Site	Depth
24. Pasaje a lo Profundo	50ft (17m)
25. Pasaje de Dos Vias	50ft (17m)
26. Cañon Profundo	60ft (20m)
27. El Salto	50ft (17m)
28. La Cuevita	50ft (17m)
29. El Gran Cañon	70ft (24m)
30. El Ancla del Pirata	55ft (18m)
31. Embudo Coral	55ft (18m)
32. Valle del Coral	60ft (20m)
33. Valle Blanco	50ft (17m)
34. Paraiso de las Levisas	60ft (20m)
35. Valle de los Tiburones	30ft (10m)
36. Paraiso de Muke	40ft (14m)
37. El Espigon	40ft (14m)
38. El Arco de los Sabalos	45ft (15m)
39. El Ancla del Rosario	40ft (14m)
40. El Reino de Sahara	30ft (10m)
41. El Jardín de la Reina	40ft (14m)
42. Los Mogotes	30ft (10m)
43. El Cangilon	35ft (12m)
44. El Oasis	35ft (12m)
45. El Retorno	35ft (12m)

Cayo Largo

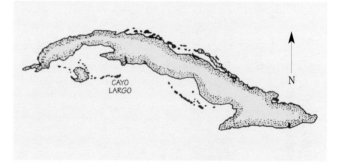

Isla De La Juventud
Special Municipality

Cayo Largo

Situated 85 miles to the south of Havana and 55 miles to the east of Isla de la Juventud, Cayo Largo is a European tourist haven with a 16-mile, white beach. This cay is particularly alluring to sun and sand lovers as well as divers. There are no locals on the island, except for a small village for employees of the hotel and dive center. But, there are 27,830 hectares of ecological reserve in Cayo Largo!

"Jutias" are indigenous to the Cayos.

The only residential building besides the airport is a tourist complex comprised of a number of all-inclusive hotels, all of which are operated by Gran Caribé or Sol Melia. A couple of hotels had been destroyed from a hurricane in 2001. All of the rooms have air-conditioning and satellite TV. Each hotel has a restaurant pool, and a bar. The food is average. Clients are sometimes assigned to a hotel and may not know which hotel they will stay in, until they arrive to Cayo Largo. Yet, all hotels are linked together and clients are free to roam around to wherever they wish. Guests are expected to eat at the restaurants of his/her own hotel for the inclusive meal plan. A brand-new option is to stay in log cabin bungalows on the water next to the marina. Puertosol owns these peaceful bungalows. Each cabin is split in half with adjoining rooms (that lock). Each side has two double beds, refrigerator, TV, private sun deck, and spacious bathrooms. All meals are included in the price of $55 per person. Divers can stay at the bungalows and walk to the dive boat in the morning (only about five minutes away). A free mini-bus service operates between the hotels and Puertosol marina/diving center. A tour guide normally accompanies groups that fly over from Havana. Room prices for the Gran Caribé hotels range from $78.00 to $187.00 per night (all-inclusive).

Puertosol owns the two dive operations in Cayo Largo. The schedule has two dives a day: one at 8:30am and the other at 2:30pm.

Puertosol has their own Bauer compressor and approximately 60 steel tanks.

Dive Prices

The Cayo Largo dive center, owned by Puertosol, runs a diving schedule of three dives a day: at 9:00am, 11:00am and 2:00pm. Night dives are offered upon request. They also offer a "full day" of diving in which divers take a 2-hour boat ride out to Cayo Blanco and have lunch onboard. Despite the long boat ride, the diving is *amazing*. It is well worth the extra time and expense.

Dive Sites

The zone is divided into three areas. The closest is located off the coast of the Playa Sirena. This area has typical coral heads, channels, ridges, and walls from 60 feet (20 meters) to 102 feet (34 meters). Brain

Cayo Largo Dive Prices

Average price for one dive	$39.00
Average price for two dives	$66.00
Average price for five dives	$149.00
Average price for ten dives	$264.00
Average price for fifteen dives	$380.00
Average price for twenty dives	$440.00
Average price for a night dive	$45.00
Average price for a resort course	$80.00
Average price for open water course (PADI, SSI))	$365.00
Average price for advanced course (PADI, SSI))	$250.00
Average price for snorkeling trip (includes boat ride to reef)	$19.00
Extra fee for full-day (Cayo Rosario) (includes lunch)	$20.00
Extra fee for full-day (Cayo Blanco) (includes lunch)	$30.00

Cayo Largo Rental Equipment Prices

Total cost for the use of an entire set of rental equipment is between $15.00 and $20.00.

Average price for only a BC jacket	$5.00
Average price for only a regulator	$8.00
Average price for a wetsuit	$5.00
Average price for mask/snorkel/fins	$6.00

All available brands of scuba equipment include: Cressi-sub (Italian) and Mares (Italian).

coral, star coral, and leaf coral form habitats for fish life such as surgeonfish, snappers, schoolmasters, schools of grunts, and other tropical fish. With a bit of luck divers can see sea turtles, lobsters, moray eels, stingrays and eagle rays. Several sunken ships can be visited including El Barco Merliza, and El Barco Rayo.

The middle area of the dive zone is located near Cayo Rosario. Coral mazes, pillars, and tunnels characterize the dive sites in this region. Most sites are found at about 60 feet (20 meters). Grouper, snappers, and schools of amberjacks are common dwellers of these waters.

The farthest diving area is located 30 miles northeast of Cayo Largo, near Cayo Blanco and Cayo Sigua. All of the dive sites in this region are splendid wall dives. Some coral walls begin as shallow as 45 feet (15 meters) and drop to more than 600 feet (200 meters). Colorful tube sponges and black coral rest on these walls. Divers may see barracuda, grouper, snappers, and spadefish, as well as other tropical fish. (See dive map on pg. 101):

El Acuario

Popular with the dive masters, El Acuario is only a 15-minute boat ride from the Cayo Largo Diving Center. This site is identified by its coral heads and conch shells. Colorful tube sponges sprout up everywhere. This coral bottom landscape can be reached at 45 feet (15 meters). Living up to its name, "the aquarium", this dive site is home to large schools of fish, including snappers, amberjacks, schoolmasters, yellowtails, and surgeonfish. Other small tropical fish such as squirrelfish, butterfly fish, and parrotfish are

Tarpon Conference

D. Tipton

also abundant. Total bottom time ranges from 40–45 minutes.

Cueva del Negro

You can reach this dive site after a 15 to 30-minute boat ride. The main attraction is a very soft, descending cave where divers enter at 72 feet (24 meters) and exit at about 100 feet (33 meters). This area is like an underwater conference room for tarpon. Divers also have the opportunity to see glassfish, angelfish, amberjacks, eagle rays, or even a sea turtle. Total bottom time is about 45 minutes.

La Montana

This site is renowned for its coral wall, comprised of five mountains of coral heads. The dive begins at 85 feet (30 meters) and drops deeper than 135 feet (45 meters). Divers can expect to see nurse sharks, gray sharks, and perhaps an eagle ray.

La Rabirrubia

A shallow dive of only 26 feet (8 meters), this site has small coral heads that dot a sandy bottom. Sea fans can be seen perched on the many types of soft and hard corals that are found here. Typical coral fish such as parrotfish and squirrel fish dart in and out scavenging for food. Every once and awhile divers can see a moray eel curiously poke its head out of a crevice. Barracuda and rays are also inhabitants of this area.

For more information on diving or to book a reservation contact:

> **Marina Cayo Largo del Sur**
> Cayo Largo del Sur
> Archipielago de los Canarreos
> Isla de Juventud, Cuba
> Ph: 534-54-8213
> Fax: 534-54-8212

The Diving Guide to Cuba Scuba

Cayo Largo is a photographer's delight.

M. Mola

Web site:
www.puertosol.cubaweb.com
Email:gcom@puertosol.cls.tur.cu

Playa Sirena
Cayo Largo del Sur
Archipielago de los Canarreos
Isla de la Juventud, Cuba
Ph: 534-54-8213
Fax: 534-54-8212
Email: gcom@psol.cls.tur.cu

Or divers can contact the Puertosol headquarters at:

Puertosol
Casa Matriz: Calle 1ra #3001
Esq. A 30. Miramar, Playa Habana,
Ph: 537-204-8563
Fax: 537-204-5928
Email: explotac@psol.mit.tur.cu
Web Site: www.Puertosol.net

Insider's Tips

Puertosol Diving Center employs four English-speaking instructors, all of whom are CMAS, ACUC, or SSI certified. During the high season the center attracts 20-30 divers.

The center has several dive boats each equipped for 20 passengers. Bottled water is available on the boats for about $1.50. Both have storage for your dive equipment.

There are plans to construct a hyperbaric chamber on Cayo Largo. Until then, if an accident occurs, divers can take a 45-minute helicopter ride to Havana.

Above the Water

For $1.00, tourists can visit the Cayo Largo Museum, a small house that exhibits the history of the island. The first settlers came from Venezuela 3,000 years ago. Much of the exhibit shows the devastation from Hurricane Michelle.

Divers are awestruck by the beautiful walls at the Cañon de Cayo Blanco dive site.   M. Mola

The Diving Guide to Cuba Scuba

Visitors can also see a sea-turtle farm, where eggs are brought to incubate. When turtles hatch and come of age (3 months old), they are released back to the ocean. The farm has turtles of all sizes. If you ask nicely, you can hold one.

Tourists can rent motor scooters or dune buggies for a fun tour of the island. However, recreation above the water is limited.

Getting There

Flights from Cuba's mainland are usually packaged through tourist agencies such as Havanatur. Divers can get to Cayo Largo from Havana, Isla de Juventud, Cienfuegos, and Santiago de Cuba. Most tourist agencies book through Aero Gaviota or Aero Caribé airlines.

Havanatur
Edificio Sierra Maestra
Calle 1ra e/ D y 2
Miramar, Playa, Ciudad de la
Habana
Ph: 537-23-9862 / 537-23-9785
Fax: 527-242-1760
Email: ramos@cimex.com.cu

Another way to make arrangements is to contact the concierge by phone or email at Melia Cohiba:

Ave Paseo e/ 1ra y 3ra
El Vedado, Ciudad de la Habana
Ph: 537-833-3636
Fax: 537-833-4555
Email: Jef_rec_mic.cohiba1
@solmelia.cma.net

The easiest and cheapest way to go to Cayo Largo is to buy an all-inclusive package at a tourist desk of any major hotel in Havana. Almost all of the agents speak

One day snorkel trip with lunch (round trip)	$124.00
Two days / one night all meals incl.	$170.00
(for a double room)	
Four days / three nights (for a double room)	$280.00
Eight days / seven nights (for a double room)	$520.00

English. Credit cards are accepted *unless* issued from an American bank.

Aero Taxi has three daily flights from Havana to Cayo Largo, which depart from Terminal Caribbean at 7:15am, 1:15pm, and 4:15pm. The flight duration is about one hour and forty-five minutes and costs about $60.00 each way. Divers can also book flights at the Inter/Lacsa office in the lobby of the Havana Libre Hotel:
Ph: 537-866-2073 / 537-866-2702
Fax: 537-833-3728

Aero Taxi has a 50-minute flight from Trinidad to Cayo Largo, that departs daily at 5:45pm. The flight returns from Cayo Largo at 2:20pm. Flights cost $50.00 each way.

Aero taxi has two flights from Varadero to Cayo Largo, which depart at 8:50am and 5:05pm. The cost is about $55.00 each way. To book a flight from Varadero to Cayo Largo, contact:
Ph: 05-861-4859

Divers can also reach Cayo Largo from Cayo Coco for about $100.00 each way. The flight is two hours. There is a 25% discount for children under 12 years of age. To book a flight, contact Cayo Coco airport:
Ph: 066-30-1245

Cayo Largo

Isolated cays create excellent areas for diving.

D. Tipton

The Diving Guide to Cuba Scuba

CAYO LARGO
Marina Puertosol

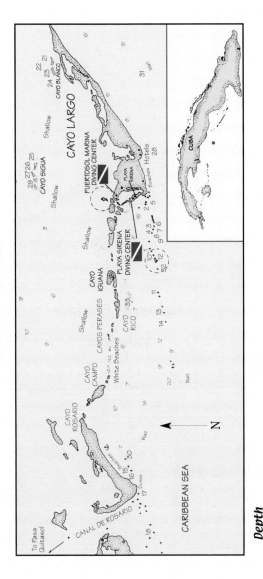

Dive Site

	Depth
1. Rabirubia	25ft (9m)
2. Canal de la Baracuda	25ft (9m)
3. Punta de Barrera	20ft (7m)
4. El Ballenato	45ft (15m)
5. Las Cuberas	35ft (12m)
6. Barco Hundido	110ft (36m)
7. Cueva del Negro	110ft (36m)
8. Pista de Ski	110ft (36m)
9. La Montaña	Wall

	Depth
10. Espondrilo	80ft (27m)
11. Cañon de Martín	80ft (27m)
12. Acuario I-II	50ft (17m)
13. Meliza Point	100ft (33m)
14. Albert Point	90ft (30m)
15. Laberinto	60ft (20m)
16. Tony Point	60ft (20m)
17. La Cabeceria	60ft (20m)
18. Tarpon Point	60ft (20m)

19. La Terraza	Wall
20. Cañon de Blanco	Wall
21. Jardín de Cazones	Wall
22. Arenazo de las Rayas	Wall
23. Cañon de Sigua	Wall
24. Abismo	Wall
25. Las Cadenas	Wall
26. Herradura de Sigua	Wall
27. La Solata	Wall

28. Pelicano	80ft (27m)
29. Cayo Sigua (blue hole)	200ft (69m)
30. Yainelis Point	60ft (20m)
31. Capricho	80ft (27m)
32. Banana Point	80ft (27m)
33. La Corona	90ft (30m)

Varadero

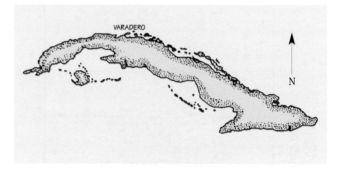

Matanzas Province

Varadero

A two-hour's drive from Havana, stretched out along 12 ½ miles of white, powdery beach, lies Varadero. Located in the Matanzas Province (Elian Gonzalez' home area), this place was developed by rich Cubans who were unable to vacation in Europe during World War I. Varadero developed into a place where affluent Cubans could dock their boats. Presently, it is a great place to visit for sun, sand, ocean, and nightlife.

A Cuban version of Cancun, Varadero is the largest resort area on the island. There are over 15,000 hotel rooms available to all types of tourists. Most hotels are all-inclusive, have their own swimming pools, restaurants, and bars. Although nearly all of the hotels are well equipped, an old favorite is Hotel Bella Costa.

Typical scene in the streets of Cuba.

There are four diving centers, that visit the same dive zone. There is Cubanacan Nautica's Barracuda Diving Center, Puertosol's ACUA Diving Center, Gaviota's Diving Center, and Superclub's Varadero Diving Center. Some hotels work directly with a specific dive center, however, clients may choose to dive with any of the four centers. You can pay through a tourist agency and then use a voucher or pay for diving when you get to the dive center. The high season for diving in Varadero is July through March. During the high season, dive centers average about 30-40 divers per day. (See dive map on pg. 109).

Cubanacan Nautica's Scuba Cuba Barracuda Diving Center

There are 30 sets of Cressi-sub equipment. The center has three Bauer compressors, which fill their 100 steel tanks. The nearest hyperbaric chamber is only 20 minutes away in Cardenas. There is one 42-foot dive boat, and one 33-foot dive boat. Both have toilets and bottled water ($1.00). For $12.00 divers can eat lobster, fish, or shrimp, freshly prepared on the boat. The lobster is scrumptious. There are also two inflatable zodiacs, which each hold six people. Barracuda diving center employs 13 instructors, all of whom speak English and are CMAS, ACUC, or NAUI certified. The center has the capacity for up to 50 divers,

but usually there are not more than 40 in high season. Out of these divers there are about 2-4 Americans who visit per month. The center normally has a two-tank dive at 10:00am. Divers can expect to be back at the hotel by around 4:00pm.

Barracuda is the main dive shop that supplies tanks for beach dives. If clients become tired of beach dives at these hotels, they are recommended to dive from Barracuda's dive boat.

For more information or to make a reservation, contact:

Scuba Cuba Barracuda Diving Center
Calle 1ra y 59
Varadero, Matanzas, Cuba
Ph: 534-566-7072
Fax: 534-566-7072
Email: ventas@aqwo.var.cyt.cu

Puertosol's Acua Diving Center

Acua has three dive boats, one with a capacity for 37 persons and two that hold 25 persons. There are toilets and bottled water ($1.00) on all the boats. A fish or chicken lunch is offered to divers for

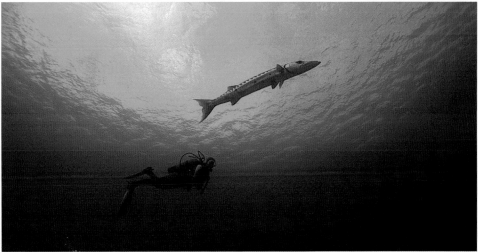

Curious barracuda are near-sighted and often swim near divers.

M. Mola

Cubanacan Nautica's Barracuda Diving Center Dive Prices	
Average price for one dive	$30.00
Average price for two dives	$60.00
Average price for ten dives	$215.00
Average price for a night dive	$50.00
Average price for a resort course	$60.00
Average price for open water course	$365.00
Average price for advanced course	$250.00

Rental Equipment Prices

The total cost to rent an entire set of equipment is $5.00 per dive. The usage of weights and weight belts is free.

Puertosol's Acua Diving Center Dive Prices	
Average price for one dive	$35.00
Average price for two dives	$50.00
Average price for ten dives	$200.00
Average price for a night dive	$40.00
(Includes the use of a dive light)	
Average price for a cave dive	$35.00
Average price for one dive at Playa Giron	$50.00
(Includes bus transportation)	
Average price for two dives at Playa Giron	$65.00
(Includes bus transportation)	
Average price for snorkeling at Playa Giron	$25.00
(Includes bus transportation)	
Average price for an open water course	$360.00
(PADI and CMAS certifications)	

Rental Equipment

The total cost for the use of an entire set of equipment is $5.00 per day. The usage of weights and weight belts is free. Acua Diving Center has 30 full sets of Cressi-Sub (Italian) equipment. The center has two Bauer compressors, which fill its 120 steel and aluminum tanks. The nearest hyperbaric chamber is located in Cardenas.

$10.00. Lobster is $20.00. There are usually no more than 30 divers per day during the high season. Acua employs eight instructors, all of whom speak English and are PADI or CMAS certified. Boats normally leave for the dive site around 9:00am.

For more information or to book a reservation, contact:

> ACUA
> Avenida Kawama No 201, e/ 2 y3
> Varadero, Matanzas, Cuba
> Ph: 534-566-8063
> Fax: 534-566-7456

Gaviota Diving Center

Gaviota Diving Center is located by Hotel Coral, which is all-inclusive. For more information or to book a reservation, contact:

> Marina Gaviota
> Autopista Sur Final
> Punta Hicacos, Cuba
> Ph: 534-566-7755
> Fax : 534-566-7756

Divers can also contact the Gaviota tour agency at:

> Agencia de Viajes Gaviota Tours
> Ph: 537-833-9780
> Fax: 537-833-2780

Puntarenas Superclub Scuba Cuba Diving Center

This dive center only services divers who are guests of the Superclub hotel. Hotel guests pay between $104.00 and $145.00 per person. This gorgeous hotel has every amenity and facility imaginable. Everything is included, even diving. There is hardly any reason to leave the hotel grounds. The center has two boats with a capacity of 11 persons. There are six instructors, all of whom speak English. All

Gaviota Diving Center
Dive Prices

Average price for one dive	$35.00
Average price for two dives	$50.00
Average price for one dive with lunch	$50.00
Average price for Saturn Cave dive	$35.00
Average price for a night dive	$40.00
Average price for a ten dive package	$200.00
Average price for two dives with lunch	$65.00
Average price for one dive at Playa Giron	$45.00
Average price for two dives at Playa Giron	$65.00

rental equipment is Sherwood (American). There are two compressors, which fill its 60 aluminum tanks. The nearest hyperbaric chamber is in Cardenas. Daily dives occur at 9:00am and 11:00am. Divers are asked to sign up a day ahead of time. If divers want to get certified, it costs between $300.00 and $360.00. ACUC, PADI, and CMAS open water certifications are all offered. For more information or to book a reservation, contact:

> Club Varadero
> Carretera Kawama
> Varadero, Matanzas, Cuba
> Ph: 534-566-8470
> Fax: 534-566-7093
> Email: ventas@aqwa.var.cyt.cu

Dive Sites

The dive zone in Varadero covers over 40 miles of coral, including nearby Cayo Piedra, Cayo Cruz, and Cayo Blanco. Diving in Varadero offers opportunities to see shipwrecks, caves, tunnels, crevices, coral walls, a blue hole, and even a moray show. Maximum depths range from 15 feet (5 meters) to 148 feet (45 meters). There are also chances to view peculiar underwater formations of stalactites and stalagmites, blind fish, and shrimp. (See dive map on pg. 109)

Barco Hundido del Caribé

This sunken boat is the stage for the moray eel show. Divers should specifically ask the dive center to make this dive. Because it is a two-hour boat trip each way to this site, divers return in the late afternoon. Having sunk in 1943 during the Second World War, this old German ship rests in about 33 feet (11 meters) of water. Divers can watch a 6½ foot-long green moray eel be hand-fed. Other inhabitants of this sunken treasure are barracuda, grouper, spiny lobsters, and angelfish. This dive is usually a little more expensive due to the amount of gas used during the boat trip. Figure at least $45.00 for the dive.

Playa Coral

This dive site can be reached from the beach. Divers can expect to see over 30 species of coral. Some coral formations are so well-developed that they protrude from the surface of the water. Heads of coral link together to form channels and connected passageways. Some passageways turn into caves. Blue cromis, parrotfish, and many other small tropical fish can be seen here. The maximum depth is about 60 feet (20 meters).

Claraboyas

Access to Claraboyas is only 10 minutes by a fast boat. Between 45-80 feet (14-20 meters), this dive site is composed of many caves, that are filled with sharks and schools of barracuda during the summer months. Many typical corals greet divers at entrances to the caves.

Ojo del Megano

This is the location of what is known as the "Blue Hole". It is 148 feet wide (40 meters) and about 230 feet deep (80 meters) in the middle of a coral platform that rests in 33 feet of water. Near this hole divers can also see a few snappers, groupers and other tropical fish.

Cueva de Saturno

Also called the Cenote, this dive site is one of a kind. Located in the natural reserve, Cienaga de Zapata, Saturn's Cave is made of limestone. Divers take a bus to this cavern flooded by both fresh and salt water. It has a small lake at the entrance and lateral gorges that reach up to 210 feet in depth. Here divers can experience stalactites and stalagmites above and below the water. Also present are blind fish and shrimp. Water is sometimes a bit cool due to the shade, so wear a wetsuit. A dive light is also required for this site. Visibility is generally good.

Las Mandarinas

This shallow site of only 33 feet (11 meters) is inhabited by a school of grunts, which are often fed by hand. The sea bottom is spotted with coral formations, sponges and sea fans. Divers can see

Shipwrecks become artificial reefs.

M. Mola

Divers can see moray eels being hand-fed by dive masters ^{M. Mola}

grouper, moray eels, and other types of small reef fish.

Above the Water

Varadero offers every type of beach and water activity one could imagine. Most hotel concierges have pamphlets and brochures detailing the area's activities. Do not miss the best disco in Varadero, La Rumba. For more details see the Cuba Handbook, by Christopher P. Baker.

Getting There

Divers can go to the concierge desk at any major hotel to book a package to Varadero. Bus transfers from Havana to Varadero generally cost about $25.00 per person each way or $35.00 round trip excluding lunch. Round trip bus fare with lunch included is $45.00. However, if you plan to dive, it is better to book the bus trip without lunch. Most buses depart for a day trip to Varadero at 7:00am from the hotels in Havana. They return around 6:30pm.

It is difficult to reserve a space for diving prior to arrival in Varadero. Therefore, even though space is normally available, it is advisable to book a package to stay overnight there. Aero Taxi has six 35-minute flights to Varadero, which usually depart Havana at 7:00am, 7:15am (two flights), 3:00pm, 4:00pm, and 4:15pm. The cost is about $30.00 each way. Aero Taxi also has flights to Varadero from Cayo Largo, Cayo Coco, and Trinidad. Contact the Inter/Lacsa office in the lobby of the Habana Libre Hotel for more information:

Ph: 537-866-2703 / 537-866-2702
537-866-2328
Fax: 537-833-3728 / 537-833-7996

There are several Melia Hotel concierges that can make arrangements for diving:

Sol Club Las Sirenas, email:
jefres@sirenas.solmelia.cma.net

Sol Club Coral, email:
depress@coral.sol.melia.cma.net

Paradisus, Varadero, email:
jefven@tpeninsula.solmelia.cu

Tryp Peninsula, Varadero, email:
clirtryp@coral.solmelia.cma.net

Tiny fish dart through coral and ambient light.

D. Tipton

VARADERO
Acua, Barracuda, Superclub, & Gaviota Dive Centers

Dive Site	Depth
1. Playa Coral	65ft (22m)
2. La Carbonera	35ft (12m)
3. Damjui Wreck	40ft (14m)
4. Saturno Cave	65ft (22m)
5. Mangle Prieto	115ft (38m)
6. Los Manchones	70ft (23m)
7. El Museo	115ft (38m)
8. El Marillo	70ft (23m)
9. Cangilones	50ft (17m)
10. El Lenquazo	115ft (38m)
11. Internacional	80ft (27m)
12. Las Mandarina	35ft (12m)
13. Las Catlinetas	55ft (19m)
14. Coral Negro	115ft (38m)
15. Las Américas	70ft (23m)
16. Melia	25ft (8m)
17. Las Claraboyas	70ft (23m)
18. El Pionero	115ft (38m)
19. Cangilones Mono	85ft (29m)
20. Carive Wreck	35ft (12m)
21. Neptuno Wreck	40ft (14m)
22. Bonaí	120ft (40m)
23. Bacunayagua	65ft (22m)

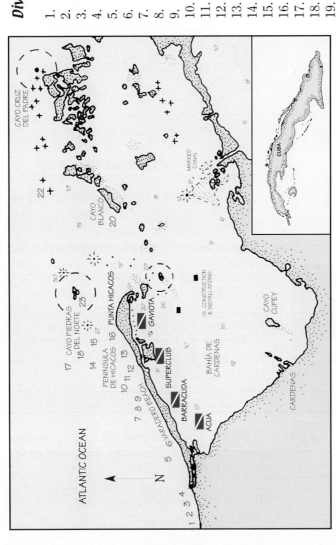

Bahía de Cochinos

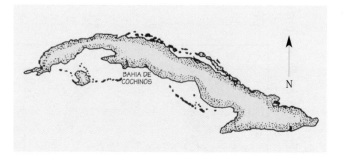

Matanzas Province

Bahía de Cochinos (Bay of Pigs)

This area is one of Cuba's premiere cave diving regions. Along the road are monuments in rememberance of tragedies from the American invasion. The Bay of Pigs is approximately a two-hour drive south of Varadero. When the Atlantic side is too rough for diving, some dive centers take divers to the calm south side at Bay of Pigs. Not only is the area calm due to its geographic location, but also because there are no boats allowed inside the bay.

The ride to Bay of Pigs is rocky like secondary back roads. In addition to the ride the bus is a bit uncomfortable because it has to carry two tanks per diver, and any other spare tanks and dive gear. Because the tanks have to lay flat, they are piled high in the aisles.

The entire bay is called Parque Natural Montemar. Due to the prohibition of boats in the bay, all dives are made from the beach. The coral walls are easily accessible because they are about 50 to 100 feet from shore. The walls begin at 30 feet and the maximum depth is about 150 feet. The coral life is healthy and bright. Shipwrecks are scattered throughout the bay.

Banana farmers

110

Barracuda's Dive Center is a dive operation in Varadero that offers trips to Bay of Pigs. Other dives can be booked with Octopus Dive Center at Playa Larga, or at Playa Girón Dive Center.

Dive Sites

As divers assemble their equipment, dive masters take orders for how many want lunch between dives. The Barracuda Dive Center offers a lunch consisting of lobster, breaded fish, shrimp, french fries and tomatoes for a total of $12.00, plus $1.00 for a soft drink.

A typical dive at Bay of Pigs includes a swim outward for about 15 minutes (depending on the swiftness of the group) to reach a coral wall. Then, at about 150 feet (50 meters) offshore, the group reassembles to descend to 100 feet (33 meters) from the surface. From there, divers swim parallel to the shoreline and slowly ascend near the wall. Total dive time is around 50 minutes.

There are no markers or buoys for the dive sites since boats do not enter the bay. Only old steel ladders or wooden signs with a dive flag sporadically placed along the wall mark the dive sites. Water clarity is usually 80-100 ft visibility.

There are approximately 10 named dive sites on the eastern side of Bay of Pigs. The west side of the bay is part of Zapata National Park. Divers are prohibited to dive on the west side. Dive masters say that the west side of the bay would require a longer swim from the beach. In addition, the wall slopes are gentler than the vertical walls on the east side of the bay.

The coral life is excellent with bright sponges of varying color and occasional giant gorgonians. Soft coral and sea fans are abundant. Typically small Caribbean fish are herded by schools of jacks. Divers can occasionally see scorpion fish, moray eels, or lobsters.

Divers exit the water from a ladder imbedded into the coral. After lunch the

Hundreds of glass fish often school together in Playa Girón. A. Nachoum

second dive is made. The second dive is often completed at dusk, but watch out for hungry mosquitos! Divers then have about a two-hour bus ride to return to Varadero unless they are staying at Villa Playa Girón or Villa Playa Larga.

Punta Perdiz

Divers can swim to this site from the coast. It is a nice wall dive because the ecological conditions in the area have favored the development of typical fish. The dive begins at around 30 feet (10 meters), and then drops off sharply to over 900 feet (300 meters).

Caribé

This site is characterized by the remains of an old German merchant ship, which sank in 1943. Divers may see angelfish, barracuda, groupers, moray eels and lobsters. Maximum depth is about 30 feet (10 meters).

Cueva el Cenote

This cave is situated in a natural reserve called Cienaga Zapata. The reserve is near the southern part of the Matanzas province. The dive site is famous for its limestone formation, which formed an underground channel to the sea, flooding it with seawater. The cave also has another entrance through a small lake surrounded by lateral gorges that reach up to 210 feet (70m) in depth. Divers can find many coral reef species of fish. Be sure to bring a dive light.

La Pared del Cenote

In front of the Cenote cave is a wall located approximately 300 feet (100 meters) from shore. The wall plunges to depths of up to 900 feet (300 meters). Divers have the opportunity to see a variety of corals, gorgonians, sea fans, sponges and tropical fish.

M. Mola

Walls and swim-throughs offer pleasurable diving.

Whalesharks have actually been encountered from this shore dive!

M. Mola

Insider's Tip

The visiblility is over 100ft (33m) during the winter.

A recommended *casa particular* is the home of Carlos Rizo and Ana:

Cienaga de Zapata, No. 39
Email: CBL917@hotmail.com

Above the Water

On the point of Bahía de Cochinos, there is a museum that displays artifacts from ill-fated U.S. agressors. There are also pictures of the location where Castro personally fired tank shells at an American Naval Ship. The museum is quite interesting for divers who enjoy historical enrichment. The hours are 8-5pm. The cost is $2 per person.

Getting There

Puertosol, Cubanacan Nautica, and Horizontes agencies can each make arrangements for tourists to dive the Bay of Pigs. Divers can stay at a hotel in Playa Girón or Playa Larga and make many beach dives. Packages to the hotel should be booked through Horizontes travel agency in Havana, because these packages usually include transportation to the Bay of Pigs.

A day trip costs about $42.00 round trip from Havana. Prices vary. Dives can be booked with Playa Girón Dive Center or Octopus Dive Center after arriving at the Bay of Pigs.

For dive information or to book reservations, contact:

Hotel Playa Girón Dive Center
Peninsula de Zapata, Matanzas
Ph: 535-839-4118 / 535-839-4110
Fax: 535-839-4117

Hotel Playa Larga
Octopus Dive Center
Peninsula de Zapata, Matanzas
Ph: 535-839-7225 / 535-839-7219

Pigs sometimes can be seen roaming the countryside of Cuba.

D. Tipton

BAHÍA DE COCHINOS
Playa Girón Dive Center

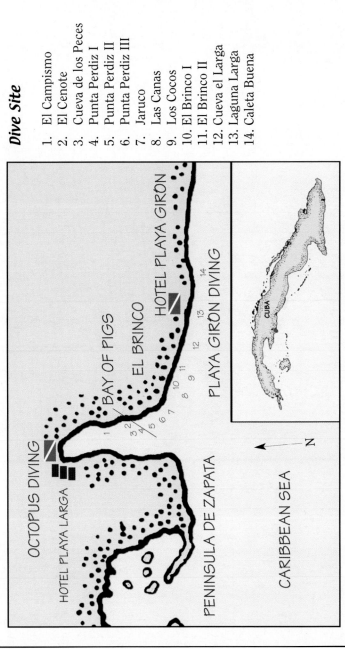

Dive Site	Depth
1. El Campismo	30ft- Wall (10m)
2. El Cenote	60ft (20m)
3. Cueva de los Peces	200ft (67m)
4. Punta Perdiz I	15ft- Wall (5m)
5. Punta Perdiz II	15ft- Wall (5m)
6. Punta Perdiz III	15ft- Wall (5m)
7. Jaruco	60ft- Wall (20m)
8. Las Canas	60ft- Wall (20m)
9. Los Cocos	60ft- Wall (20m)
10. El Brinco I	125ft (42m)
11. El Brinco II	125ft (42m)
12. Cueva el Larga	80ft (27m)
13. Laguna Larga	80ft- Wall (27m)
14. Caleta Buena	80ft- Wall (27m)

Background: W. Houghton, Top Left: E. Macao, Bottom Left: W. Houghton, Right: M. Mola

Central Cuba

Cienfuegos Province

Cienfuegos

Named after a Spanish descendant, Governor Don José Cienfuegos, this city has often been called "La Perla del Mar" (The Pearl of the Sea). This city has parks, plazas, churches, restaurants, nightclubs, palaces, and all roads lead to the sea. Divers have the chance to explore Cuban culture above and below the water.

There are two hotels located near diving centers. Hotel Faro Luna hosts Cubancan Nautica's Faro Luna Diving Center while Hotel Rancho Luna hosts Puertosol's Whale

Cienfuegos

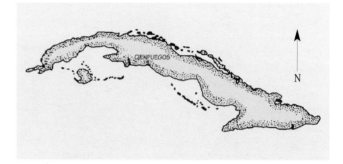

Shark Diving Center. Faro Luna is the result of a joint venture between a Barcelona company and a Cuban company. Whale Shark is a joint venture between an Italian company and a Cuban company. Both centers are well equipped and visit the same dive zone.

Rated as three stars, Cubanacan's Hotel Faro Luna was constructed in 1992 and has 42 rooms. All rooms are air-conditioned, have private baths, satellite TV, radio, telephone, mini-bar, and safety deposit boxes. Facilities include a swimming pool, lobby bar, concierge, medical service, pharmacy, currency exchange, and car rentals. The hotel restaurant serves average cuisine. Room prices cost between $39.00 and $56.00 depending on the season. The dive center is about 1 mile away on a gravel road. For more information or to make a reservation, contact:

Dominos is a favorite past-time in Cuba.

> **Hotel Faro Luna ACUC**
> Carretera Pascaballo km. 18
> Cienfuegos, Cuba
> Ph: 534-324-5134
> Fax: 534-324-5134
> Email: dcfluna@acuc.cfg.cyt.cu

For about the same price, divers can stay in a much larger four-star hotel. Horizontes' Hotel Rancho Luna has 225 air-conditioned rooms with private bathrooms, safety

118

deposit box, telephone, and radio. Facilities include an Olympic-sized swimming pool, two restaurants, snack bar, lobby bar, pool bar and grill, two beach bars, coffee-shop, game room, concierge, massage services, motor-scooter and car rentals, and medical services. The dive center is next to a beach bar. Room prices range from $34.00 to $54.00 per night, including breakfast. The hotel is alive with natives because Cubans can pay with Cuban pesos at this hotel. For more information or to book a reservation, contact:

Central de Reservas Hoteles
Horizontes (open 24 hours)
Ph: 537-833-4042
Fax: 537-833-3722
E-mail: crh@s1.hor.cma.net
Web site: www.horizont.cu

Divers can also contact Hotel Rancho Luna at:

Faro Luna ACUC
Carretera de Rancho Luna
Cienfuegos, Cuba
Ph: 534-324-5134
Fax: 534-324-5134
Email: dcfluna@acuc.cfg.cyt.cu

Faro Luna has 25 full sets of equipment, all of which are of the brands Cressi-sub

Faro Luna Diving Center
Dive Prices

Average price for one to three dives (per dive)	$25.00
Average price for four dives (per dive)	$94.00
Average price for six dives (per dive)	$138.00
Average price for eight dives (per dive)	$180.00
Average price for ten dives (per dive)	$220.00
Average price for fifteen or more dives (per dive)	$20.00
Average price for a resort course	$60.00
Average price for an open water course (ACUC certification)	$375.00
Average price for snorkeling trip	$10.00

Rental Equipment

The total cost to rent an entire set of equipment is $22.00 per day.

Average price for only a BC jacket	$5.00
Average price for only a regulator	$10.00
Average price for mask/fins/snorkel	$2.50
Average price for only a wetsuit	$5.00

(Italian) and Subaqua (Spanish). The usage of weights and weight belts are free. The center has a Colti-sub compressor and a Bauer compressor, which fill their 70 steel tanks. The dive center has two 24-foot boats, equipped for 10 people each. This center annually attracts about 1500 divers, of which only about 20 are Americans.

5,700 kilometers of shoreline beckons divers.

D. Tipton

Cienfuegos

Dives are scheduled for 9:00am, 11:00am, 2:30pm, and 4:00pm each day. All dive sites are between 10 and 15 minutes from the dive center. The nearest hyperbaric chamber is in Havana. In case of an accident, Faro Luna provides a helicopter service.

Whale Shark has 25 full sets of rental equipment, all of which are of the Italian brand Coltri-sub. The dive center is also insured by DAN of Europe. Whale Shark provides a helicopter service for emergencies. The center employs three instructors all of whom speak English. The dive center has four Coltri-sub compressors, which fill their 60 steel tanks. Two of the compressors are full size and two are portable to take on the dive boat. Dives are usually conducted at 9:30am and 2:00pm.

There is one 33-foot dive boat with two 225 horse-powered engines, which some-

Whale Shark Diving Center Rental Equipment

The total cost to rent an entire set of equipment is $12.00

Average price for only a BC jacket	$5.00
Average price for only a regulator	$5.00
Average price for mask/fins/snorkel	$5.00
Average price for a wetsuit	$5.00
Average price for a dive light	$5.00
Average price for a compass/depth gauge	$3.00
Average price for a dive knife	$2.00
Average price for a dive computer	$10.00

times doubles as a live-aboard. The boat is also equipped with three 5-liter tanks of pure oxygen. Examples of live-aboard packages are as follows:

One option is a trip to Cayo Dios, which costs $400.00. The maximum diver capacity is six people. This price includes breakfast and lunch. Divers catch their own lobsters for dinner (Omar guarantees it!). The price also includes trolling for deep-sea fish and snorkeling.

A second option is a trip to Cayo Largo, which costs $400.00. The maximum diver capacity is six people. The price includes breakfast, lunch, and dinner. Diving is unlimited. For more information or to book a reservation, contact:

Whale Shark Diving Center
Carretera de Pasacaballos, Km.17
Cienfuegos, Cuba
Ph: 534-324-5134
Fax: 534-324-5128
E-mail: whaleshark@ip.etecsa.cu
or mpsolcfg@ip.etecsa.cu

Dive Sites

Rancho Luna and Whale Shark Diving Centers visit over 30 sites along the coral reef. Particular to this area are wide coral

Whale Shark Diving Center Dive Prices

Average price for to four dives (per dive)	$25.00
Average price for five dives (total)	$123.00
Average price for six dives (total)	$140.00
Average price for ten dives (total)	$230.00
Average price for fifteen dives (total)	$335.00
Average price for twenty dives (total)	$410.00
Average price for a resort course	$50.00
Average price for a night dive	$30.00
Average price for snorkeling trip	10.00
Average price for open water course (NAUI & PADI certifications)	$310.00 - $325.00
Average price for advanced course (NAUI & PADI certifications)	$260.00 - $270.00
Average price for medic first aid (PADI certification)	$150.00
Average price for rescue course (NAUI & PADI certifications)	$450.00
Average price for divemaster course (NAUI & PADI certifications)	$550.00

M. Mola

channels between 35 feet (12 meters) and 120 feet (40 meters). These channels descend upon walls hosting flat and column-shaped corals, bright sponges, and medium-sized sea fans. Many species of corals can be found here including elkhorn and brain coral. Divers can expect to see barracuda, grouper, snapper, grunts, chubs, parrotfish, surgeonfish, angelfish, nurse sharks, sea turtles, eagle rays, or even a whale shark. This dive zone provides opportunities for wreck diving, wall diving, cave diving, and pinnacle diving.

Near the bay, a monumental coral formation has been discovered. It has been named "La Dama del Caribé," which means "The Lady of the Caribbean."

La Corona

Located at the entrance of the Cienfuegos' Bay, this site has profound coral channels that lead the diver to a coral wall covered with sponges, black coral, and sea fans. The maximum depth is 115 feet (35 meters), although shallow dives can be made here as well. Curious barracuda, nurse sharks, tarpon, and snapper frequent this area. Occasionally a whale shark may swim through this region.

Grunt City

This dive site is characterized by a large coral head, which resembles a cathedral. It holds worship to hundreds of grunt fish. The dive masters have been known to feed bananas to the grunts . This site is a shallow dive with a maximum depth of about 45 feet (15 meters).

Camaronero II

This sunken shrimp boat lies in 60 feet (18 meters) of water. The 58-foot ship is constructed of steel. Now covered in bright sponges and coral, the ship allows divers to safely explore and penetrate many compartments including the engine room.

D. Tipton

Barracuda and small fish often cruise the outskirts of the wreck.

El Laberinto

This dive site is quite versatile. Divers can dive between 25 feet (8 meters) and 120 feet (42 meters). The labyrinth consists of large capes of coral, arising from the sand. Many caverns and pathways exist. Lobsters, crabs, and morays cleverly hide in crevices. Small parrotfish and blue cromis dart in and out of coral heads.

Punta Sabanilla

Resting in 90 feet (30 meters) of water, this dive site is noted for its deep channels. The coral bottom has well-developed sponges, gorgonians, and sea fans. Mullusks and crustaceans add to its beauty.

Above the Water

Save some time to explore the downtown area. Along with historical sites, Cienfuegos also has Cuba's only nuclear power plant in the making. In May of 1999 Russians announced a joint venture to help Cubans complete this project. It's worth seeing. Bars and entertainment also tend to be pretty good. For more details check out the *Cuba Handbook*, by Christopher P. Baker.

M. Mola

Insider's Tip

For a good *casa particular*, divers can try:

Aida Moejon
No. 5820 e/ 58 y 60
Cienfuegos
Email: CBL917@hotmail.com

Getting There

Divers can inquire about Cienfuegos at the concierge desk of any major hotel. Havanatur is the only agency that can book bus excursions to Cienfuegos and Trinidad. Round trip from Havana to Cienfuegos is about $53.00 per person.

Music is in the soul of Cubans

D. Tipton

CIENFUEGOS
Faro Luna & Whale Shark Dive Centers

Dive Site	Depth	Dive Site	Depth
1. El Nucleo	50ft (17m)	17. Rancho Luna I	35ft (12m)
2. Boya Recalo	40ft (14m)	18. Rancho Luna II	35ft (12m)
3. La Corona	50ft (17m)	19. Punta Barrera	40ft (14m)
4. Barco Arimao	60ft (20m)	20. El Bajo	15ft (5m)
5. Cable Ingles	25ft (9m)	21. Barco Punto Itabo	40ft (14m)
6. Barco Rio Club	30ft (17m)	22. La Guasa	50ft (17m)
7. El Coral	25ft (9m)	23. La Piedra	40ft (14m)
8. Los Palos	45ft (16m)	24. El Camino	40ft (14m)
9. Patana I	60ft (20m)	25. Carboneros	45ft (16m)
10. Camaronero I	25ft (9m)	26. El Fariot	40ft (14m)
11. Las Torres	55ft (19m)	27. El Molino	45ft (16m)
12. Laberinto	40ft (14m)	28. Campo Tiro	50ft (17m)
13. Patana II	35ft (12m)	29. Playitas Afuera	60ft (20m)
14. Camaronero II	40ft (14m)	30. Playitas Adentro	40ft (14m)
15. Camaronero III	40ft (14m)		
16. Las Esponjas	40ft (14m)		

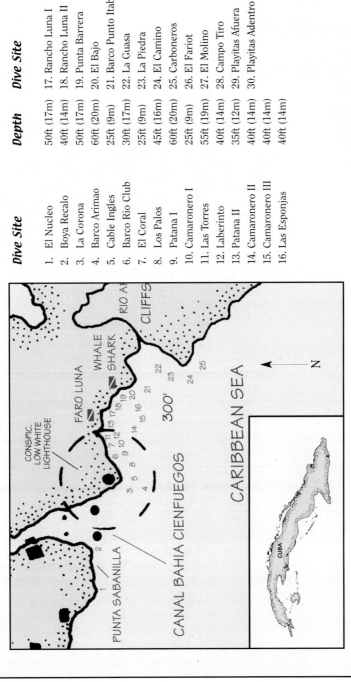

Guajimico

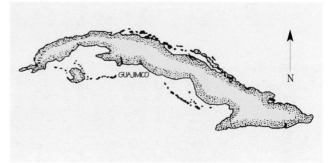

Cienfuegos Province

Guajimico

Half way between Cienfuegos and Trinidad, lies Guajimico, a small ecological village on a Caribbean inlet. At the entrance is a statue of the Indian who bore this tribal name.

Situated on the 42nd kilometer of the highway, Hotel Villa Guajimico is surrounded by a tranquil environment at the mouth of the River La Jutia. This small natural hamlet is rated as three stars. There are 51 air-conditioned cabins, of which 17 are triples, and 34 are doubles. Each has its own private bathroom, safety deposit box, telephone, and satellite TV. A restaurant overlooking the water is also on the premises. Other hotel facilities include a swimming pool with a bridge overlooking the bay, a small beach, an outdoor snack bar, a game room, a concierge, room service, and medical service. The high season for Americans is July 15-August 31, and December 22-January 3rd. Depending on the season, number of meals, and size of the cabin, room prices range from $14.00 to $46.00 per night. The experience in this village camp is a bargain. Owned by Cubamar, Guajimico has its own dive center and 13 dive sites. Six more sites are waiting for official approval. The

Cubans net fishing

A. Houghton

center has a staff with two Cuban instructors and one French instructor. All speak English. If you book your reservation early with the Cubamar travel agency, diving is only $20.00 per dive including rental equipment. If you show up without a reservation, dives will cost $5.00 extra. A normal dive schedule has a dive at 9:30am, 11:00am, and 4:00pm.

Dive Prices	
Average price for one dive	$20.00 to $25.00
Average price for two dives	$50.00
Average price for a night dive	$30.00
Average price for a resort course	$20.00
(divers only dive to about 15 feet)	
Average price for a package of dives	Negotiable

Rental Equipment

Use of rental equipment is included in the dive price. There are 50 sets of new equipment, most of which are of the American brand Seaquest. Guajimico has four German compressors, which fill its steel tanks. Although the center has two dive boats with a diver capacity of 20 and 30 people each, there are usually never more than 9 divers a day. Both vessels have toilets and bottled water. The nearest hyperbaric chamber is located in Havana. Helicopter service is provided.

Above the Water

Some of the options offered at Villa Guajimico are: a city tour of Trinidad, a tour of Cienfuegos, an excursion to the mountain-top cascade of Salto de Caburni, a picnic in the mountains, a horseback ride to la Hacienda La Vega, and a sea safari.

Getting There

Guajimico is accessible by road from either Cienfuegos or Trinidad. Divers can buy packages from Cubamar with transportation included. For more information, or to book a reservation contact:

Cubamar
Calle Paseo, no. 306, e/ 13 y 15
Vedado, Havana, Cuba
Ph: 537-866-2523 / 537-866-2524
Fax: 537-833-3111 / 537-830-1308
Email:
cubamar@cubamar.mit.cma.net

Havanatur offices usually can book one day in advance for an early morning bus departure. The cost is about $29.00 each way.

To contact Guajimico Hotel directly:

Villa Guajimico
Carretera de Cienfuegos
a Trinidad, Km 42
Cienfuegos
Ph: /Fax: 537-434-8125

D. Tipton

Visitors are permitted a two month stay on a tourist visa.

W. Houghton

GUAJIMICO
Guajimico Dive Center

Dive Site	Depth
1. Boca Ambuila	15-50ft (5-17m)
2. Dama Axul	65ft (22m)
3. Farallon I	50ft (17m)
4. Farallon II	50ft (17m)
5. Guanito	40ft (13m)
6. Paraiso	55ft (19m)
7. La Guanabana	10ft (3m)
8. Los Loros	35ft (12m)
9. Acuario I	20ft (7m)
10. Los Cabezos	50ft (17m)
11. Boca Naranjo	15-50ft (5-17m)
12. Acuario II	25ft (8m)
13. La Ceiba	Wall
14. La Piscina	15ft (5m)
15. La Posa	35ft (12m)
16. Punta Arriba	Wall

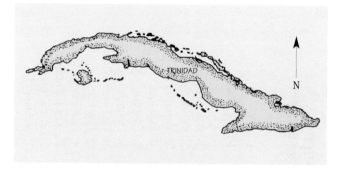

Sancti Spiritus Province

Trinidad

Pertaining to the Sancti Spiritus province and founded by Diego de Velasquez in 1514 near the shores of the Guarabo river, Trinidad has it all: the historic city, the mountains, and the sea. This region, only one-hour's drive from Cienfuegos, is an above and below the water delight for explorers. Trinidad is a great place for divers who want to have a taste of Cuban culture, history, and diving.

Walking the streets of Trinidad is like returning to the Spanish colonial era. The only evidences of the 20th century are the countless buses filled with tourists. Due to tourism motivated by these historical sites, Cuban residents are prohibited to change any outer construction of their homes or businesses. Money can only be spent on restoration to preserve this city. Trinidad is like a living museum.

Conventional transportation

W. Houghton

Convenient and economical accommodations are *casas particulares*, which are private Cuban homes. Many Cubans happily rent a room or even their whole house for $25.00 or less to tourists. You can choose from many homes, because locals will approach you to rent private rooms. Throw in a couple extra bucks and most families will cook for you too!

Divers have the option of two hotels in Trinidad. Hotel Costasur, located on Punta Maria Aguilar, has about 135 comfortable rooms. All are air-conditioned and have a private bathroom. Prices range from $45.00 to $70.00 per night.

Situated on a nice sandy beach, Hotel Ancon is named after a large rock formation that simulates a horse's hind leg. Comprised of nearly 280 air-conditioned rooms with private bathrooms, this hotel has a swimming pool, seven bars, a game room, and concierge service. Depending on the season, room prices range from $73.00 to $145.00 per night. Puertosol owns this dive center.

Rental Equipment

The average price for the use of an entire set of rental equipment is between $15.00 and $20.00. All of the gear is of the

Dive Prices	
Average price for only one dive	$30.00
Average price for only two dives	$50.00
Average price for a package of ten dives	$230.00
Average price for a night dive	$35.00
Average price for a resort course	$70.00
Average price for non-divers to ride on boat	$5.00
Average price for open water course (PADI certification)	$365.00
Average price for advanced course (PADI certification)	$235.00

Italian brand, Spirotechnique. The center has about 35 full sets of rental equipment. It also has a Bauer compressor, which the center uses to fill its 180 steel and aluminum tanks.

Dive Sites

There are 21 dive sites off the coast of Trinidad. Large coral heads, platforms, ridges, and sandy channels characterize diving near the western coast of Playa

Marine research shows that Cuban reefs are healthy.

E. Macao

Maria Aguilar. Moving eastward, the coral reef has walls and drop-offs. Finally, the most eastern diving zone is near Cayo Blanco. Tunnels, tall coral fingers, and sandy passageways classify this zone. Depth ranges from 15 feet (3 meters) to 99 feet (33 meters).

Popular dive sites have large, colorful sponges and many species of soft and hard corals. Small tropical fish are sparsely found in and around coral heads. (See dive maps on pg. 134-135)

For more information or to book a reservation, divers should contact:

> **Blanco Cay**
> Peninsula de Ancon
> Trinidad, Sancti Spiritus, Cuba
> Ph: 534-819-6205
> Fax: 534-819-6205
> Email: marinastadad@ip.etcsa.cu
> Also contact:
>
> **Puertosol Marina Chain**
> Calle 1ra, No. 3001, esq. A30
> Miramar, Habana, Cuba
> Ph: 537-204-5923
> Fax: 537-204-5928
> Email: psolger@psol.mit.tur.cu
> or comerc@psol.mit.tur.cu
> Website:
> www.puertosol.cubaweb.cu

Live-Aboard

A comfortably equipped and well-staffed live-aboard offers diving in Trinidad. The ship also visits Jardines de la Reina, Maria la Gorda, Cayo Largo, and Varadero. It has a capacity for up to 10 divers. All trips are five days long. Costs are $1500 per day for the entire boat. The price includes everything, even fresh lobster and fish dinners. For more information or to book a reserva-tion contact one or more of the following agencies:

> Da Silva Tours, Canada: 403-263-1699
> Regal Holidays, England:
> 013-53-778-096
> Cubana, Belgium: 02-640-35-60
> Blue Wave, Belgium: 056-51-70-03
> Subexplore, France: 01-40-39-99-33

The easiest method to book a reservation is via email at:

> trisub.sc@skynet.be
> or dionisio@stage.cha.cyt.cu

Insider's Tips

Some divers call Ancon "Cayo Blanco Area". The nickname is derived from a small island in the bay that contains two of the named dive sites. The Ancon Nitrox Dive Center has been popular for over a decade. Divers can see tunnels, caves, wide varieties of coral fingers, and giant gorgonians. There are shallow non-current dives for beginners, as well as challenging dives for skilled divers.

Center for Marine Research, Univ. Havana

The author exploring coral heads   M. Mola

Hotel Ancon Diving Center employs five instructors, four who speak English. All of the instructors are CMAS or PADI certified. The center has two boats for 12 and 22 passengers and has the capacity for 80 divers, but seldom more than 25 in the high season. The nearest hyperbaric chamber is in Cardenas, which is about 165 miles away from Trinidad.

Puertosol plans to begin a joint venture with a French company to start a liveaboard service. Clients will embark in Trinidad and dive as far out as Los Jardines de la Reina (The Queen's Gardens).

Marina Puertosol de Cayo Blanco offers a number of water-sport activities such as: deep-sea fishing, sunset cruises, and snorkeling excursions.

Cubanacan Nautica is opening a Scuba Cuba Dive Center at the new four star Brisas Hotel in 2003.

A suggested *casa particular* in Trinidad is la casa de Carlos e Iraida:

>Calle Piero Guinart, No. 36 Altos
>2 Flor e/ Pedro Zerquera y
>Anastasio
>Cardenas, Cuba
>Email: CBL917@hotmail.com

Above the Water

There are a multitude of historic places to see such as: The Museum of Architecture, The Museum of History, The Museum of Decorative Arts, La Iglesia de Popa (a church), a cigar factory, and many walking tours around the city's plazas. Shopping at the market is also a fun way to find well-made souvenirs for reasonable prices. See the *Cuba Handbook*, by Christopher P. Baker for more details.

Getting There

Divers can buy a bus ticket to Trinidad from any Havantur Agency in hotel lobbies. Buses leave from most major hotels in Havana at round 8:00am. The bus fare costs $36.00 each way. If you plans to do a day trip, it makes for a long day. Packages that include lunch are available for under $100.00.

AeroTaxi has daily flights from Havana to Trinidad, which depart at 7:00am, 12:45pm, 1:15pm, and 4:00pm. The average flight time is one hour and fifty minutes and costs about $50.00 each way.

Flights can be booked at the Inter/Lacsa office in the lobby of the Havana Libre Hotel at :

>Ph: 537-866-2703 / 537-866-2702
>Fax: 537-833-3728 / 537-833-7996

The Trinidad office can be contacted at:

>Ph: 534-819-4406

Trinidad can also be reached by Aero Taxi from the following areas:

Varadero has a one-hour flight to Trinidad for $45.00 each way. It leaves at 7:50am and 4:50pm.

Cayo Coco has a fifty-five minute flight to Trinidad for $50.00 each way. It leaves at 4:35pm. Ph: 533-830-1245

Cayo Largo has a fifty-minute flight to Trinidad for $50.00 each way. It leaves at 2:20pm. Ph: 534-819-8100

TRINIDAD
Ancon Nitrox Dive Center

Dive Site	Depth
1. Paraiso de las Esponjas	Wall
2. Jardín Colgante	Wall
3. El Tunel Profundo	100ft (33m)
4. El Laberinto	100ft (33m)
5. La Pared de Neptuno	100ft (33m)
6. El Camino de Triton	35ft (12m)
7. El Tunel de Gran Azul	100ft (33m)
8. La Pared de Punta Gorda	100ft (33m)
9. La Pared de la Torre	100ft (33m)
10. Las Piedras	100ft (33m)
11. Maria Aguilar	100ft (33m)
12. Bajo de Maria Aguilar	100ft (33m)
13. La Roca de los Corales	100ft (33m)
14. Las Gorgonias	100ft (33m)
15. Fondo de Omar	40-120ft (13-40m)

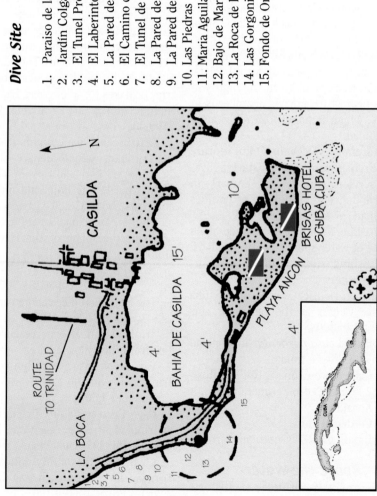

TRINIDAD
Ancon Nitrox Dive Center (Continued)

Dive Site	Depth	
16. Los Canales	50-100ft	(17-33m)
17. Barcos Hundidos de Ancon	50-100ft	(17-33m)
18. La Pared Negra	50-100ft	(17-33m)
19. Barcos Hundidos de las Mulatas	25-120ft	(8-40m)
20. Los Corales	Wall	
21. La Corona de los Sabalos	50-125ft	(17-42m)

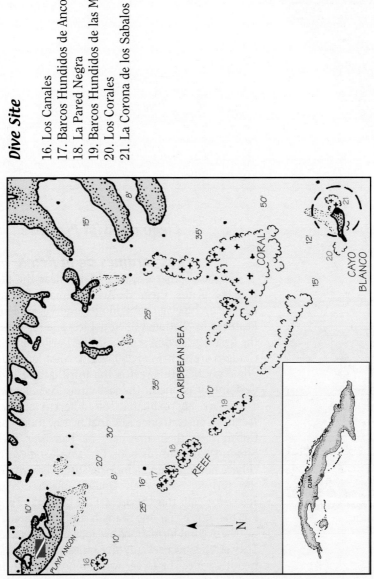

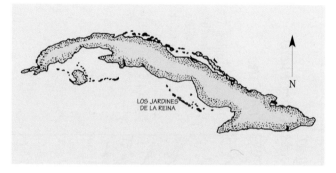

Ciego de Avila Province

Los Jardines de la Reina

Off the southern coast of Cuba near the provinces of Sancti Spiritus, Ciego de Avila, Camaguey, and Granma, lies the archipelago containing hundreds of deserted keys. Featured in "National Geographic," and regarded as one of the best kept diving secrets in the Caribbean, the Queen's Gardens are a chain of 250 virgin, coral, unsettled islands. Some say that this reef is the third largest in the world. Certainly it is one of the last virgin reefs known to man. There are approximately 60 different species of fish. Jacques Cousteau once said that he saw more fish on these Cuban reefs than anywhere he had ever been. Author Simon Charles in his book *Cruising Guide to Cuba* says, "I have never dived in a more beautiful environment below the surface." And even Doug Paulson of *Sport Diver Television* calls this Cuban reef the best in the entire world. For me, it is by far one of my favorite dive areas in Cuba!

World class boat fishing in Queen's Garden

D. Tipton

These coral formations are located forty miles offshore. They stretch over seventy-five miles and at times are twenty miles wide. The larger westernmost part of the gardens is called the Doce Leguas, where divers have the opportu-

136

nity to see marine turtles everywhere. In 1996, this vicinity was declared a protected area, thereby shielding these pristine waters for future divers to enjoy these marine riches. Access is somewhat restricted. Commercial fishermen have been banned from all areas except the outermost extremities. The best way to experience this gorgeous marine area is by two live-aboard boats. Jucaro, a small village with old fashion houses and 2000 inhabitants, is the boarding point for both live-aboards.

The Hotel Flotante is also called La Tortuga "The Turtle". It was built eight years ago, staffed by Cubans and managed by two Italians. La Tortuga provides seven cabins, each equipped with their own shower, toilet, and air conditioning. The ship, with a maximum capacity for fourteen people, has good communication with the outside world by a satellite telephone. All of the employees speak English. Because the Queen's Gardens are a protected area, the ship's anchor cannot be used on the reefs. In fact, a $5,000 fine will be imposed for doing so. La Tortuga has a capacity for up to twenty-two divers. The ship has two Bauer compressors (k 15, k 14) which allows for filling empty tanks. Full sets of rental equipment are available, which are of Mares, Aqua-Lung, or Speedo-Technic brands. Dive lights are also available. Prices start at $110 per day per customer and include meals. Dives are scheduled two times per day. Programs are usually seven days or fourteen days long departing on a Sunday morning and returning on a Saturday.

The Halcon, a non-diver sport fisherman live-aboard ship, is 72 feet long and has a motor with 450 horse-power. Aboard the Halcon, there are six cabins, three bathrooms, air-conditioning, and opportunities for exclusive fly-fishing cruises. Food usually consists of local fish, shellfish, fruit, pasta, rice and flan. It is delicious. Water, soft drinks, beer, rum, and wine are offered. Laundry is available on a daily basis. Also available is the Explorador, a more economic, less spacious diver's live-aboard

Both divers and fishermen enjoy tarpon.

M. Mola

with a maximum capacity for eight people and a cost of only $700 per person.

Dive Sites

The Queens Gardens is the best place to see healthy fish-life. The quantities and sizes of the fish exceed all other diving locations in Cuba. La Tortuga visits an infinite number of dive sites. Sixty sites are easily located. All the diving along the wall is great. Some sites are marked with buoys.

There are three impressive underwater shows that divers do not want to miss. The first dive is a silky shark feeding show. Up to fifty or sixty sharks participate in this show. All of them are about 3 feet (1 meter) up to 8 feet long (2½ meters). Divers have the opportunity to touch these sharks. The show takes place in 45-75 feet (15-25 meters) of water. Sometimes divers can see silkies in just 15 feet (5 meters) of water while the dive master places small scraps of fish on the surface.

Another great dive show is the caribbean reef sharks. Dive masters first encountered these sharks years ago at 200 feet. They kept feeding them at gradually shallower depths and now they congregate at 90 feet (30 meters). The sharks are quite bulky and broad reaching up to 12 feet (4 meters) in length. This is a great dive that encourages the adrenaline glands to flow. Do not forget your camara.

The other show worth seeing is a goliath grouper fish feeding. Anywhere from three to six goliath groupers show up for this dive. All of the groupers are over a hundred pounds. One mammoth grouper weighs in at about 450 pounds! After feeding, the groupers follow the dive group for the rest of the dive. This site is teeming with fish. Occasional eagle rays can also be seen. (See dive map on pg. 143)

Puente Escondido

This site has a reef that creates a submerged bridge 45 feet long (15 meters). Schools of large tarpon live under it. In the shallower water there are many tropical reef fish such as grunts, angelfish, black durgeon, groupers and barracudas. Maximum depth is 60 feet (20 meters).

El Dafil

This site has a maximum depth of 105 feet (35 meters). The area has many coral heads beginning at 30 feet (10 meters) with white sandy canals extending to the wall at 90 feet. (30 meters). There are many groups of black coral, cubera snappers, yellowtail snappers, black groupers, tiger groupers and dog snappers.

Peruano I

This sea floor has a vertical wall between 30-65ft (10-22 meters) with some small caves. Afterward, it returns to a sandy floor. Thriving coral share this site with bright sponges, which reach 3 feet (1 meter) in height. Divers can also appreciate the abundance of tarpons, moray eels and rays. Maximum depth is 90 feet (30 meters).

Vincent

Great coral pillars lead divers to a wall. A tunnel perforates one of these pillars that juts upward. Excellent fish life can be found such as goliath groupers, sharks, devilfish and eagle rays. The maximum depth is about 120 feet (40 meters).

Divers are guaranteed to see 20-40 silky sharks at a time.

D. Tipton

Los Jardines de la Reina

Goliath groupers reach up to 450 lbs.   E. Macao

Montaña Rusa

Beautiful coral canyons create a picturesque painting in a diver's eye at a depth of 66-105 feet (22-35 meters) near the corner of a wall. At times these canyons form tunnels at great depths. Goliath groupers, snappers, king fish, schools of horse-eyed jacks, jack crevalles and silky sharks live there. Maximum depth is 120 feet.

El Farallon

This area has a great coral formation, which is 40ft high (13 meters), with many narrow canyons. Schools of tarpon, some goliath grouper, devilfish, turtles and sharks inhabit this site. Maximum depth is 95 feet (32 meters).

Avalon

A sandy bottom weaves between coral formations and a deep canyon at 120 feet (40 meters). Divers can expect to see great quantities of fish including: devilfish, eagle rays, dog snappers, snappers, some sharks and sometimes hammerheads. This area is subject to strong currents and thus it is necessary to dive at high tide. Maximum depth is 40 feet.

Neptuno's Garden

This site is formed by elegant corals beginning at 30 feet and has many wide, sandy channels that flow towards the wall. Fish life is abundant with dog snappers, cubera snappers, black groupers, and king mackerel. Maximum depth is 105 feet (35 meters).

Puente Grande

Here the coral wall forms a bridge that protects a large school of tarpon. Divers can also observe Nassau groupers, black groupers, turtles and cubera snappers. Maximum depth is 55 feet (18 meters).

El Quebrado

In February this site is a favorite spawning ground for many tiger groupers. There are also black grouper, rock hind grouper, Nassau grouper and silky sharks that live in

    The Diving Guide to Cuba Scuba

this area. Maximum depth is 120 feet (40 meters).

Five Sea

This is an excellent shallow site in 60 feet (20 meters) of water. Between the rising coral mounds is the wreckage of a small American boat 45 feet (15 meters) long. After 20 years of resting on the bottom, this wreck has been colonized by corals and is home to small arrow crabs and shrimps. Large overhangs are adorned with black coral trees and soft branching corals. Red sea-whips corkscrew downward from the ceiling. Tropical fish are everywhere. Maximum depth is 60 feet (20 meters).

Cabeza de la Cubera

This site rises from a sandy bed into several mounds and canyons. One of the biggest groupers ever seen in Los Jardines de la Reina was discovered recently on this reef. Lush corals grow on the mounds. Within the cracks are green moray and tiger moray eels. Many varieties of grouper and snapper are inquisitive enough to closely approach divers. Maximum depth is 65 feet (22 meters).

El Tunel Azul

The entrance to this tunnel is on the vertical wall at 150 feet. A solitary jack crevalle often follows divers everywhere during the dive. Out in the blue: eagle rays, sharks and schools of barracuda cruise the premises. Large sweeping banks of coral rise to within 45 feet of the surface at high tide. Maximum depth is 150 feet (50 meters).

Coral Negro I

This is a rush of a dive, which provides many exciting experiences with numerous silky sharks. Over and alongside the drop-off, large eagle rays swim parallel to the wall. Black coral forests clump together with other soft bright corals. Small reef fish are abundant. Maximum depth is 120 feet (40 meters).

Pequeño Paraiso

This site is comprised of islands of dark rock coral set amongst white sand. The beautiful green moray and tiger moray have made homes here. Stingrays can be found half buried in the sand. There are numerous large grouper. Gorgonians and soft coral trees wave in a slight surge. During the day, lobsters stay hidden. Brain corals and large finger coral complete the background of this dive. Maximum depth is 60 feet (20 meters).

La Gruta del Tarpon

This site has a cave with a large opening at 30 feet (10 meters), which drops to 45 feet (15 meters) where many tarpon school together and swim rapidly. Divers should be ready with their camera. Also inhabiting this area are rays, moray eels, schools of snapper, and large grouper. Maximum depth is 60 feet (20 meters).

Las Cruces

This casual dive has a sea bed and a swim-through cave where black sands provide special photographic effects. Divers will see jacks, snappers, moray eels, barracuda and smaller reef fish. Maximum depth is 55 feet (18 meters).

Divemaster, Noel, holding a silky shark.   M. Mola

During the fishing season live-aboard trips run from a Friday to the following Saturday. The season is generally from October 27 to Aug 31. A normal week includes five full days of fishing and one to two half days, depending on your schedule and mode of transportation.

Tipping the Staff

Many divers and fisherman like to show their appreciation for the excellent customer service by giving tips. In general, the average fisherman tips $100 to their guide and $100 for the Hotel Flotante (Tortuga) staff to be split among the bartenders, waitresses, cooks, cabin attendees, etc. Divers usually tip $20-$25 per dive instructor, $10-$15 per crewmember, and $30-$100 for the Hotel Flotante (Tortuga) staff to be split.

Insider's Tips

All fishermen and divers are required to pay a $90 park fee. During the month of September, the live-aboards are usually closed. During winter months divers have the best chance to see whale sharks.

World-class fishing can be experienced in these areas via the Halcon. Among their clients has been college basketball coach, Bobby Knight, formerly of Indiana University and now at Texas Tech. Tarpon, bonefish, permit, mutton snappers, jack crevelle, horse-eye jacks, barracudas, and sharks are abundant. It is also not uncommon to find kingfish, tuna, and wahoo. Fishing hours are totally at the discretion of the clients. The fishing day normally begins with breakfast at 7:00am, departing for fishing from 7:45am on. Many people elect to return to the boat for a nice lunch. Most of the flats are within fifteen minutes of the boat. Clients can fish late into the afternoon if they wish. In Los Jardines de la Reina, the morning winds often calm down in the afternoons. Fishing in the late afternoon can be superb, especially for bonefish.

Getting There

You must book a reservation before arriving in Jucaro to board La Tortuga, Halcon, or Explorador. It is advisable to book early, as cabins are usually full. Packages include airfare, transfers, and live-aboard fees. These packages are the most cost efficient. From January 15 – July 31 charter flights from Havana to Ciego de Avila are available. The best way to book a reservation is to contact the manager online at:

> Filippo Invernizzi
> (Italian manager)
> Pepe Omegna (Italian Manager)
> Fax: +1 928-222 1631
> Web page: www.avalons.net
> Email: avalon@avalons.net

LOS JARDINES DE LA REINA
Avalon Dive Center

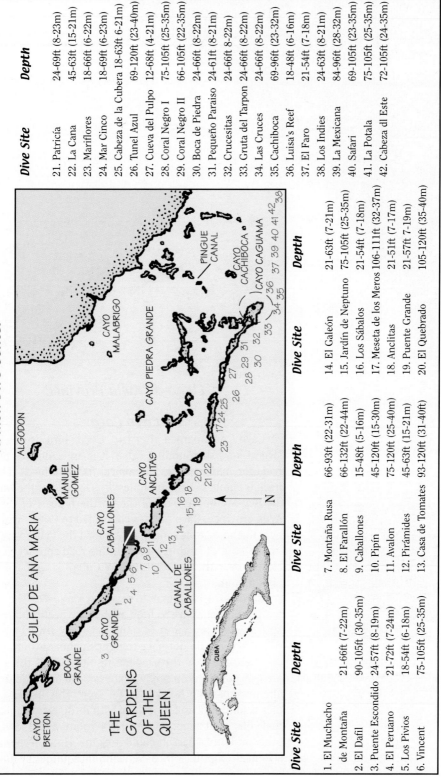

Dive Site	Depth
1. El Muchacho de Montaña	21-66ft (7-22m)
2. El Dafil	90-105ft (30-35m)
3. Puente Escondido	24-57ft (8-19m)
4. El Peruano	21-72ft (7-24m)
5. Los Pivios	18-54ft (6-18m)
6. Vincent	75-105ft (25-35m)

Dive Site	Depth
7. Montaña Rusa	66-93ft (22-31m)
8. El Farallón	66-132ft (22-44m)
9. Caballones	15-48ft (5-16m)
10. Pipín	45-120ft (15-30m)
11. Avalon	75-120ft (25-40m)
12. Pirámides	45-63ft (15-21m)
13. Casa de Tomates	93-120ft (31-40ft)

Dive Site	Depth
14. El Galeón	21-63ft (7-21m)
15. Jardín de Neptuno	75-105ft (25-35m)
16. Los Sábalos	21-54ft (7-18m)
17. Meseta de los Meros	106-111ft (32-37m)
18. Anclitas	21-51ft (7-17m)
19. Puente Grande	21-57ft 7-19m)
20. El Quebrado	105-120ft (35-40m)

Dive Site	Depth
21. Patricía	24-69ft (8-23m)
22. La Cana	45-63ft (15-21m)
23. Mariflores	18-66ft (6-22m)
24. Mar Cinco	18-69ft (6-23m)
25. Cabeza de la Cubera	18-63ft 6-21m)
26. Tunel Azul	69-120ft (23-40m)
27. Cueva del Pulpo	12-68ft (4-21m)
28. Coral Negro I	75-105ft (25-35m)
29. Coral Negro II	66-105ft (22-35m)
30. Boca de Piedra	24-66ft (8-22m)
31. Pequeño Paraiso	24-61ft (8-21m)
32. Crucesitas	24-66ft 8-22m)
33. Gruta del Tarpon	24-66ft (8-22m)
34. Las Cruces	24-66ft (8-22m)
35. Cachiboca	69-96ft (23-32m)
36. Luisa's Reef	18-48ft (6-16m)
37. El Faro	21-54ft (7-18m)
38. Los Indies	24-63ft (8-21m)
39. La Mexicana	84-96ft (28-32m)
40. Safari	69-105ft (23-35m)
41. La Potala	75-105ft (25-35m)
42. Cabeza dl Este	72-105ft (24-35m)

Cayo Coco

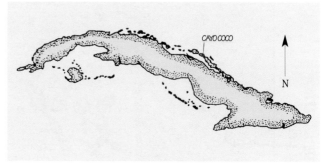

Ciego de Avila Province

Cayo Coco

Cayo Coco, named after the "Coco" bird, is one of the largest keys surrounding Cuba. It is an ecological promenade for many species of tropical fish and birds. The key itself is about 144 square miles. It is located in the Jardines del Rey Archipelago off of the northern coast of Ciego de Avila province. Cayo Coco is connected to Cuba's mainland by a 13 and ½ mile long bridge, called the Pedraplen. Built in 1988 out of landfill material, this road appears to hover closely over the sea, escorted by Cuba's largest colony of pink flamingos.

Cayo Coco is similar to a young Varadero. The white, powdery beaches are as long as they are beautiful. In their entirety, they are about 14 miles in length. Divers who visit this sanctuary do not have to fight the hoards of tourists.

There are only three operating hotels, but three more are expected to crop up by next year. The most deluxe and all-encompassing hotel is Hotel Tryp. This massive complex is like a Cuban Disneyland with its diverse ethnic colonial villages. It supports over 1,000 rooms along with every other amenity a person could imagine. Hotel Tryp makes a strong attempt to combat vengeful mosquitoes by fumigat-

Ribbons of road connect the cayos.

W. Houghton

ing the premises during dusk and dawn. It would be smart to lather on the repellent anyway.

The hotel grounds display six gigantic swimming pools. In addition to over ten bars and restaurants, guest activities include: six tennis courts, bad-mitten, beach volleyball, basketball, water sports, ping pong, pool tables, gym, sauna, day-care center, bicycle rentals, car and motor-scooter rentals, nightly entertainment shows, massages, disco/night club, gift shops, ice cream stands, film developing centers, conference rooms, pharmacy, and 24-hour medical services.

All-inclusive prices range from $185.00 for a double room during the low season to $250.00 during the high season (December 21st – January 3rd). If you elect not to go all-inclusive, rooms range from $100.00 for a double room in the low season to $148.00 during the high season. One, two and three-week packages are also available. Prices vary.

Cubanacan Nautica's Coco Diving Center is located just outside of Hotel Tryp on the beach. Divers meet at the center at 9:00 in the morning. After registration, three dive boats leave at 9:30 am. Two dives are usually made: one deep and one shallow. After the second dive, boats return to the center around 12:30. Sometimes there is a third dive at 2:30, but it is usually filled with beginner resort divers who are restricted to a maximum depth of 30 feet (10 meters) and a bottom time of only 40 minutes. An easy way to make arrangements is to con-

Dive Prices	
Average price for one to four dives (per dive)	$30.00
Average price for five dives	$140.00
Average price for ten dives	$250.00
Average price for fifteen dives	$360.00
Average price for twenty dives	$440.00
Average price for Open Water Course	$365.00
Average price for Advanced Course	$250.00
Average price for a Resort Dive	$60.00
Night dives are not offered	

Sting rays are timid because they are unfamiliar with divers.

M. Mola

tact the concierge at Sol Club Cayo Coco at: depress.smcoco1@solmelia.cma.net

Rental Equipment

The cost for an entire set of rental equipment is only $5.00. There are 22 BC jackets, 28 regulators, 12 sets of masks/fins/snorkels, and 16 wetsuits available at the center. Coco Diving Center has a 1996 Bauer compressor and a 1998 Bauer compressor which fill their 90 tanks.

Dive Sites

Cayo Coco's coral reef extends for over 20 miles. There are 21 dive sites. Most of the reef lies in 33 feet of water (11 meters), causing coral bands to form. These bands are hosts to abundant schools of fish. Many have described the waters of Cayo Coco as an aquarium of fish. (See dive map on pg. 151).

Divers can expect to see a wide array of fish including tarpon, jacks, spadefish, grunts, angelfish, file fish, black durgeon, dog fish, surgeon fish, schoolmasters, snappers, large groupers, sharks, eagle rays, barracudas, and dolphins.

La Jaula

Located near La Jaula lighthouse, this dive site takes about 25 minutes to reach by boat. The depth ranges from 33-99 feet (11-33 meters). Divers have the opportunity to discover enormous, attractive gorgonians, and sponges of all shapes, sizes and colors. Also common to the area are black and Nassau groupers, large snappers, schoolmasters, stingrays, and eagle rays. A lucky diver may even spot a nurse shark, reef shark, or sea turtle.

Las Coloradas

At 36 feet (12 meters), this zone has a very sporadic sea bottom, with small caves, tunnels, and crevices. Divers who thoroughly investigate the crevices are destined to see an occasional lobster or any other surprise. A gigantic coral formation is home to many sea fans, anemone, inquisitive tarpon, schools of grunts, yellow-tail

An arrow crab perched on coral polyps

E. Macao

Sea fan M. Mola

snappers, large parrot fish, angelfish, and other small tropical species.

Casasa

This shallow dive site sits in just 15 feet (5 meters) of water. Between the rows of coral there are sandy canals, which often attract stingrays, schools of grunts, sea turtles, and nomadic barracuda.

Los Tiburones

This dive site has a maximum depth of 48 feet (16 meters). In this region, large coral formations form narrow passageways where reef sharks like to find shelter. Other fish such as groupers, snappers, bar jacks, and barracuda like these coral formations.

Insider's Tips

The best times for diving in Cayo Coco is during the months of May, June, July, August, and September. These months seem to be ideal for optimum weather conditions.

If you are considering deep-sea fishing while in Cuba, this is a great spot.

Although during the high season the center averages about 22-24 clients, the dive center has the capability of servicing 30 divers. Only about 10-15 divers visit per day during the low season. All of the employees speak English.

There are three certified ACUC instructors employed by the diving center. Certification for the open-water course requires four days. Only two days are required for the advanced course.

The nearest hyperbaric chamber is located in Cardenas, Matanzas, which is about a two-hour helicopter ride from Cayo Coco.

A professional under water video photographer is available every day to accompany divers and videotape their dives. The cost is $30.00 for one dive and $40.00 for two or more dives. Prices may vary.

For more information on diving, or to book a reservation at Hotel Tryp contact:

> **Coco Scuba Cuba**
> Cayo Coco
> Ciego de Avila, Cuba
> Ph: 533-330-1311
> Fax: 533-330-1386
> Email: idania@club.tryp.cma.net
> or gerencia@marlin.cav.cyt.cu

Divers can also contact Cubanacan Nautica's headquarters at:

> **Cubanacan Nautica**
> Calle 184, No. 123,
> Reparto Flores, Playa
> La Habana, Cuba
> Ph: 537-833-6675
> Fax : 537-833-7020
> Email:
> commercial@marlin.cha.cyt.cu
> Website: www.cubanacan.cu

Cayo Coco

Also available to book reservations is:
> Blue Diving
> Melia Cayo Coco
> Ciego de Avila, Cuba
> Ph: 533-330-8179
> Fax: 533-330-8180
> Email:
> en20@bluediving.cav-cyt.cu

Above the Water

There are a variety of excursions in which divers can participate.

Getting There

Divers may visit any major hotel's concierge desk to book a tourist package to Cayo Coco. Divers can book a flight with Cubana Airlines for about $120.00 per person, round trip. It is smart to book ahead, because this particular flight has a tendency to sell out completely.

The taxi from Cayo Coco airport to the hotel is approximately $20.00 one way. If you book a package with Havanatur, it is convenient to have them confirm an advance reservation for the taxi ride.

Aero Taxi has three daily flights from Havana to Cayo Coco, which cost about $100.00 each way. Flight departures are at 7:15am, 1:15pm, and 3:00pm. The office phone number of Aero Taxi in Cayo Coco is 033-301245.

Aero Taxi has four flights from Varadero to Cayo Coco, departing at 8:50am, 3:50pm,

Sample Excursion Package	
Havana day tour by plane	$150.00
Havana overnight by plane	$259.00
Trinidad by plane	$99.00
Trinidad overnight by bus	$140.00
Catamaran full day	$55.00
Catamaran half day	$35.00
Glass bottom boat	$25.00
Boqueron Jeep-Horse safari	$63.00
Boqueron by plane	$81.00
Moron full day	$40.00
Moron half day	$25.00
Cayo Coco Discovery	$20.00
Evening at La Cueva	$19.00
Deep sea fishing	$98.00
Deep sea fishing half day	$58.00
Bass Fishing	$98.00
Mayajigua by bus	$53.00
Aerial Cayo tour	$33.00
Jeep Safari Loma de Cunagua	$65.00
Cuba Trails overnight	$179.00

Cayo Coco is an area of many secluded mangroves.

D. Tipton

The Diving Guide to Cuba Scuba

Anemone

E. Macao

and 5:05pm. The flight is one hour and twenty-five minutes and costs $80 each way. To book tickets in Varadero, contact: Ph: 05614859 or 05667540 or 05612929

From Trinidad to Cayo Coco, the flight is about 55 minutes and costs $50.00 each way.

Aero Taxi also has a two-hour flight from Cayo Largo to Cayo Coco, which departs at 2:20pm. The cost is $100 each way. To book tickets from Cayo Largo contact: 05-48100.

One of the most convenient ways to get to Cayo Coco is to book a total package from a Canadian tour agency that includes the hotel, airfare, and ground transfers. For more information refer to listings in the back of this book.

Camagüey Province

Cayo Crúz

Between Cayo Coco and Cayo Romano is a small island called Cayo Crúz. This area opened during the year 2000 for divers. Look for this area to be developed in the near future.

Getting There

You must go through Cayo Coco to get to Cayo Crúz. Please refer to the Cayo Coco Section for flight information.

The dive center is nestled on the calm secluded beach.

W. Houghton

CAYO COCO
Coco Dive Center

Dive Site	Depth
1. Jaula I	100ft (33m)
2. Jaula II	100ft (33m)
3. Jaula III	55ft (19m)
4. Jaula IV	55ft (19m)
5. Loma del Puerto I	50ft (17m)
6. Loma del Puerto II	100ft (33m)
7. Triton I	100ft (33m)
8. Triton II	40ft (13m)
9. El Penon	80ft (27m)
10. Las Coloradas	40ft (13m)
11. El Cayuelo	100ft (33m)
12. Bautista I	55ft (19m)
13. Bautista II	100ft (33m)
14. Casas I	50ft (17m)
15. Casasa II	85ft (29m)
16. Los Canalones	20-60ft (7-20m)
17. Los Mogotes	55ft (19m)
18. Los Tiburones	50ft (17m)
19. Los Robalos	50ft (17m)
20. Blue Hole	120ft (33m)

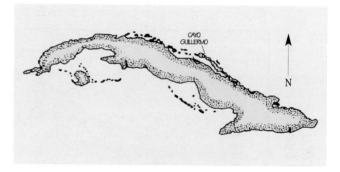

Ciego de Avila Province

Cayo Guillermo

W. Houghton

Cayo Guillermo is situated to the northwest of Cayo Coco. A narrow channel called "La Pasa Guillermo" (William's Pass) separates the two cays. This newly developed, all-inclusive beach is home to four large hotels, including the five-star Sol Melia, Iberostar Daiquiri, Villa Cojimar, and Sol Club Cayo Guillermo. Each offers beach diving. All dive boats visit the same 20 dive sites. In October of 2002 the Sol Melia began to include diving in their all-inclusive price. In addition to the hotels, the main dive shop called "Cuba Divers", is jointly owned by Puertosol and a German operator, located to the north of the channel. Cuba Divers offers efficient diving, excellent new equipment, and PADI standards of operation.

The Cuba Divers center has one dive boat, 41 feet long. Three instructors are employed at the center, and have the authorization to certify divers in CMAS, ACUC, and PADI.

Rental Equipment

In addition to 25 sets of SeaQuest rental equipment, and over 40 tanks, Cuba Divers center also has its own

Bauer compressor. Underwater cameras are available for rent. In case of emergency, the center is a two-hour helicopter ride from the hyperbaric chamber in Cardenas, Matanzas.

Dive Prices

Prices are similar among all the dive centers. Prices vary depending on the number of dives purchased in a package.

Average price for one dive	$35.00
Average price for two dives	$60.00
Open Water Course	$365.00
Resort Dive	$90.00

Dive Sites

There are 20 dive sites where divers can expect to see coral formations, caves, and an occasional shipwreck. Typical diving is between 45ft and 80 ft (16-20 meters). Barracudas, nurse sharks, stingrays, eagle rays, and turtles are sometimes seen in these coral territories. Dives are made at 9am and 2pm. Night dives are not offered because the coast guard prohibits this activity. (See map on pg. 156)

El Acuario

A 25-minute boat ride from shore, the site is nestled in 45 feet (15 meters) of water. Divers can see lobsters, morays, and rays around colorful corals.

Media Luna

This site has a small reef at 50 feet (17 meters) followed by sand canyons and then another reef. The formations resemble a half moon. Eagle rays usually swim near the end of the second reef.

Just chillin'

W. Houghton

Cayo Guillermo

D. Tipton

Servimar

This wreck dive begins in about 64 feet (21 meters) of water. Tropical fish have adopted homes in this wreck while moray eels swim in the open. Coral formations make a great setting here for pictures.

Coco

A secret site known only by the boat captain, this place is the ultimate in Cayo Guillermo for tons of fish, lobsters, nurse sharks, rays, grouper, etc. The reef platform begins at 30 feet (15 meters) and is the only place the boat sets anchor. The area is full of fish and vegetation. The German owner compares this site to the Maldive Islands.

El Perro

Nice coral heads trimmed with sandy fingers, tropical fish, and lobsters are set in depths beginning at 48 feet (16 meters).

El Capitan

This deep dive is a computer Deco-Dive beginning in about 90 to 105 feet.

La Morena

On a shallow dive of about 33 feet to 45 feet (11-14 meters), lucky divers may see schools of snapper, grunts, and jacks and an occasional moray eel. This is a nice spot for photography.

Insider's Tips

Cayo Guillermo is not yet a protected zone, however, dive centers are trying to work with local fisherman to ask them not to take fish near dive sites. It is unlikely to see a buoy marking the dive sites since fisherman were used to fishing nice dive areas.

Nonetheless, fish life seems to be healthy.

Jungle tours with snorkeling are also offered for $35 per person. It is a two hour excursion across the mangrove channels of Cayo Guillermo. Snorkeling equipment, soft drinks, life jackets, guide, lockers, and transfers are included in the price. Departure times are 9am, 11am, 1pm and 3pm.

The hotels host several water sports, including snorkeling, jet-skis, catamarans, and diving. Nightlife is a bit sterile, but hotels do their best to entertain guests.

Deep-sea fishing is good in Cayo Coco. For more information on fishing or diving contact:

Cuba Divers
Cayo Guillermo, Moron
Ciego de Avila, Cuba
Web Site: www.cuba-divers.com
Email: info@cuba-divers.com

Sol Club Guillermo Scuba Cuba
Green Moray Diving Center
Hotel Sol Club
Cayo Guillermo
Ciego de Avila, Cuba
Ph: 533-330-1760
Fax: 533-330-1328
Email:
gernecia@marlin.cav.cyt.cu or
depress@cguille.solmelia.cma.net

Jardines Del Rey
Rotonda Villa Oceano
Cayo Guillermo
Archipielago, Jardines del Rey
Moron, Ciego de Avila, Cuba
Ph: 533-330-1738
Fax: 533-330-1737
Email: psol@cayo.cco.tur.cu

Melia Cayo Guillermo
Scuba Cuba
Hotel Melia
Cayo Guillermo
Ciego de Avila, Cuba
Ph: 533-330-1627
Fax: 533-330-1328
Email:
gerencia@marlin.cav.cyt.cu

Getting There
Cayo Guillermo is accessible through Cayo Coco. You can drive through Cayo Coco or fly into Cayo Coco airport. The Máximo Gómez International Airport, near the provincial capital of Ciego de Ávila, receives medium-sized and large direct planes daily. Please refer to the Cayo Coco chapter for flight information.

W. Houghton

Cayo Guillermo

Dive Site

1. La Propela
2. Barrera Felipe
3. Felipe
4. La Angelica
5. La Morena
6. La Gorgonia
7. La Finca
8. El Perro
9. Los Magotes
10. El Pargo
11. Media Luna I
12. El Aguaji
13. Media Luna II
14. Media Luna III
15. El Acuario I
16. El Acuario II
17. Los Meros
18. La Jaula I
19. La Jaula II
20. Los Meros

Ancient cayos waiting to be discovered

D. Tipton

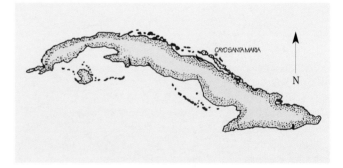

Ciego de Avila Province

Cayo Santa Maria

Cayo Santa Maria is located on Cuba's Atlantic coast, north of Cayo Romano, just off the northern coast of Villa Clara Province. This territory is a diamond in the rough. The area's first hotel with 420 rooms was opened in 2002. It is an all-inclusive Melia Hotel. Cayo Santa Maria is in its infant stage. Many of the dive sites have yet to be named.

The dive center, owned by Gaviota, employs two dive masters. Both speak English and are ACUC certified. There are two available boats, each 21-feet long. The center is open until 5:00pm. The dive schedule usually begins the first dive around 9:00am, the second dive at 11:30am, and the third dive at 2:00pm.

Many Cubans learn to salsa when they learn to walk.

W. Houghton

Dive Prices		
Average price for one dive	$45.00	Average price for six dives $240.00
Average price for two dives	$70.00	Average price for resort dive $55.00
Average price for four dives $128.00		

Rental Equipment

All equipment is of the Italian brand Cressi-Sub. There are 50 steel tanks available, all of which are 10 or 12 liters air capacity. The cost for a complete set of rental gear is $20.00 per day. It may be possible to negotiate rental prices when purchasing a dive package. There are no dive lights for rent. The dive center has one Bauer compressor. The nearest hyperbaric chamber is located in Mantanzas, Cuba.

Dive Sites

The diving in Cayo Santa Maria is virtually untouched. Pristine seabeds offer much to be explored. There are 10 sites that are newly discovered.

La Cueva Sin Nombre

Just a 10-minute boat ride from shore, this cave has a capacity to hold up to 12 divers at one time. The cave varies in depths measuring to 30 feet (10 meters), 54 feet (18 meters), and 90 feet (30 meters). Divers can expect to see small schools of tarpon, an occasional black tip shark, and other typical Caribbean fishes. The average bottom time is dependent on dive tables and experience.

A Legendary Sunken German U-Boat Submarine from World War II

This is another great wreck for history buffs, adventurers, and curious divers. Locals often speak of this wreck and believe that it could possibly be the missing U-boat from Keele, Germany. Germany has recorded a missing U-boat from World War II, which they believe sank somewhere off the coast of Cuba. The wreck site is thought to be located less than an hour's boat ride from shore in about 54 feet (18 meters) of water. Divers have the opportunity to experience the ship while it is still completely intact. Yet few locals actually know how to locate this site.

Queen Angel fish

E. Macao

Insider's Tips

A one-year old live aboard vessel is currently operating in Cayo Santa Maria. Owned by Rumbos, this floating hotel has the capacity for 16 divers. There are 6 employees that work aboard the ship, all of whom speak English. The ship has a Bauer compressor, 20 tanks, and 6 sets of Mares rental equipment. The cost for an entire set of rental gear is about $20.00. For more information or to make a reservation contact :

Cubanacan Nautica
Calle 184, No. 123,
Reparto Flores, Playa
La Habana, Cuba
Ph: 537-833-6675
Fax : 537-833-7020
Email:
commercial@marlin.cha.cyt.cu
Website: www.cubanacan.cu.

Las Brujas Diving Center
Cayo Las Brujas
Villa Clara, Cuba
Ph: 534-220-4199
Fax: 534-220-7599
Gaviota
Email: gaviota@nwgaviot.vma.net
Website: www.gaviota.cu

Getting There

Divers can reach Cayo Santa Maria by flying to the newly built Santa Clara airport. At the time of publication of this book, it is possible for divers to book direct charter packages from some Canadian travel agencies.

For reservations, divers can contact the Sol Cayo Santa Maria concierge at:

Reflections in a mangrove cayo

D. Tipton

W. Houghton

Sol Cayo Santa Maria
Cayo Santa Maria, Caribbean
Villa Clara, Cuba
Ph: 534-235-1500
Fax: 534-235-1505
Email: cayostamaria@
tpeninsula.solmelia.cu
www.solmeliacuba.com

Divers can book a trip to Cayo Santa Maria through any Rumbos travel agency in Havana. There is a Rumbos agency in the lobby of the Riviera Hotel (next to the Melia Cohiba) and the Habana Libre Hotel. Although the Rumbos travel agency can reserve the airline ticket, divers still have to go to Rampas Street to pick up the tickets.

Divers can book an airplane ticket from Havana to Cayo Romano, and then take a $20.00 taxi ride from Cayo Romano to Cayo Santa Maria. Both Cubana and Aero Gaviota airlines have daily flights to Cayo Romano for about $120 round trip.

It is advisable to book your packages in advance, because flights are sometimes sold out, especially during the winter months.

E. Macao

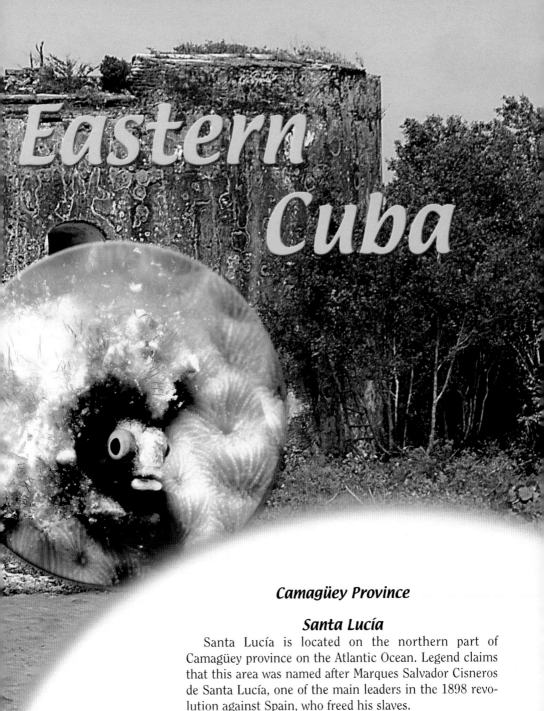

Eastern Cuba

Camagüey Province

Santa Lucía

Santa Lucía is located on the northern part of Camagüey province on the Atlantic Ocean. Legend claims that this area was named after Marques Salvador Cisneros de Santa Lucía, one of the main leaders in the 1898 revolution against Spain, who freed his slaves.

Santa Lucía has a blanket of 12½ miles of white powdery beaches, which are protected by a large coral reef. It is one of the most coveted dive areas on the island. Its rich waters are a spectacle of nearly any diver's preference.

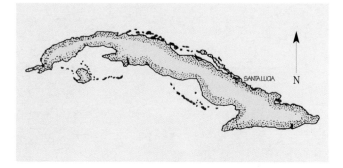

Santa Lucía has vintage sunken Spanish galleons, adventurous shark shows, historic submerged artifacts, and excellent fish life. And, except for five hotels, there is very little infrastructure outside an occasional fishing village that lines the sandy coast of Santa Lucía. Some hotels close during slow months, so it is a good idea to check in advance to plan vacations.

Club Amigo Mayanabo

Rated as three stars, this all-inclusive club has had recent renovations since its construction in the 1970's. There are 213 rooms and 12 suites with air-conditioning, telephones, satellite TV, and safety deposit boxes. Amenities that are offered include: a large swimming pool, children's pool, gym, two restaurants, two bars, tennis court, non-motorized water sports, game room, animated entertainment, bicycles, fitness center, gift shop, post office, scooter and car rentals, medical service, and a concierge desk. The average price per person is $75.00 per night, all-inclusive. For more information or to book a reservation contact:

Wreck of the Mortera

M. Mola

> Club Amigo Mayanabo
> Playa Santa Lucía, Nuevitas
> Camagüey, Cuba

Ph: 533-236-5168
Fax: 533-236-5176
E-mail: aloja@
mayanabo.stl.cyt.cu

Club Amigo Caracol

This three-star hotel has 150 bunga-lows. Each bungalow has one bedroom and a living room. Some have ocean views. Other amenities are: two restaurants (one which is buffet style), two bars, grill, swim-ming pool, jacuzzi, volleyball, tennis, water sports, daily entertainment. For prices and more information, contact:

Vita Club Caracol
Playa Santa Lucía, Nuevitas
Camagüey, Cuba
Ph: 533-236-5158
Fax: 533-236-5307
E-mail: aloja@caracol.stl.cyt.cu

Villa Tararaco

This two-star motel has 30 rooms and one suite, all of which are air-conditioned.

Other amenities are: a restaurant, bar, snack bar, night club, game room, water sports, daily entertainment. There is also a convention room on the second floor. The price is only $25.00 per day, which includes breakfast. For more information, contact:

Villa Tararaco
Playa Santa Lucía, Nuevitas
Camagüey, Cuba
Ph: 533-236-4100
Fax: 533-236-5166

Club Santa Lucía

This three-star club has 249 rooms, of which 56 are junior suites, 40 regular suites, and 12 bungalows. Salsa lessons are given at the pool with 6 full time dance instructors! Guest amenities include: two restaurants, snack bar, three bars, swim-ming pool, miniature golf, volley ball, water sports, day-care center for children, disco/night club, game room, conference room, and daily entertainment. For prices and more information, contact:

Dieppa's spacious diving boat makes diving easy.

W. Houghton

Club Santa Lucía
Playa Santa Lucía, Nuevitas
Camagüey, Cuba
Ph: 533-233-6109
Fax: 533-236-5147
Email: aloja@clubst.stl.cyt.cu
Or gerente@clubstl.cyt.cu

Brisas Santa Lucía

Rated as four stars and the most luxurious of hotels here in Santa Lucía, Brisas has 412 rooms and 8 suites. All are air-conditioned. The lay out of the hotel's structure consists of a series of buildings, each having 8 rooms. The best building is number six because it is on the beach near the dive shop. There is one restaurant buffet, three bars, snack bar, sauna, gym, tennis, volleyball, disco/night club, day-care for children, daily animation, and a large pool with a swim-up bar. Rates are anywhere from $78.00-$120.00 per night which includes breakfast and dinner. The hotel has 220-volt current, so bring your own 110-220 volt converter. Also, bring a ground plug converter (3 prongs as opposed to 2 prongs) because the hotel only has two prong outlets.

Reservations can be made through any travel agent on the island. The travel agent can include arrangements for connecting flights and transfers from Camagüey. For more information or to make a reservation, also contact:

Brisas Santa Lucía
Playa Santa Lucía, Nuevitas
Camagüey, Cuba
Ph: 533-236-5160
Fax: 533-236-5142

Future plans hold more opportunities for 7,000 hotel rooms, but it will take a lot of time to fulfill these plans. Until then, this untarnished region offers comfortable accommodations and thrilling diving.

Just outside of the Brisas Santa Lucía hotel is Scuba Cuba Sharks' Friends Diving Center, owned by Cubanacan Nautica. The daily schedule of diving varies, but a typical schedule begins with a first dive at 9:00 in the morning, a second dive at about 11:00 am, followed by a dive at 1:00pm. Occasionally there is a dive offered at 3:00pm. There

José Dieppa, celebrating his 38th birthday by feeding a bullshark with a fish from his own mouth!

are three dive boats, each with the capacity of ten people. There is also one larger boat that holds 25 divers. For most dives, guests are asked to put on their gear and wade out to the boat. Next, they must take off their gear, put it in the boat, and then cleverly hoist themselves over the edge into the boat. There are no ladders, so keep your fins on to help propel yourself into the boat.

Recently, José Dieppa, a local man who grew up in the shores of Santa Lucía, established a new dive shop, which is a joint venture with Ecotur, Dadopado International, S.A. Dieppa speaks English well and is very experienced, well known and well-liked by the locals. Dieppa helped to establish diving centers in Cayo Coco, Marea del Portillo, Guardalavaca, Covarrubia, Marina Hemmingway and Santa Lucía. In his 20+ years of diving, Dieppa has dived with revered divers such as "National Geographic's" Al Giddings. The new dive shop is located at Club Santa Lucía. The dive boat, "DADO I", is equipped for up to 25 people, complete with fresh water, kitchen, bathroom and sleeping quarters. Depending on the season, deliciously fresh lobster, rice and fried plantains are available for lunch (starting at $12 per person). Guests board the boat near the Mortera wreck where bull sharks live. However, soon they may be able to board the ship directly from a hotel dock. Transportation is provided free of charge from the hotels to the docks. Dive schedules run at 9am and 2:30pm. Night dives are offered from 8pm. Also, Dieppa can arrange transportation to and from the airports and hotel accommodations. Prices are very reasonable. For example, a 7 day-6 night hotel stay, including 12 dives, food, and airport transfers is as low as $500 per person in the low season (at the Club Santa Lucía Hotel).

Dive Prices

Prices are similar for both dive centers, however Sharks' Friends recently lowered their rates:

Average price for one-four dives	$31.50
Average price for four-nine dives (per dive)	$29.40
Average price for ten-fourteen dives (per dive)	$26.95
Average price for fifteen-nineteen dives (per dive)	$25.20
Average price for twenty or more dives (per dive)	$23.10
Average price for a night dive	$42.00
Average price for shark show	$70.00
(Well worth every penny!)	
Average price for open water course	$390.00
Average price for advanced course	$250.00
Average Price for a resort course	$63.00
Weights and weight belts are free.	

Rental Equipment

The average cost for the use of an entire set of rental equipment is about $18.00 per day. The usage of weights and weight belts are free. The Sharks' Friends Center has 27 BC jackets, 27 regulators, 12 sets of masks/fins/snorkels, 33 wetsuits, and 10 dive lights. Most of the dive equipment is of Spirotechnique or Technisub, both of which are Italian brands. Sharks' Friends also has two Bauer compressors, which fill their 110 tanks. Dieppa's Dive Center has 45 full sets of Italian "Oceanways" rental equipment and 80 tanks.

Dive Sites

There are approximately 37 dive sites off the shores of Santa Lucía. Sites range from 21 feet (7 meters) to 105 feet (35 meters) offering glimpses of shipwrecks, remains of an old Spanish fort, caves, tunnels, and large coral heads. These territories are home to a myriad of marine animals, such as grouper, stingrays, manta rays, barracuda, snapper, and sea turtles. One other animal dominates this area… the shark. Sharks' Friends Diving Center received its name for a reason…its electrifying shark show. If you are searching for one of the most thrilling dives in Cuba, you have found it. (See map on pg. 173)

Shark Show at Nuevo Mortera

This spot was discovered about ten years ago by José Dieppa and is one of few places in the world where divers watch unprotected dive masters feed nine and ten-foot bull sharks. As many as fourteen sharks can be seen at a time. No clients have ever been injured on this dive.

Divers may only enter the sharks' world on certain days depending on the strong currents created by the tides. Because this site is located at the channel of Bahía de Nuevitas, divers must wait until the Atlantic tide is even with the tide of the channel, thus creating a window of about one hour's time without current. "Even tide" varies from day to day and usually falls every twelve hours. However, there are some days when "even tide" falls at nighttime. Because this dive is only made during daylight hours, there are days when the shark show is not possible. Interested divers should ask the center when the next show will be, and sign up in advance because the show books up fast.

The sharks' channel is about a ten to fifteen-minute bus ride away from the dive center. The bus stops in front of a pile of rocks, upon which two cement planks are carelessly resting. A mere 50 feet away lie the buoys of the shipwreck Mortera, marking the shark's lair. Upon arriving, divers

Lacero feeds his shark friend.   E. Macao

are instructed to assemble their gear and wait for instructions by two dive masters. They tell divers to descend over a sloping bottom until they reach a sandy bottom in about 82 feet (27 meters) of water. Then, divers should calmly kneel on the sand, arms folded and stay very still. The instructions are simple, the thrill and rush of adrenaline are sensational. Here is what I experienced:

As I prepared my gear, stood on the plank, and stared at the buoys, I wondered "Where are they right now? Are they waiting for us?" Then I tried to convince myself not to worry. After all I was diving with "Sharks' Friends".

One divemaster, armed with a bag of dead fish and a harpoon, jumped in ahead of the group. We all carefully watched his bubbles make their way to the anchored buoys as he swam out. Soon after, we faithfully leaped in. I quickly deflated my BC to sink to the bottom, which was only about 15 feet (3 meters). Swiftly, we initiated our journey following Lazero, our divemaster, and the sloping bottom downward. "No sharks yet", I thought to myself. The first dive master was waiting for us at the wreck site, already flashing dead fish around in the water. We swam to the wreck, all the while my eyes searching fiercely into the blue water. "Clang, Clang, Clang", I heard the dive master noisily banging on his tank as if it were the dinner bell. Suddenly, I saw a large shadow off in the horizon. My heart began to pump faster. False alarm, it was only a large 200-pound black grouper.

We finally caught up to the divemaster and dutifully assumed our positions on our knees, almost as if we were kneeling at the altar. My father, camera and flash in hand, laid on his belly in the sand inches away from the sharks' dinner. Several seconds went by and then I saw it. A nine-foot, 1,000-pound bull shark emerged from the deep blue limits. And then came another. "Are they hungry today?" I wondered to myself. The first two appeared shy and timid, as if they were sizing us up. Then, hesitantly, one bull shark took the fishy carcass from the divemaster's hand. Cautiously, he pulled back his hand to avoid any confusion of where the fish ended and his hand began. More sharks showed up to participate in the show. Soon I counted four, then five. One was a 10-foot, 1,200-pound tiger shark!

They began their promenading circle: first in front of, then beside, then behind us. My loyal father always focused on whichever shark was taking the fish out of the divemaster's hand. He paid no attention to the other four circling sharks. I could see him concentrating on perfectly framing, zooming, and timing the shot. It was like clockwork. His camera flashed every time the shark's jaws opened to swallow another fish. I could see he was oblivious to the other inquisitive characters swimming about us. Then one bull shark decided that my father's tank was more interesting than bloodstained fish, so it swam closer to take a better look. Lazero, promptly made a noise that sounded like a loud bark, which startled the shark and made him swim off. Not more than three minutes went by when it reappeared, this time coming in even closer to my father's tank! Lazero barked loudly again, but the shark ignored him. Finally Lazero swam directly over to my father, put his hand on his tank, and fiercely barked. The shark lost interest and swam away.

After we were out of fish, Lazero led our group through the beautiful Mortera wreck, covered with orange and yellow elephant ear sponges. We stopped to pet Margarita, the 6-foot friendly green moray eel. The other divemaster stayed behind with his harpoon to ward off any pursuing shark. We weaved our way in and out of

Fresh lunch between dives!   W. Houghton

portholes and sometimes our brave guard would be stationed outside the opening with his harpoon. As the current began to increase we headed back to shore. In 40 minutes we packed in a thrilling shark show and a great wreck dive.

Las Ánforas

This dive site is located close to what once was a Spanish fort that guarded the entrance to the Bahía de Nuevitas Bay. Sunk in the 1800's, this wreck is so old that nearly every inch is covered with colorful marine growth. Antique pitchers, bottles, and clay vessels can be discovered in these waters at about 81 feet (27 meters). The historic artifacts make this site a nostalgic dive.

Poseidon

This site is made up of stunning coral ridges, which form marine terraces and platforms. Maximum depth ranges from 54 feet (18 meters) to 96 feet (32 meters). Divers have opportunities to see grouper, tarpon, minute coral fish, as well as other tropical fish.

Nuestra Señora Virgen de Altagracia

The main attraction of this dive site is a steel tugboat, dating back to the early 20th century, in perfect condition. José Dieppa sank it. Nearby, a coral wall juts down into the blue abyss. The walls are lined with brightly quilted patchworks of sponges. The site is an excellent opportunity for photos. A good playground for tropical fish, this wreck lies in about 81 feet (27 meters) of water.

Cueva Honda

There is an impressive cave at this site. It tends to shelter tarpon and big groupers. The maximum depth is about 96 feet.

For more information on diving, or to book a reservation contact:

Scuba Cuba Sharks' Friends
Diving Center
Brisas, Santa Lucía
Playa Santa Lucía
Camagüey, Cuba
Ph: 533-2236-5182
Fax: 533-2236-5182

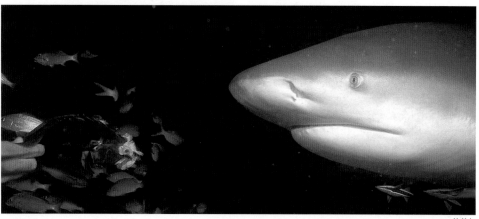

M. Mola

Adrenaline "junkies" flock to this site.

E. Macao

José Dieppa
Dadopado International, SA
Club Santa Lucía
Playa Santa Lucía, Nuevitas
Camagüey, Cuba
Ph: 533-2233-6109 ext. 542
Fax: 533-2236-5147
Email:
dieppasub@cmg.colombus.cu

Divers can also contact Cubanacan
Nautica's headquarters at:

Cubanacan Nautica
Calle 184, No. 123,
Reparto Flores, Playa
La Habana, Cuba
Ph: 537-833-6675
Fax: 537-833-7020
Email:
commercial@marlin.cha.cyt.cu
Website: www.cubanacan.cu.

Insider's Tips

Scuba Cuba Sharks' Friends Diving Center draws about 48 divers per day in the high season. In the low season, there are 12-28 divers per day. Four of the six instructors speak English. The Center also offers a day trip excursion to Los Jardines de la Reina. It requires many hours each way by transfer, but allows for two dives in the beginning area of the cayos in Queen's Gardens. The price is between $89-$99. Cubanacan Nautica also offers Catamaran and fishing trips in Santa Lucía.

During the months of January and February, there is only a 50% chance of diving due to high winds. The best diving in Santa Lucía is between October and April. However, shark season is best during summer months because the channel is cooler than open water temperatures. Also, for several months in the winter (January-February), the sharks sometimes disappear. Dive masters proclaim that Santa Lucía attracts many hammerheads during the breeding season. Visibility averages 60-75 feet.

The nearest hyperbaric chamber is in Santiago de Cuba, and a helicopter is provided. The center also employs a medical specialist.

Santa Lucía

Above the Water

A fun local flavor Cuban club is the Mar Verde located on the Carretera Tararaco, Santa Lucía. Divers can feel the rhythm from around 10:30pm to 2am.

Ph: 533-233-6205

Divers can explore the historic scenes of the city of Camagüey, which is only about one hour's drive away from Santa Lucía. For more details, refer to the *Cuba Handbook* by Christopher P. Baker.

Getting There

Santa Lucía is serviced by both Cubana Airlines and Air Gaviota. Divers can fly to either Camagüey or Holguin. Airfare from Havana to Santa Lucía costs about $60 each way. International charter flights and packages are available through some Canadian Travel Agencies.

Santa Lucía has numerous ancient wrecks.

M. Mola

SANTA LUCÍA
Scuba Cuba Sharks' Friends & Dieppa's Dive Center

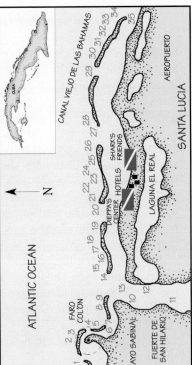

	Dive Site	Depth		Dive Site	Depth
1.	Mantas	100ft (33m)	21.	Divers' Den	100ft (33m)
2.	Maternillo	100ft (33m)	22.	Poseidon I	100ft (33m)
3.	La Corona	90ft (30m)	23.	Hector's Coral Garden	100ft (33m)
4.	Las Palmas	90ft (30m)	24.	Posidon II	100ft (33m)
5.	El Cable	90ft (30m)	25.	Poseidon III	100ft (33m)
6.	Playa Bonita	70ft (23m)	26.	Poseidon IV	100ft (33m)
7.	Joventina III	90ft (30m)	27.	Cañon I	100ft (33m)
8.	Joentina II	70ft (23m)	28.	Cañon II	100ft (33m)
9.	Joventina	70ft (23m)	29.	Cañon III	100ft (33m)
10.	Sharks	40ft (13m)	30.	II Susto	90ft (30m)
11.	Las Ánforas	55ft (18m)	31.	Este 120	85ft (28m)
12.	Mortera Wreck	90ft (30m)	32.	La Copa	90ft (30m)
13.	Biosca Stone	90ft (30m)	33.	Valentina	100ft (33m)
14.	La Poza	35ft (12m)	34.	Cañon IV	100ft (33m)
15.	Black Coral	70ft (23m)	35.	Neptuno	100ft (33m)
16.	Sabinal Wreck	55ft (18m)			
17.	Alta Gracia Wreck	90ft (30m)			
18.	Escalón	65ft (22m)			
19.	Cueva Chiquita	100ft (33m)			
20.	Cueva Honda	100ft (33m)			

Covarrubias

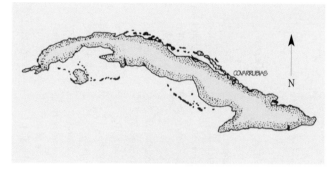

Las Tunas Province

Covarrubias

Covarrubias is an hour's drive from Santa Lucía. With pristine diving, a brand new hotel, good management, and excellent food, Covarrubias is just beginning to get discovered by tourists. The dive center, now managed by Puertosol, resides inside Villa Corrubias Hotel, which opened as part of the Gran Caribé hotel chain.

Creative Cuban skateboard

The isolated hotel is 50 kilometers from any village. Guests are free to relax in this remote resort. The meals are above average by Cuban hotel standards. The cost is $70.00 for a double room in the low season (Dec.- June) and $96.00 in the high season (July – Nov.). Prices are subject to vary. Children who are two years or younger can stay for free. Children between the ages of two years and twelve years stay for half price. Everything is all-inclusive, which makes this hotel one of the best bargains in Cuba. Transportation from Holguin to Covarrubias is included if the hotel package is purchased from a travel agent. Booking through a travel agent is advisable. Otherwise, expect to pay $50.00 each way for a taxi or $55.00 per day for a rental car. Diving can be arranged through the hotel after you arrive.

José Dieppa discovered and named virtually all of the dive sites in Covarrubias. Depending on the size and preference of the dive group, dives are usually scheduled for 9:00am and 2:00pm.

Dive Prices

Average price for one dive (includes all equipment)	$45.00
Average price for two dives (includes all equipment)	$70.00
Average price for four dives	$128.00
Average price for six dives	$240.00
Average price for a resort course	$55.00
30-minute boat trip	$8.50
Snorkel safari (per hour)	$13.00
Fishing trip (per hour)	$15.00
Night dives and beach dives are not available at this dive center.	

Dive Sites

There are 27 dive sites in Covarrubias. From the shore, all are within a three-minute ride in a rubber Zodiac boat. A larger dive boat is in the plans. The fish life is average for Cuba. (See map on pg.179)

La Punta

Three minutes from the shoreline, this dive site is for all divers. The maximum depth ranges from 24 feet (8 meters) for beginners and 71 feet (27 meters) for experienced divers. There is an abundance of black coral and also many other types of coral. Divers can expect to see a number of groupers, squirrelfish, typical Caribbean red fish, and other reef fish.

La Cueva Chiquita

This dive has exceptional fish life. The site is located 1½ minutes from shore with a maximum depth of 54 feet (18 meters). Big and small fish like to swim through and around the coral tunnels. La Cueva Chiquita provides a good opportunity for quality photos. The average bottom time is about 45 minutes.

El Puente

This site is Dive master Heribero Alberro Vasquez' favorite spot. It is about two minutes from shore. The maximum depth is 81 feet (27 meters). There are

M. Mola

D. Tipton

plenty of gorgonians, sponges, and colorful coral. Divers can expect to see lobsters hiding in coral crevices and barracuda curiously gliding through the water.

For more information or to book a reservation, contact:

Villa Covarrubias
Playa Covarrubias
Puerto Padre, Las Tunas
Ph: 533-814-6230
Fax: 533-236-5305

For direct booking, divers can contact Puertosol at

Casa Matriz.
Calle 1 era #3001 a 30
Miramar, Playa,
Ciudad de La Habana, Cuba
Ph: 537-204-5923
Fax: 537-204-5924
Email: comerc@psol.mit.tur.cu
comerc@psol.mit.tur.cu
Website:
www.Puertosol.cubaweb.cu

Insider's Tips

One client of Covarrubias Dive Center said, "This dive company is the friendliest on the island, and that is a tough call where so many friendly people live here in Cuba. The divemasters put your gear together and load it onto the boat for you. All you have to do is wade out in the water and climb aboard the boat."

Covarrubias offers more than 320 days of good diving. Two instructors are employed at the Puertosol dive center. Both speak English. There is one 15-foot zodiac boat and usually no more than six divers per day in the high season, which make the dives seem more pristine. In the future two brand new dive boats will be available.

Courses for open-water certification are offered by ACUC and SSI.

Above the Water

The nearest nightlife is in Puerto Padre, which is about a 50-minute drive by car.

Getting There

For more information, check any major hotel for a tourist package to Covarrubias. Airfare from Havana to Covarrubias on Aero Caribé or Cubana airlines costs about $70.00 each way. Ground transportation from the airport to the hotel is about $25-30 each way.

Spiney Lobster

E. Macao

D. Tipton

COVARRUBIAS
Villa Covarrubias Dive Center

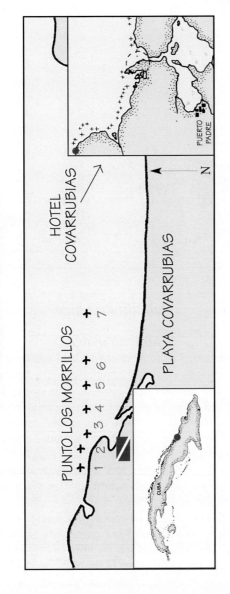

HOTEL COVARRUBIAS

PUNTO LOS MORRILLOS

1 2 3 4 5 6 7

PLAYA COVARRUBIAS

PUERTO PADRE

CUBA

N

Dive Site

1. La Punta
2. Cueva Chiquita
3. El Puente
4. Los Perros
5. The Wall
6. Acuario
7. Covarrubia

Depth

71ft (24m)
54ft (18m)
81ft (27m)

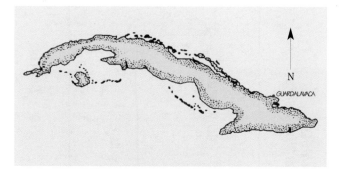

Holguin Province

Guardalavaca

Guardalavaca is an area of flat land between Holguin and Covarrubias on the Atlantic coast. This area was very important to raising cattle. However, it is said that a cattle rancher had to be careful of the pirates who occasionally landed on the beach because they would steal the cattle. Captain Morgan (the man the rum is named after) was the most famous for stealing cows in this region. Therefore, whenever a local Cuban saw a pirate approaching the beach, he would yell to his neighbor, "Hey, guard the cow!"

The beach at Guardalavaca is white, clean, and sun-drenched. The sand is trimmed by a forest of sea grape trees. Within the grove of sea grapes is a myriad of tiny open-air bars, some of which are open twenty-four hours a day. Hotels are perched on sheer cliffs overlooking local barbeques on the beach. Divers can purchase snacks, food, beer, rum, and mixed drinks. A Coca-Cola costs one dollar. A rum and Coke is also one dollar.

If you are looking for a cheap dive vacation, this is a superb area to visit. Hotel Atlantico has great all-inclusive packages. Canadians and Englishmen usually vacation at

La Roca Disco has excellent music.

D. Tipton

Guardalavaca. They go there because they can have a two-week vacation for about $750 per person, which includes round trip airfare, transportation to the hotel, room, unlimited food and beverages. Those who are interested may book the same package from any Toronto travel agency.

There are two dive centers in Guardalavaca: Gaviota's Sea Lovers Dive Center and Cubanacan Nautica's Eagle Ray Dive Center. Gaviota is located on Playa Guardalavaca in front of the Hotel Rio de Mares, which is owned by a Spanish family connected to the Melia hotel chains. Eagle Ray is located near Playa Esmeralda and Hotel Atlantico. During the high season, December through March, there are usually between five to eight divers per day at both dive centers. Eagle Ray employs five divemasters and two boats. Gaviota has three divemasters and one boat. Both dive centers tend to have the same schedule with dives beginning at around 9:00am, 11:00am, and 2:00pm. Occasional night dives are also offered. Both dive centers visit the same sites. However, Gaviota's dive center has a slightly shorter boat ride to the preferred dive sites. Cubanacan Nautica's dive center visits a different site each day in order to give divers a variety and to cause less impact to the reef. Both centers have similar prices. (See dive maps on pgs. 184-185).

Dive Prices

Average price for one dive	$30.00
Average price for two dives	$60.00
Average price for a package of ten dives	$250.00
Average price for a package of twenty dives	$440.00
Average price for a night dive	$40.00
(includes dive light)	

Rental Equipment

Both Cubanacan Nautica and Gaviota dive centers have Cressi-Sub and Mares Italian brand rental equipment. Eagle Ray rents a full set of gear for $5.00 per day. Gaviota rents a full set for $10.00 per day. Both centers use steel tanks and have two Bauer compressors.

Dive Sites
La Corona

La Corona is a three-minute boat ride from Sea Lover's and a seven-minute boat ride from Eagle Ray Dive Center. You can dive this site in 42-46 feet (14-18 meters) and float along the top of the reef. If divers wish to see the coral wall, the maximum depth is around 120 feet (40 meters). Divers can expect to see brain coral, black coral, red coral, antler coral, and fingers of various types of coral. Local fish-life includes grouper, barracuda, angelfish, moray eels, and an occasional octopus or reef shark. The average bottom time ranges from 40 to 50 minutes.

Canto Azul

This site is a three-minute boat ride from Gaviota's dive center. The dive is quite similar to La Corona's wall dive. The average depth and bottom time depends on divers' experience.

La Sirena

This site is a two-minute boat ride from the Eagle Ray Dive Center. Divers enter a cave-like tunnel at around 79 feet (40 meters) and exit the tunnel through the coral wall at about 110 feet (37 meters). Small reef fish and stingrays inhabit this

Blue Tang graze on tiny coral particals.   D. Tipton

area. The average bottom time is about 40 minutes.

El Acuario

This site is two minutes from Eagle Ray Dive Center. It has a long reef parallel to the shore. Classified as a shallow dive, this area can be reached in 12-65 feet (4-22 meters) of water. It is an excellent dive for beginners and is often used as a "checkout" dive by divemasters in order to judge the experience of divers. Divers can expect to see various types of hard and soft coral and typical Caribbean reef fish such as parrotfish and grunts.

Canto Bonito

In this area there is a wall that drops from a depth of 45 feet to a maximum depth of 105 feet. Divers can see lobster, crab, octopus, and small coral fish.

Pesquero

This site boasts a coral bottom teeming with sponges, gorgonians and fish. Its major attraction is numerous colonies of the highly-valued black coral. Maximum depth is about 120 feet.

Casa Coral

This site has a coral barrier with abundant fauna, small coral fish, diverse coral species, large gorgonians and sea fans. Maximum depth is only about 30 feet.

For more information or to book a reservation contact:

Cubanacan Nautica's
Eagle Ray Dive Center
Playa Guardalavaca
Holguin, Cuba
Ph: 532-843-0316
Fax: 532-843-0815
Email: Cubanacan.nautical
@guard.gvc.cyt.cu

Gaviota Sea Lover's Dive Center
Playa Esmeralda
Carretera de Guardalavaca
Holguin, Cuba
Ph: 532-843-0030
Fax: 532-843-0065

Insider's Tips

A helicopter is available to take divers to the nearest hyperbaric chamber in Santiago de Cuba. There is also a helicopter day trip, that takes tourists out to sight see. Cubanacan Nautica's Dive enter offers a snorkeling safari for five dollars per hour. The price includes a boat ride and rental gear.

When staying in Holguin, consider a *casa particular*:

Miriam Gave de Peralta
Avenida Libertadores No. 22
Esq. Avenida Rosveldt,
Rpto. Peralta
Email: CBL917@hotmail.com

Above the Water

One of the popular disco dance clubs on the island is located in Guardalavaca. It is called "La Roca", meaning "The Rock". Located just 200 yards down the beach from Hotel Atlantico, this open-air dance club is carved out of rock in the side of a cliff. Tourists climb about 30 stone steps up to the entrance, pay a $2.00 cover charge, and dance the night away to Cuban salsa music. Hundreds of Cubans also attend, and are more than willing to show you how to shake and bend your spinal cord on the dance floor in ways you never thought possible.

Getting There

Holguin is served by two airlines from Havana: Aero-Caribbean and Cubana. A one way flight from Havana to Holguin costs $80.00. Rental cars are available at the international terminal in Holguin, but if you land through a domestic flight, you can call the Havanauto car rental agency in the international terminal. The agency will bring the car and the paperwork to the domestic terminal after you have chosen the type of car you desire. Be sure to grab a map. Divers then drive the rental car to Guardalavaca.

You also have the option of taking a taxi from the Holguin Airport to Guardalavaca. The cost is $30.00 one way. If you are planning to stay for several days in Guardalavaca, then a taxi is a cheaper mode of transportation. Once divers reach Guardalavaca, a car will not be necessary.

If you fly to Holguin on a package booked through a Cuban travel agency, the transfer to the hotel will be via bus. The transfer cost will be included in your package.

Divers can also book packages through any Canadian travel agency that does business with Cubanacan. Packages include roundtrip airfare from Havana to Camagüey (usually about $80.00 each way), transfers from Holguin to Guardalavaca, and hotel with all-inclusive meals, which normally would cost $80.00 without a package.

Some Canadian charter flights fly directly into the international airport at Holguin and completely bypass Havana.

M. Mola

GUARDALAVACA
Sea Lover's & Eagle Ray Dive Centers

Dive Site		Depth
1.	Casa Coral	35ft (12m)
2.	Aquario	50ft (17m)
3.	Canto Azul	50ft (17m)
4.	Cueva No. 1	115ft (38m)
5.	Cueva No. 2	130ft (43m)
6.	Cueva No. 3	80ft (27m)
7.	Coral Negro	115ft (38m)
8.	La Corona	80ft (27m)
9.	Punta Ingles	65ft (21m)
10.	Canto Bonito	115ft (38m)
17.	Sirena	103ft (34m)
18.	Coral Garden	15-50ft (5-17m)
19.	Canto Izzy	30-100ft (10-33m)
20.	Loma Jorge	25-80ft (8-27sm)

GUARDALAVACA
Sea Lover's & Eagle Ray Dive Centers (Cont.)

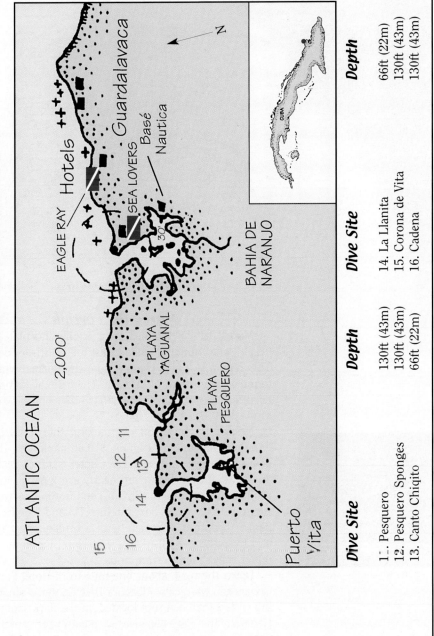

Dive Site	Depth
11. Pesquero	130ft (43m)
12. Pesquero Sponges	130ft (43m)
13. Canto Chiqito	66ft (22m)

Dive Site	Depth
14. La Llanita	66ft (22m)
15. Corona de Vita	130ft (43m)
16. Cadena	130ft (43m)

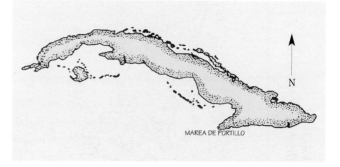

MAREA DE PORTILLO

N

Granma Province

Marea del Portillo

Marea del Portillo lies on a scenic chocolate-colored beach, one hundred miles east of Santiago de Cuba. This region is a nice change from the normal white sand found over most of Cuba's coast. The main attraction is the beautiful scenery. Divers have few other options except to scuba dive.

D. Tipton

Nestled up in a cliff overlooking the ocean is Hotel Farallon del Caribé. At about $70.00 per night, this gorgeous, architecturally attractive hotel is a nice deal. There are views of the ocean from nearly every perspective. The rooms are comfortable with air-conditioning, private bathroom, safety deposit box, satellite TV, and telephone. The pool is beautiful, complete with a bridge and a swim-up bar. Everything is all-inclusive at Hotel Farallon, and the buffet is fresh and scrumptious.

Down the road, about one mile from Hotel Farallon is Cubanacan Nautica's Albacora Dive Center, a small building with a thatched roof located on the dark sandy beach. Generally there are two dives each day at the center: one at 9:00am and the other at 4:00pm.

Dive Prices	
Average price for one to four dives (each)	$25.00
Average price for five dives	$120.00
Average price for ten dives	$220.00
Average price for fifteen dives	$320.00
Average price for twenty dives	$400.00
Average price for a night dive	$40.00
Average price for a resort course	$50.00

Rental Equipment

The total cost to rent an entire set of equipment is $10.00 per day. The usage of weights and weight belts are free. Albacora Dive Center has twenty full sets of equipment, all which are of the Italian brand Cressi-sub. The center also has four dive lights. Albacora has one Bauer compressor, which fills their twenty steel tanks.

Dive Sites

The dive zone at Marea del Portillo continues from Santiago's coast. Therefore the diving here is similar to the reef at Santiago where large coral heads, ridges, trenches, walls, and shipwrecks are prevalent.

At the most western point, Cabo Cruz, divers can see a reef filled with elkhorn coral, brain coral, species of soft coral, and small tropical fish such as grunts, yellowtails, surgeon-fish, schoolmasters, and a few barracuda. (See dive map pg. 191)

Red Snapper

This dive site is only ten minutes from the Albacora Dive Center. The maximum depth is about 80 feet (25 meters). Divemasters sometimes call the site *el acuario* (the aquarium), due to the number of small blue cronies, red snapper, barracuda, grouper, and moray eels found here.

There are large colorful sponges in this aquarium.

Punta del Inglés

Located twenty minutes from the dive center, this site is characterized by its great coral found at 65 feet (21 meters). Several pairs of French angelfish are common to the area, as well as green and spotted moray eels, grouper, and barracuda. Dive masters say that during January and February, divers sometimes have the opportunity to see a whale shark.

La Tortuga

This shallow dive is fifteen minutes from the dive center in about 40 feet (13 meters) of water. Dive masters estimate that 80% of the time divers will find small sea turtles in this area. The site also displays a variety of corals and small fish. Total bottom time is usually one hour.

M. Mola

Grouper

187

Cabo Crúz

Divers can find anything from a coral barrier peppered with lobster, to cubera snapper, to barracuda to gorgonians, sponges and sea fans. Divers may also spot several stray cannons from a shipwreck. The maximum depth is about 95 feet (32 meters).

Black Coral

True to its name, this site has a large population of black coral colonies. Baracudas, trumpetfish, and cubera snappers are sometimes seen here. The maximum depth is about 100 feet (33 meters).

Boca del Toro

This area is the habitat for many fish and coral species, gorgonians, sponges and sea fans. The maximum depth is about 100 feet (33 meters).

For more information or to make a reservation, contact:

Albacora Scuba Cuba
Playa Marea del Portillo
Pilon, Granma, Cuba
Ph: 532-359-7139
Fax: 532-359-7080
Email: economia@marlin.grm.cu

Insider's Tips

The winter months are the best times to dive Marea del Portillo because visibility is good, the rain is scarce, and the water is calm. Whale sharks can also be seen during the winter. At one time, Jacques Cousteau even filmed whale sharks at Marea del Portillo.

Albacora employs one dive master and two instructors. Both instructors speak English and are CMAS certified. The center has the capacity for 30 divers per day, but

M. Mola

M. Mola

usually has about 12 during the high season. There are three dive boats that are between 21 and 24 feet. Each holds eight divers.

The nearest hyperbaric chamber is in Santiago de Cuba. If there is a diving accident, Albacora offers a helicopter service. While the helicopter service is free to Cubans in a medical emergency, it can be quite expensive to foreigners.

Other available water-sport activities include deep-sea fishing ($42.00 per hour), snorkeling boat trip ($5.00), water skiing ($1.00 per minute), and a sea safari ($7.00 per hour). The dive center also offers a dive trip to see the sunken "Cristóbal Colón" shipwreck, which is only a 45-minute drive from the dive center.

Getting There

Divers must fly to Santiago de Cuba, which costs about $160 round trip from Havana. Then, drive westward to Marea del Portillo. The scenic drive will take about $2\frac{1}{2}$ hours. Another way is to get there is to fly to Holguin, and then also drive $2\frac{1}{2}$ hours.

Divers can also buy trip packages through most Cuban travel agencies or through any Canadian travel agency that does business with Cubanacan. Packages include meals, roundtrip air-fare, rooms, and transfers from Holguin.

Cuban culture is rich with rhythm.

D. Tipton

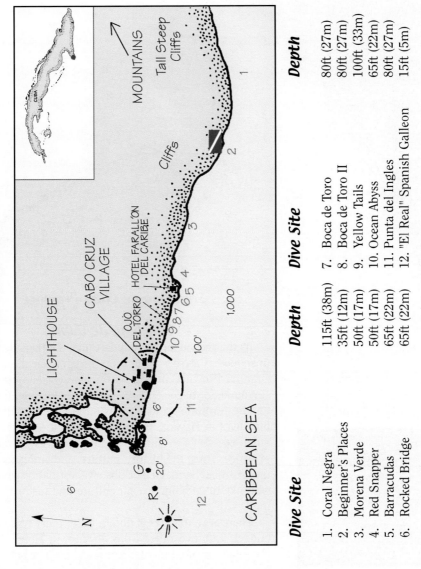

MAREA DEL PORTILLO
Albacora Dive Center

Dive Site   **Depth**

1. Coral Negra   115ft (38m)
2. Beginner's Places   35ft (12m)
3. Morena Verde   50ft (17m)
4. Red Snapper   50ft (17m)
5. Barracudas   65ft (22m)
6. Rocked Bridge   65ft (22m)

Dive Site   **Depth**

7. Boca de Toro   80ft (27m)
8. Boca de Toro II   80ft (27m)
9. Yellow Tails   100ft (33m)
10. Ocean Abyss   65ft (22m)
11. Punta del Ingles   80ft (27m)
12. "El Real" Spanish Galleon   15ft (5m)

Santiago de Cuba

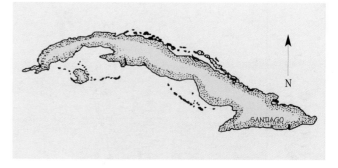

Santiago de Cuba Province

Santiago de Cuba

As the second largest city in Cuba, Santiago de Cuba, is unspoiled. Castro's revolution began near here in the Granma Province in the Sierra Maestra Mountains that surround Santiago. This region was nicknamed the cradle for the revolution and Cubans often joke that the "baby" now lives in Havana. Intimate beaches are tucked among quiet coves. Few tourists venture to this eastern-most province. Thus, the history, culture, and ambiance are left undisturbed. Santiago de Cuba is a destination for tourists who like to combine Cuban culture and history with diving.

D. Tipton

There are a number of hotels, fit for every type of tourist budget. Just two miles from downtown, Hotel San Juan is behind the monumental San Juan Hill. The hotel is comprised of villas, which clump about 25 rooms together. There are 112 rooms all total. Each room is equipped with a private bathroom, satellite TV, air-conditioning, and a safety deposit box. The hotel facilities include a swimming pool, pool-side bar, concierge, rental cars, restaurant, evening music and entertainment. Room prices range from $40.00 to $60.00 per night. For more information or to book a reservation, contact:

Hotel San Juan
Avenida Siboney y Calle 13
Santiago de Cuba
Ph: 532-264-2478
Fax: 532-233-5015

The Coralia Club Bucanero is all-inclusive, except for the diving. The hotel is situated in the Sierra Maestra Mountains overlooking a cliff that juts into a small inlet. The scenery is gorgeous and the diving is nice too. All of the rooms have air-conditioning, private bathroom, satellite TV, and a safety deposit box. The hotel has a large, beautiful pool. A buffet-style restaurant is located next to the pool. A cliff-top bar is situated directly over the beach. Average room prices are between $60.00 and $114.00 depending on the season. For more information or to book a reservation, contact:

Coralia Club Bucanero
Carretera Arroyo La Costa Km 4½
Baconao, Santiago de Cuba
Ph: 532-265-4596
Fax: 532-268-6108
Email:
jcarpeta@bucaner.scu.cyt.cu

There are many more hotels than the two previously described. Also, divers may want to consider staying in a *casa particular* (private home).

Dive Sites

The three dive centers in Santiago de Cuba are all owned by Cubanacan Nautica. Each dive center has its own dive zone. Fish life seems to be a bit sparse in all of the zones, however the coral is interesting and healthy. All of the dive centers have access

Blue Nudebranch.

M. Mola

Center for Marine Research, Univ. Havana

to the hyperbaric chamber in Santiago de Cuba.

Bucanero Diving Center

Bucanero Diving Center is located in the Coralia Club Bucanero. The hotel was damaged by a hurricane in 1998. The stone structure remained in tact, and the entire hotel was renovated in 1999. The gorgeous structure boasts tennis courts with ocean views, and outstanding meals. The beautiful canyon behind the hotel is a bird sanctuary. All inclusive packages must be purchased from French travel agencies or directly through the hotel. There are three instructors, all of whom speak English and are ACUC certified. The center has one Mako compressor which fills its 40 steel tanks. There are 15 sets of Cressi-sub rental gear. It costs $5.00 per day to rent an entire set of equipment. The diving capacity is 15 people a day. However, usually there are only between 3 and 6 divers per day. Diving takes place from a 21-foot, 12-passenger dive boat. The dive schedule is flexible, but normally there is one dive at 9:30am and one dive at 11:00am. Divers who are not

staying at the hotel can pay $15.00 for lunch and all you can drink until 5:00pm. All of the 21 dive sites can be reached by boat in about 5-10 minutes. The Bucanero dive zone is famous for its many shipwrecks and its wall diving. (See dive map on pg. 200)

La Cueva

This site is worth a visit due to its interesting coral formations. The cave opening begins at about 30 feet (10 meters) of water. Coral continues to protrude through the surface of the water. Divers can find large canyons, colorful sponges, black coral and small tropical reef fish at this site. Maximum bottom time runs between 45-50 minutes.

La Pared

Divers have the opportunity to see a large coral wall in conjunction with a deep drop-off over 120 feet (30 meters). The wall is a host to many hard and soft corals, small reef fish, and black coral. Maximum bottom time is about 45 minutes.

El Colón

This is a special dive trip offered by Bucanero. Due to visibility, the best time for this dive is between February and June. Divers take a two-hour bus ride outside of Santiago de Cuba near Sierra Mar, where the shipwreck lies in about 85 feet (27 meters) of water. Divers swim about 45 feet from the shore to begin their dive. El Cristóbal Colón, sunk in 1898 by American war power, still holds much of its original shape. Tarpon and small reef fish also dwell in this area. Maximum dive time is about 45 minutes. (For more details see the next chapter)

Piedra de Ariguas

This dive site is located in about 85 feet (27 meters) of water. The area is best known for a coral wall with a small cave. Yellowfin groupers enjoy this cave along with smaller coral fish. Maximum dive time is about 45 minutes.

Bucanero Diving Center Dive Prices	
Average price for one to four dives (per dive)	$30.00
Average price for five dives (total)	$140.00
Average price for ten dives (total)	$250.00
Average price for 20 dives (total)	$440.00
Average price for a night dive	$40.00
Average price for resort course	$60.00
Average price for open water course (ACUC certification)	$365.00
Average price for advanced course (ACUC certification)	$250.00

For more information or to book a reservation, contact:

Bucanero Scuba Cuba
Carretera de Baconao, Km 21
Santiago de Cuba
Ph: 532-268-6363
Fax: 532-268-6070

Sigua Diving Center

The Sigua Diving Center is located about 20 miles east of downtown Santiago de Cuba. The Sigua Diving Center has an office nearby the Los Corales Hotel, a Cubanacan managed hotel owned by the LTI chain. For more information or to book a reservation at this office, contact:

Los Corales-Carisol Hotels
Carretera de Baconao
Playa Cazonal
Santiago de Cuba
Ph: 532-268-6177
Fax: 532-268-6177

There are four instructors at Sigua, all of whom speak English and are ACUC certified. The center has one Bauer compressor, which fills its 25 new Italian steel tanks. There are 15 sets of Cressi-sub rental equipment. The cost of rental gear is included in the price of the dive. The center's diving capacity is 10 divers, but usually there are no more than 3-7 divers per day. Diving takes place from a 21-foot, 10-passenger dive boat. Dives are normally made at 9:30am and 11:00am. The Sigua Center visits 23 dive sites. Much of the mountain landscapes seem to sink into the sea, forming interesting coral formations. Shipwreck and wall diving are the best sites in this zone. (See dive map on pg. 202)

Guarico

Located just 3 minutes from shore, a small steel shipwreck. The Guarico lies in about 45 feet (15 meters) of water. Brightly colored sponges and small coral tend to congregate on the frame of the ship. Divers can expect to see two to four black groupers, each weighing in at about 25 pounds. Some will eat out of the diver's hand. Also inhabiting this area are moray eels, queen angelfish, and juvenile blue parrotfish.

Morrillo Chico

This site is reachable by a one-hour boat ride from the Sigua Diving Center. Found in about 65 feet (22 meters) of water, this point has a little bit of everything. Divers have the opportunity to see moray eels, groupers, and some tarpon. Conch shells can be seen slowly trudging across the sand. Many sponges and small, brightly colored reef fish also like this area. Maximum bottom time is about 45 minutes.

La Pared

Only a three-minute boat ride from shore, this wall falls to nearly 100 feet (33 meters). Black coral is abundant, as are red snapper, trigger fish, grouper, and sometimes sea turtles. Maximum bottom time ranges from 45-50 minutes.

Ferry

This dive site boasts the wreck of a 100 foot merchant ship. It rests in about 110 feet (35 meters) of water. Divers have the opportunity to swim through the cabins and over the bridge. Impressive goliath grouper cruise these waters also. Maximum dive time is about 45 minutes.

Open Water

At this site there are coral outcroppings with attractive shapes of large gorgonians and sea fans. A variety of coral fish also populate the area. The maximum depth is 50 feet (17 meters).

Spring Carol

This site preserves the remains of a floundered vessel. Divers may find this wreck attractive due to the black groupers, parrotfish, and other tropical fish that inhabit this area. The maximum depth is about 75 feet (25 meters).

Sigua Diving Center Dive Prices	
Average price for one to four dives (per dive)	$30.00
Average price for five dives (total)	$140.00
Average price for ten dives (total)	$250.00
Average price for a night dive	$40.00
Average price for a resort course	$60.00
Average price for open water course (ACUC certification)	$365.00
Average price for advanced course (ACUC certification)	$250.00

For more information or to book a reservation, contact:

Sigua Scuba Cuba
Carretera de Baconao, Km. 40
Playa de Sigua, Santiago de Cuba
Ph: 532-263-56165
Email: root@carisol.scu.cyt.cu

Sierra Mar Diving Center

The Sierra Mar Diving Center is located at the SuperClub Sierra Mar Hotel, about 35 miles (62 km) west of Santiago. The hotel was built in 1990 with the help of Delta of Canada. It was opened personally by Fidel Castro and is owned by Cubanacan.

The hotel is all-inclusive. Room prices range from $83.00 to $133.00 depending on the season. The Sierra Mar Hotel closes during the summer, but divers can still dive at the Center during these months if they notify Cubanacan Nautica. The hotel is laid out on the side of a gorgeous mountaintop, overlooking the sea.

Sierra Mar's Diving Center Dive Prices	
Average price for one to four dives (per dive0	$30.00
Average price for five dives (total)	$140.00
Average price for ten dives (total)	$250.00
Average price for twenty dives (total)	$440.00
Average price for a night dive	$40.00
Average price for the COLON ship wreck dive	$60.00
Average price for an open water course (ACUC certification)	$240.00
Average price for a advanced course (ACUC certification)	$250.00
Average price for a resort course	$60.00

For more information, or to book a reservation, contact:

Sierra Mar Scuba Cuba
Hotels Super Sierra Mar
Carretera Chivirico, Km 60
Guama, Santiago de Cuba
Ph: 532-262-6337
Email: sierramar@smar.scu.cyt.cu

The Dive Center is located on the beach below. There are two instructors employed at the center. Both speak fluent English and are ACUC certified. The center has one Bauer compressor, which fills its 30 steel tanks. There are 20 full sets of Cressi-sub rental equipment. The cost of usage for an entire set is $5.00 per day. Total diver capacity is 20 divers per day. However, there are never more than 5-10 divers at a time. Diving takes place from two dive boats. Both are 21-feet long and hold 10 people. Dives are usually made at 9:00am and 11:30am. The center visits 20 dive sites. The diving here is characterized by several important shipwrecks, coral gardens, and wall dives. The famous 1898 Colón shipwreck is only one hour from the dive center.

Paradise

This dive site is located 5-10 minutes away from the dive center. Divers descend to a coral reef, which leads to a cliff and a drop-off. The dive offers opportunities to see large coral heads, tube sponges, snapper, grouper, barracuda, and parrotfish. Maximum depth is 90 feet (30 meters). Total dive time is about 35 minutes.

The Maze

A 10-15 minute boat ride takes divers to this maze of coral heads. Resting in about 87 feet (28 meters) of water are big coral heads intertwined in a maze-like formation. Spade fish, trigger fish, amber jacks, barracuda, grouper, and yellow-tail snappers can also be seen here. Maximum dive time is about 35 minutes.

Conch Reef

Famous for its plentiful population of queen conches, this area has a relatively nice population of fish for Santiago de Cuba. The coral reef is a host to a number of hard and soft corals. Maximum depth is about 45 feet (15 meters). Total dive time is about 40 minutes.

Mandinga Reef

The bottom emerges from a depth of 105 feet. There is a wide variety of small tropical fish.

For more information or to book a reservation contact:

Centro de Buceo Sierra Mar
Carretera de Chivirico, Km. 60
Guama, Santiago de Cuba
Ph: 532-262-6436/532-269-1446
Fax: 532-268-6108

Hotel Daiquiri

Yes! This is the spot where the daiquiri rum drink was invented. According to Christopher Baker, author of *Cuba Handbook*, "The copper firm's chief engineer, Jennings S. Cox first created the now world famous cocktail that Hemingway once immortalized in his novels. Cox had arrived in 1898, shortly after the Spanish American War, to find workers at the mines anxious about putatively malarial drinking water. Cox added a heartening tot of local Bacardi rum to boiled water, then decided to give this mixture an added snap and smoothness by introducing lime juice and sugar". About 25 years later, a bartender at the famous Floridita Bar in Havana added shaved ice to the drink to make it what it is today.

The hotel can be reached by travelling east 16 miles on Carretera de Baconao and then turning right at the sign indicating the Daiquiri Hotel. Follow the road to Playa El Indio. The hotel has 94 rooms ranging from $35-45 and 62 suites ranging from $55-60 per night.

In 1999, Hotel Daiquiri was closed, and the Daiquiri divemasters moved to Cubanacan Nautica's other two dive shops: Sigua (east) and Bucanero (west). It is possible that Hotel Daiquiri could re-open. However, in the meantime, Daiquiri's dive sites are close enough to the Bucanero Dive Center, that they are still available for eager divers. (See dive map on pg. 201)

Large eyed squirrel fish

Center for Marine Research, Univ. Havana

Fruit Cuba

This interesting shipwreck, with history dating from the turn of the century, can be found at about 130 feet (43 meters) on a sandy bottom.

El Casco and El Tanque

These shipwrecks can be accessed from the beach. The ships lay in a depth of only about 50 feet (17 meters). They have become perfect artificial reefs for small tropical fish that inhabit these shelters in the sand.

For more information on Hotel Daiquiri contact:

Hotel Daiquiri
Carretera de Baconao Km 25
Daiquiri, Santiago de Cuba
Ph: 532-262-4849 / 532-262-4724

Above the Water

Santiago offers many historical sites as well as cultural evening entertainment. La Casa de La Trova is the best place to hear Cuban music. It costs tourists one dollar to enter. Many famous musicians have played here, including a few groups who have even won a Grammy award, such as the Buena Vista Social Club. For more details, see the *Cuba Handbook*, by Christopher P.Baker.

Insider's Tips

Driving west from Bucanero (toward Santiago de Cuba), the road comes to a "T". Turn left toward Playa Siboney. When the road ends at the beautiful beach, turn right (into the village of Siboney). Ask the locals or look to your left for a *paladar* restaurant. From the cliff enjoy the view of Cubans swimming in the surf, while you eat tasty lobster swilled with a couple

D. Tipton

Tropical fish in Santiago

of delicious cold beers, all for less than $15.00.

A suggested *casa particular* just a block from the Cathedral in Santiago de Cuba is:

Teresa Puig Macias
Calle Mariano Corona, No. 863 A
E/ San Carlos y Santa Rosa
Email: CBL917@hotmail.com

Getting There

Divers can book a package to Santiago de Cuba through any concierge desk at major hotels in Cuba, or book a direct flight from Canada. Roundtrip airfare between Havana and Santiago de Cuba is about $160.00.

SANTIAGO DE CUBA
Bucanero Dive Center

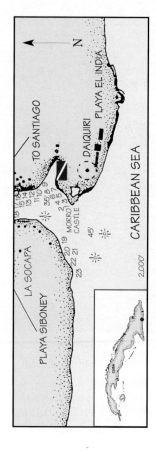

Dive Site	Depth
1. El Pico	115ft (38m)
2. El Tanque	75ft (25m)
3. Juragua I	55ft (19m)
4. Juragua II	115ft (38m)
5. Punta Azul	80ft (27m)
6. El Espejo	80ft (27m)
7. Canto Suave	60ft (20m)
8. Piedra de los Arigues	90ft (30m)
9. Punta Bucanero	12-40ft (4-13m)

Dive Site	Depth
10. La Playa	12ft (4m)
11. Piedra de los Pargos	130ft (43m)
12. El Cañon	45ft (15m)
13. Peladero	60ft (20m)
14. La Pared	50ft (17m)
15. Punta Cubera	50ft (17m)
16. La Cueva	25ft (8m)
17. Los Janaos	130ft (43m)
18. Punta Gaviota	100ft (33m)

Dive Site	Depth
19. Siboney	40ft (13m)
20. Cantera	130ft (43m)
21. Paso Prieto	130ft (43m)
22. La Cabana	130ft (43m)
23. Caballo Blanco	130ft (43m)

SANTIAGO DE CUBA
Daiquiri Dive Center

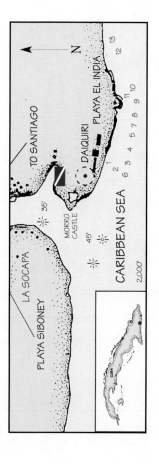

Dive Site

	Dive Site	Depth
1.	El Tanque	7-50ft (2-17m)
2.	El Ancla	20-60ft (7-20m)
3.	Jardín de Coral I	20-65ft (7-22m)
4.	Jardín de Coral II	20-65ft (7-22m)
5.	Canto Suave	115ft (38m)
6.	Gran Piedra	80ft (27m)
7.	Balcon	60ft (20m)

Dive Site

	Dive Site	Depth
8.	Las Penas	100ft (33m)
9.	Baconao	80ft (27m)
10.	Fruit Cuba	130ft (43m)
11.	El Casco	50ft (17m)
12.	Los Mogotes	80ft (27m)
13.	Islotes	50ft (17m)

SANTIAGO DE CUBA
Sigua Dive Center

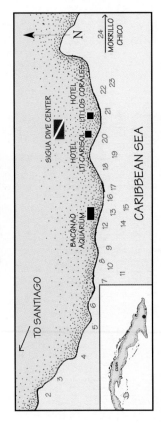

Dive Site

Dive Site	Depth
1. Playa Larga	50ft (17m)
2. Playa Larga	100ftII (33m)
3. Los Cobos	60ft (20m)
4. La Goleta	60ft (20m)
5. La Kawama	85ft (29m)
6. Sifomas I	25ft (8m)
7. Caracoles	40ft (13m)
8. Open Water	35ft (12m)
9. Guarico	50ft (17m)
10. Sponge City	80ft (27m)
11. La Pared	115ft (38m)
12. Sifomas II	35ft (12m)

Dive Site

Dive Site	Depth
13. Mogotes	45ft (15m)
14. Spring Carol	80ft (27m)
15. Ferry	115ft (38m)
16. Cangilones	20-70ft (7-23m)
17. Chopa's Town	40ft (13m)
18. Coral Garden I	45ft (15m)
19. Coral Garden II	80ft (27m)
20. La Turbina	20-65ft (7-22m)
21. Cazonalito I	15ft (5m)
22. Cazonalito II	15ft (5m)
23. Cazonalito III	45ft (15m)

The Diving Guide to Cuba Scuba

Scenic coastline along the road to Santiago de Cuba.

The Wreck of Cristóbal Colón

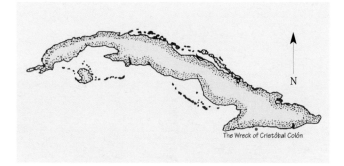

The Wreck of Cristóbal Colón

Santiago de Cuba Province

The Wreck of the Cristóbal Colón

A two-hour bus ride outside the city of Santiago de Cuba, the wreck of the Cristóbal Colón is a submerged capsule of history. Wreck divers, history buffs, and divers looking for something unique, will not want to miss this dive.

The 6,840-ton Cristóbal Colón was sunk during the Spanish-American war in 1898. The Colón was the finest armored cruiser in the Spanish fleet. She was a modern and speedy ship, almost brand new. Some historians claim that the Colón was so new that its heavy guns had not yet been mounted. Many sources have said that all she had in defense were fake, wooden dummies. However, according to Deborah Bachrach, author of *The Spanish-American War*, the Colón was carrying 10 light guns, 10 medium guns and 2 large guns. Furthermore, divers can see spent cannon shells lying near the wreck of the ship, proving that the Colón did have ammunition to defend itself.

The Cristóbal Colón was the third ship to leave the Santiago Bay on July 3rd, 1898. The battle created much confusion, allowing the opportunity for her to speed out of the tumultuous area. At first it seemed that the ship might escape the battle unharmed. But, after the Colón used up

Divers have a rocky walk to the beach dive.

W. Houghton

the last of her high-grade Cardiff coal and was forced to switch to coal of less quality, her speed was greatly inhibited. The Colón's lack of speed and crucial error of the captain, Admiral Serveras, who commanded the Colón to hug the shore rather than head for the open ocean, led to a terrible outcome. By 2:00pm the American fleet spotted the Colón and came within firing range. The retreating Colón ran itself onto the rocks and took down its flag. Most Spanish sailors jumped ship and escaped to the beach. An American salvage crew quickly went aboard, and later tried to tow the Colón off the rocks. Some say that the Americans wanted to bring the Colón back to display it as a trophy, but it sank as soon as it was pulled from the rocks and turned toward the open sea. This is the reason that divers will see the stern of the Colón facing the beach and the bow pointing toward the open ocean.

To access the wreck of the Colón, divers must first put on all their dive equipment and climb down a hill. Then, they must cross 50 yards of slippery china stones to reach the edge of the water. Divers should remember to carry their fins to wade across rocks. The divemaster enters the water first. Divers should carefully enter the ocean by waiting for a wave to crash, and then diving into the next wave. After swimming about 15 feet (3 meters) divers may begin their descent along a gentle sloping bottom. During the snorkel out to the ship, pounding waves drag the little china stones across the foot of the beach. The noise is so poignant that it sounds as if the stones are falling above you! The stern of the Colón, without propellers, appears in less than one minute. It rests in about 30 feet (10 meters) of water. Divers can swim the entire length of the wreck and descend to about 130 feet (42 meters) to the anchor,

Divers can see old cannons from the Cristóbal Colón wreck. M. Mola

205

which seems colossal in size. The bottom of the bow lies in about 120 feet (40 meters). Divers can swim across the deck in about 60 feet (20 meters) to the first huge cannon. Bullets and cannon shells rest on the lower decks. The entire ship is covered with tiny crustaceans, small corals, and sponges.

In 1985 Pedro Soberats Trigueros, the Cuban pioneer of diving, described the fish life at the wreck of the Colón as "like an aquarium". Pedro Soberats was a highly regarded diver who discovered many new dive site areas and spent his life in the waters around Cuba. He even introduced the wreck to Jacques Cousteau. Soberats said that the wreck was home to schools of sharks such as bull, tigers, and hammerheads. Yet before he recently passed away, Soberats visited the wreck in May of 1999 and did not see one shark. He believed that all of the sharks were fished out by "palangre", which is a Cuban term for "trawler lines". Trawler lines are fishing line with many hooks. These lines extended up to five miles long into the ocean. Local Cubans ate the sharks as fast as they were caught. The use of trawler lines is illegal now, but that has not stopped the over-fishing of the area. In 1996, licenses were granted to fisherman to use spear guns. As a result, enforcement of the regulations has been difficult.

Although fish life has seemed to dwindle over the years, resident groupers and tarpons can be seen patrolling the wreck on most days. Tarpon only appear at the beginning of the dive. Visibility is better on a clear day. October through April is the best season to see this awesome wreck because there is less chance for rain and the seas are calmer. If rain occurs, the Mula River clouds up the waters surrounding the wreck for several days. When the visibility is good, the Colón provides a great opportunity for photos. From mid-April to September heavy rains decrease visibility. The presence of Caribé is also possible during this time. It is highly recommended to experience the wreck of the Colón as a boat dive rather than a shore dive, if possible. The shore is not sand, but small pebbles. The waves can be brutal on some days. A crashing wave could smash a diver onto the rocks and cause serious injury. Almost all dive centers in Santiago make bus trips to the Colón. Cubanacan Nautica's dive centers usually charge about $60.00 for the dive. The wreck dive is for moderate to experienced divers only.

For more information or to book a reservation, contact any dive center in Santiago de Cuba.

Insider's Tips

Sometimes the visibility can be a lot clearer 15 feet (3m) below the surface due to tides. It is normal to not always see the boat while snorkeling out to the site. The best visibility is usually in the morning.

Getting There

Divers may rent a car and drive to the area of the wreck. But, the most cost efficient way to dive the Colón is to book through Sigua, Buccanero, or Sierra Mar dive centers. Refer to the section on Santiago for more details about these dive centers and for information on how to contact them.

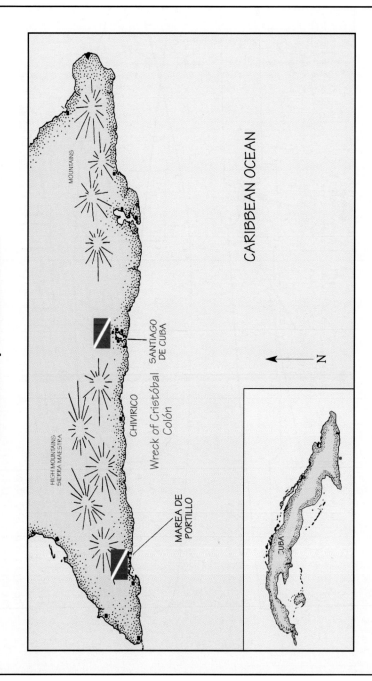

Granma Province
The Wreck of Cristóbal Colón

MOUNTAINS

HIGH MOUNTAINS
SIERRA MAESTRA

CHIVIRICO

Wreck of Cristóbal
Colón

SANTIAGO
DE CUBA

MAREA DE
PORTILLO

CARIBBEAN OCEAN

N

CUBA

WRECK OF THE CRISTOBAL COLÓN
(Drawing of wreck layout)

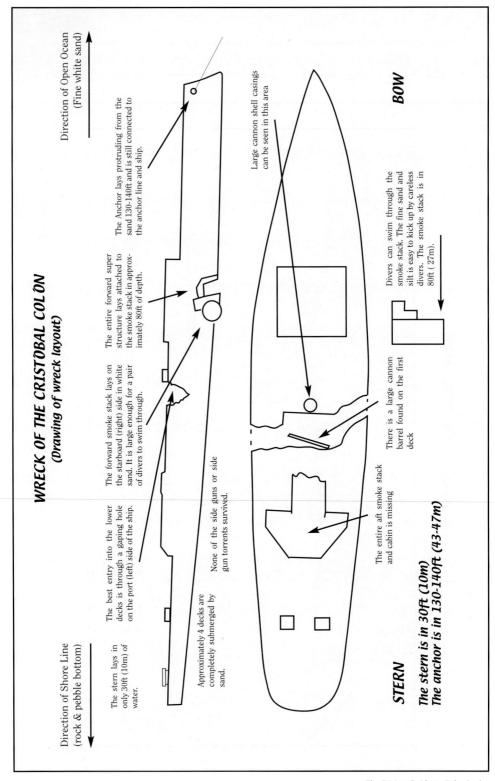

Direction of Shore Line
(rock & pebble bottom)

Direction of Open Ocean
(Fine white sand)

The Anchor lays protruding from the sand 130-140ft and is still connected to the anchor line and ship.

The entire forward super structure lays attached to the smoke stack in approximately 80ft of depth.

The forward smoke stack lays on the starboard (right) side in white sand. It is large enough for a pair of divers to swim through.

The best entry into the lower decks is through a gaping hole on the port (left) side of the ship.

None of the side guns or side gun torrents survived.

The stern lays in only 30ft (10m) of water.

Approximately 4 decks are completely submerged by sand.

Large cannon shell casings can be seen in this area

Divers can swim through the smoke stack. The fine sand and silt is easy to kick up by careless divers. The smoke stack is in 80ft (27m).

BOW

There is a large cannon barrel found on the first deck

The entire aft smoke stack and cabin is missing

STERN

The stern is in 30ft (10m)
The anchor is in 130-140ft (43-47m)

208   The Diving Guide to Cuba Scuba

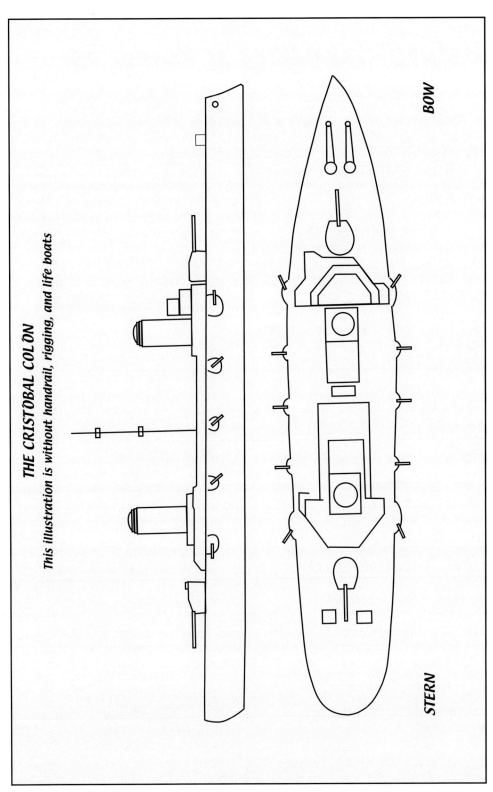

THE CRISTOBAL COLÓN

This illustration is without handrail, rigging, and life boats

BOW

STERN

These websites and contacts are available for further information about Cuba. The Internet is the best place to find the most current information. These sites and contacts can assist to inform and familiarize the diver.

Scuba Diving in Cuba

http://www.cubascuba-thebook.com - IN ENGLISH, this site has updates, current information, editorials, traveler's tips and experiences for divers.

http://www.cubatravel.cu/en/productos/nautica.asp# - Overview of diving from the Ministry of Tourism of Cuba.

http://www.diving-cuba.com/divesites.htm - Gives detailed information on the marinas and diving centers of Puertosol.

http://www.cubanacan.cu/INGLES/Nautica/BUCEO.HTM - Lists the contact information for all the dive centers of Cubanacan Nautica's (Scuba Cuba).
ONLY IN SPANISH.

http://havanacuba.com/scuba/default.htm - Cubatravel works in conjunction with Caribbean Diving Center LTD., and Puertosol's highly trained personnel.

http://www.diveguide.com/p1720.htm - Jardines de la Reina (Queen's Gardens) official website.

http://www.cuba.tc/Blue%20Reef_DivingCenter.html - Blue Reef diving center in Havana, Cuba.

http://www.netssa.com/diving.htm - Diving in Guajimico village between Cienfuegos and Trinidad.

http://www.oceanus.com.mx/html/oceanus.html - Oceanus live aboard goes to Isla de Juventud, Cayo Largo and Maria la Gorda. It is a fully legal diving trip for Americans!

Cuba's Official Web-site

http://www.cubatravel.cu/ - Official site of the Ministry of Tourism of Cuba.
GREAT SITE IN ENGLISH

http://www.cubaweb.cu/
ONLY IN SPANISH, but interesting information on cuban music, how to fly inside Cuba, rent a car on the internet, questions and suggestions, news and magazines, travel and tourism, fairs and events.

http://www.cubagob.cu/
ONLY IN SPANISH, this is the official site of the Cuban government. Addresses exterior relations, economic development, and social development.

US Government Web Resources

http://usembassy.state.gov/posts/cu1/wwwhmain.html - U.S. Interest Section in Havana, Home page.

http://www.travel.state.gov/cuba.html - Official Travel Consular sheet.
Fax: (202) 647-3000

http://www.state.gov/www/regions/wha/cuba/ - Updated official information from the U.S. treasury department on current news, rules, and events. VERY IMPORTANT http://www.odci.gov/cia/publications/fact-book/geos/cu.html - CIA FACTBOOK gives population, geographic location, growth statistics, cultural facts, etc.

Cuba Information

http://www.cubanacan.cu/INGLES/ - The Cubanacán Group is a holding company of tourism and trade that hosts around 40 per cent of international tourists visiting Cuba. It has 9 offices in different countries of Europe and the Americas.

http://www.cubatrade.org – US-Cuba Trade and Economic Council focuses on food and agricultural businesses and exports.

http://www.seekon.com/L/CAR/CC/Cuba/ - infinite information all about Cuba.

http://www.canfnet.org/ - CANF Website Cuban-American National Foundation updated News and Cuban affairs.

http://www.geocities.com/TheTropics/Shores/5902/cubaguid.htm - Money and language, dangers and annoyances, accommodations, getting there, internal transportation, eating, miscellaneous and special considerations for Americans, things to do, places to visit, not so budget information, links to other web sites about Cuban travel (VERY, VERY USEFUL INFORMATION. WELL WORTH READING)

http://www.cubana.cu/ -
IN SPANISH ONLY, Cubana Airlines is a Republic of Cuba government-controlled airline, which provides regularly, scheduled and chartered services throughout North America, Central America, Caribbean, South America, and Europe.

http://www.cybercuba.com/ - Good Information on Cuba, too.

http://www.cubasolidarity.ca/01tours/traveltips.html - Focuses on educational tour programs, but gives good insights on preparations, packing, and what to expect when traveling to Cuba.

http://www.USCuBA.ORG - A newly developed business organization for Americans who want to establish business in Cuba.

http://www.globalexchange.org/tours/auto/byCountry.html#Cuba - Global Exchange is a licensed Cuba Travel Service Provider. In addition, specific educational travel licenses are obtained from the U.S. Treasury Department for each Reality Tour. This site lists a complete updated schedule of legal trips to Cuba.

http://www.cubaupdate.org - Center for Cuban Studies of New York gives travel information and schedules of legal travel events to Cuba.

http://www.cubanacan.cu/ - ENGLISH & SPANISH Tourism, Hotels, News, Tips, Links, (Cubanacan is the largest Republic of Cuba government-controlled company involved in the tourism industry, comprised of tour operators, hotels, restaurants, vehicle rental, air charters, travel agents, retail, agriculture, and other enterprises.)

http://www.lanic.utexas.edu/la/cb/cuba/ Really good Information, Too much to list it all, general, arts, human rights, business, news, directories, tourism.

http://www.dtcuba.com/eng/default.asp
Excellent source of general information on Cuba.

http://www.latinworld.com/caribé/cuba/index.html - Latin America on the net- A business oriented website on Cuba. Addresses culture, business, music, traditions, sports, education.

http://www.fiu.edu/~fcf/gen.info.cuba.html
General information on the island of Cuba.

http://www.cuba.com/facts.htm
Facts about Cuba.

News Agencies
http://www.granma.cu - ONLY IN SPANISH, Granma International is the official newspaper of the Government of the Republic of Cuba. The newspaper is printed weekly in five languages.

http://www.radiohc.org -
Radio Habana Cuba, daily articles and archives in English and in Spanish.

http://www.miami.com/mld/miamiherald/ -
Type in Cuba in the search box to bring up archived articles from the Miami Herald newspaper.

Solidarity Organizations
http://www.ifconews.org/ -
Interreligious Foundation for Community Organization, Pastors for Peace.

http://www.jewishcuba.org
Judaism in Cuba.

http://www.afrocubaweb.com - Afro-Cuba website with lots of information on race in Cuba, Afro-Cuban culture, José Martí, etc.

http://www.cubamer.org - Cuban American Alliance Education Fund (Progressive Cuban American Group) Educational trips. Legislature information, and more.

http://www.igc.org/cubasoli/ - Solidarity organization for Cuba's national health care system and other news.

http://www.igc.org/cubasoli/uscumedi.html – US/Cuba medical projects.

Cuban Cities
http://search.yahoo.com/bin/search?p=Varadero - Information on Varadero, Cuba. (Cuba's equivalent to Cancun, Mexico)

http://www.cubatravel.cu/en/destinos/la_habana.asp - Overview of Havana from the Ministry of Tourism.

http://www.cuba.tc/Havana/CubaHavanaHotels.html - Information on most cities in Cuba along with hotels in each area.

http://www.netssa.com/cienfuegos.html - Great pictures and info on Cienfuegos.

http://www.1000traveltips.org/santiago.html - Information on getting to Santiago to Cuba; what to do; where to go.

http://www.1000traveltips.org/trinidad.htm
Information on Trinidad.

Weather

http://www.usatoday.com/weather/fore-cast/international/caribbean-temps-index.htm - Caribbean & Cuba temperatures.

http://www.1uptravel.com/weather-fore-cast/cuba.html - Forecasts for most areas in Cuba in Celsius.

Maps

http://www.scubaspots.com/Listings.asp?Location=Cuba - map of Cuba and selected cities.

Travel Agencies

http://www.nashtravel.com/hotels/cayole-visa.html - A. Nash travel is a Canadian travel agency specializing in Cuba.

http://www.marazulcharters.com/ - U.S. legal travel agency for group tours.

http://www.globalexchange.org/ - Legal travel agency offers "reality tours" to Cuba

http://www.macqueens.com/macqueens.html - Travel agency quoted by the NY times to have the best cycling tours in Cuba.

http://www.cubalinda.com - American owned travel agency located in Havana (registered in the Bahamas) with rights to book trips to and within Cuba.

http://www.diving-cuba.com/aboutus.htm Partnership travel agencies with Cuba.

http://www.cancun.com/tours/divermex/ Mexican Divers Travel Agency.

Airlines

http://www.destinationcuba.com/airfare.html - Flight schedule for airlines from the U.S, Jamaica, Mexico or Grand Cayman that fly to Cuba.

http://www.worldheadquarters.com/cuba/transportation/ - Contact information for airlines in Cuba.

http://sancristobaltravel.com/cuba-travel-flights-to-cuba.html - flight schedules from Cancun to Havana and from Nassau to Havana.

http://www.usacubatravel.com/domestic.html - domestic flight schedules within Cuba.

http://climate.envsci.rutgers.edu/lidar/charter.htm - Charter flights to Cuba.

Casa Particular

http://www.caspar.net/casa/cuba.htm CASABLANCA, the *casa particular* in Havana where Author Amy Houghton stays.

Hotels

http://www.cubanacan.cu/INGLES/HOTE-LES/hoteles_cubanacan.html - Unlimited hotels of every luxury levels with complete descriptions and contact information.

http://hotelroomsplus.com/cuba/cuba.htm - Hotels listed by regions in Cuba.

http://www.1click2cuba.com/menu.html - information and pictures on hotels in Cuba. Does not provide opportunities to make reservations.

Restaurants

http://www.lahabana.com/dining/index.shtml - Lists popular state owned restaurants and a few private *paladares* in Havana.

Car Rentals

http://www.cuba.tc/Havanatur/havanauto.html - Havana Autos, even includes a toll free number to call from the U.S. or Canada!

http://www.cuba.tc/Gaviota/GaviotaCarRental.html - Car rentals from Gaviota tour group picks you up at the airport.

Havanautos

Center of Reservations
Havana, Cuba
Ph: 537-204-0647 / 537-204-0648

Havanautos José Martí Airport
Terminals I and II
Havana, Cuba
Ph: 537-833-5215 / 537-833-5197

Panautos

José Martí Airport
Terminal II
Havana, Cuba
Ph: 537-80-3921

Transautos

Havana, Cuba
José Martí Airport
Center of Reservations
Ph: 537-204-5532

W. Hougthon

Useful Dive Terms

Mask	Máscara	mah-scar-uh
Fins	Patas Ranas / Aletas	pah-tahs rah-nuhs
Snorkel	Snorkel	snor-kehl
BC Jacket	Chaleco Compensad	chah-lay-ko come-pen-say-door
Regulator	Regulador	ray-guh-luh-door
Full Wet Suit	Isotérmico Largo	eee-soe-tear-me-ko lahr-go
"Shorty" Wet Suit	Isotérmico Corto	eee-soe-tear-me-ko core-toe
Knife	Cuchillo	coo-chee-yo
Weight Belt	Cinto de Plomos	seen-toe day ploe-moes
Weight	Plomos / Las Pesas	ploe-moes / las pay-suhs
Tank	Tanque	ehl tahn-kay
Rental Gear	Equipo de Renta	eh-keep-o day rent-uh
Depth Gauge	Profundimetro	pro-fune-dee-meh-troe
Air Pressure	Manometro de Aire	mahn-o-meh-tro day eye-ray
Maximum Depth	Profundidad Maxima	pro-fune-dee-dahd max-ee-muh
Bottom Time	Tiempo del Fondo	tea-em-poe del fone-doe
Safety Stop	Parada de Seguridad	par-ah-dah day say-gur-ee-dahd
Dive Master	Guía de Buceo	gee-yah day boo-say-o
Dive Boat	Barco de Buceo	bar-koe day boo-say-o
Dive Sites	Sitios de Buceo	seat-ee-yos day boo-say-o
Divers	Buceadores	boo-say-uh-door-ays
Dive Shop	Centro de Buceo	cen-tro day boo-say-o
Resort Course	Curso Resort	coor-so ray-sor
Open Water	Mar Abierto	mar ah-bee-yer-toe
Advanced	Avanzada	ah-vahn-sah-dah
Hyperbaric Chamber	Cámara Hiperbárica	kah-mar-uh ee-pear-bar-ee-kuh
Emergency	Emergencia	eh-mer-hen-see-ya
Please, help me	Por favor, ayúdame	pore fuh-vore, eye-you-duh-may
Sandy Bottom	Fondo Arenoso	fone-doe ah-ray-no-so
Coral Bottom	Fondo Coralino	fone-doe co-rah-leen-o
Tunnel	Tunel	too-nell
Cave	Cueva	quay-vah
Cavern	Caverna	cah-bear-nuh
Beach	Playa	ply-ya
Shark	Tiburón	tea-bur-rone
Nurse Shark	Tiburón Gata	tea-bur-rone gah-tuh
Eel	Morena	more-ray-nuh
Barracuda	Baracuda	bar-ruh-coo-duh
Sea Turtle	Tortuga	tore-too-guh
Lobster	Langosta	lang-goe-stuh
Shrimp	Camerones	kah-mare-row-nays
Crab	Cangrejo	kahn-gray-ho

Useful Dive Terms

Conch Shell	Caracol	car-ruh-cole
Snapper	Pargo	par-goe
Grouper	Mero	mare-o
Jewfish	Chema	kay-muh
Angel Fish	Pez Angel	paze on-hell
Fish Life	Vida de Peces	vee-duh day paces
Sea Fans	Abanicos	ah-bahn-ee-kos
Ship Wreck	Barco Hundido	bar-ko un-dee-do
Coral Wall	Pared Coralina	par-red core-rah-lee-nuh
Night Dive	Buceo Nocturno	boo-say-o noke-turn-o
Wind	Viento	vee-yen-toe
Waves	Olas	o-lahs
Current	Corriente	core-ree-yen-tay
Temperature	Temperatura	tem-per-rah-tour-rah
Meters	Metros	meh-troes
Feet	Piés	pee-yahs
Kilos	Kilos	kee-los
Pounds	Libres	lee-brays
To The Right	A La Derecha	lah dare-ray-chuh
To The Left	A La Izquierda	lah ee-skee-yer-duh
Wait!	Espérate	spare-eh-tay
Let's Go!	Vámanos	ba-mah-nose
Mermaid	Sirena	see-ray-nuh
Beer	Cerveza	sair-vay-suh
Rum	Ron	rrrrun
Party	Fiesta	fee-yes-tuh
Let's Dance!	Bailamos	bye-lah-mose
Hang-over	Resaca	ray-sock-uh
Nap	Siesta	see-yes-tuh

E. Macao

Scuba Certification Schools

ACUC International
(American Canadian Underwater
Certification)
Anastro 25
Ph: 341-766-8412
Fax: 341-766-8651
Madrid, Spain 28033
ACUC certifications can be obtained at
the following dive centers in Cuba:
La Aguja, City of Havana
Maria la Gorda, Pinar del Rio
Bucanero, Santiago de Cuba
El Colony, La Isla de la Juventud
Cayo Blanco, Sancti Spiritus
Cayo Guillermo, Ciego de Avila
Cayo Largo, Isla de la Juventud
Acua, Matanzas
Sharks' Friends, Camagüey
Sierra Mar, Santiago de Cuba
Sigua, Santiago de Cuba
Faro Luna, Cienfuegos
Coco Dive Center, Ciego de Avila

PADI
(Professional Association of Diving
Instructors)
P.O. Box 7005
Rancho Santa Margarita, California.
USA 92688
Ph: 1-800-PAY-PADI
PADI certifications can be obtained at
the following dive centers in Cuba:
Cuba Divers, Cayo Guillermo
Whale Shark, Cienfuegos
Acua, Matanzas
Ancon, Trinidad
Sea Lovers, Holguin

NAUI
(National Association of Underwater
Instructors)
9942 Currie Davis Drive
Tampa, Florida USA 33619
Ph: 1-800-553-6284
NAUI certifications can be obtained at
the following dive centers in Cuba:
Whale Shark, Cienfuegos
Acua, Matanzas

SSI
(Scuba Schools International)
2619 Canton Court
Fort Collins, Colorado USA 80525-4498
Ph: 1-800-892-2702
SSI certifications can be obtained at the
following dive centers in Cuba:
Sea Lovers, Holguin
Cayo Largo, Isla de la Juventud
Marina Tarara, City of Havana
La Aguja, City of Havana

CMAS
(Confederation Mundial des Activities
Subaquatiques)
France
CMAS certifications can be obtained at
the following dive centers in Cuba:
Abalone, Ciego de Avila
Acua, Matanzas
Cayo Blanco, Sancti Spiritus
Cayo Guillermo, Ciego de Avila
El Colony, La Isla de la Juventud
Guajimico, Cienfuegos

**NO CERTIFICATION SCHOOLS
AVAILABLE IN THE FOLLOWING AREAS**
Diving World, Cayo Levisa
Club Varadero-Superclub, Matanzas
Gaviota, Matanzas
Playa Giron, Matanzas
Octopus, Matanzas
Blue Scuba Club, La Habana

Center for Marine Research, Univ. Havana

Cuban Dive Centers

Acua/ Puertosol
Ave. Kawama No. 201 e/ 2 y 3
Varadero, Matanzas
Ph: 534-566-8063
Fax: 534-566-7456
Email: darsena@psolvar.get.tur.cu

Aguja/ Cubanacan Nautica
Residencial Turistico Marina Hemingway
5ta Avenida y 248
Playa Santa Fe, Ciudad de la Habana
Ph: 537-204-1150
Fax: 537-204-5280
Email: alain@puertomh.cha.cyt.cu

Albacora/ Cubanacan Nautica
Playa Marea del Portillo
Pilon, Granma
Ph: 532-359-7139
Fax: 532-359-7080

Avalon/ Puertosol
Cayo Caballones, Archipielago Jardines
de la Reina
Jucaro, Ciego de Avila
Email: avalon@avalons.net
Ph: +1 928-222-1631
Website: www.avalons.net

Barracuda/ Cubanacan Nautica
Calle 1ra. y 59
Varadero, Matanzas
Ph: 534-566-7072
Fax: 534-566-7072
Email: ventas@aqwo.var.cyt.cu

Beaches - Varadero/ Cubanacan Nautica
Hotel Beaches
Carrretera Las Americas, Km. 3
Varadero, Matanzas
Ph: 534566-8470
Fax: 534-566-7093
Email: ventas@aqwo.var.cyt.cu

Blue Diving/ Cubanacan Nautica
Melia Cayo Coco,
Ciego de Avila
Ph: 533-330-8179
Fax: 533-330-8180
Email: enzo@bluediving.cav-cyt.cu

Blue Reef/ Cubanacan Nautica
Playa El Salado
Villa Cocomar
Carretera Panamericana Km 23½
Caimito, La Habana
Ph: 537-680-8290 ext 72
Fax: 537-24-1149

Blue World/ Gaviota
Playa Pesquero
Carretera de Guardalavaca
Holguin
Ph: 53-243-0030
Fax: 53-243-0065

Bucanero/ Cubanacan Nautica
Hotel Bucanero
Carretera de Bacanao Km 21
Arroyo la Costa
Santiago de Cuba
Ph: 532-268-6363
Fax: 532-268-6070

Cayo Blanco/ Puertosol
Hotel Ancon, Carretera Maria Aguilar,
Playa Ancon, Casilda
Trinidad, Sancti Spiritus.
Ph: 53-419-6205
Ph: 53-419-6205
Email: marinastdad@ip.etecsa.cu

Cayo Guillermo
Hotel Sol Club, Cayo Guillermo,
Ciego de Avila
Ph: 533-330-1760

Fax: 533-330-1328
Email: gernecia@marlin.cav.cyt.cu or
depress@cguille.solmelia.cma.net

Cayo Largo/ Puertosol
Marina Cayo Largo del Sur
Archipielago de los Canarreos, Isla de la
Juventud
Ph / Fax: 53-454-8213
Email: gcom@psol.cls.tur.cu

Club Habana
5ta Ave. e/ 188 y 192
Repto. Flores, Playa
Habana
Ph: 537-204-5700
Fax: 537-204-5705

Copacabana Hotel
Calle 1ra. No. 4404 e/ 44 y 46
Playa, La Habana,
Ph: 537-204-1037
Fax: 537-204-2846
Email: commercio@copagca.cma.net

Coco/ Cubanacan Nautica
Hotel Tryp Cayo Coco,
Cayo Coco, Ciego de Avila
Ph: 533-330-1323
Fax: 533-330-1328
Email: gerencia@marlin.cav.cyt.cu

Cuba Divers/ Puertosol
Rotonda Villa Oceano,
Cayo Guillermo
Archipielago Jardines del Rey
Moron,Ciego de Avila
Ph: 533-330-1738 / 533-330-1740
Fax: 533-330-1737
Email: info@cuba-divers.com
Website: www.cuba-divers.com

Jose Dieppa
Dadopado International, SA
Club Santa Lucía
Playa Santa Lucía, Nuevitas
Camagüey, Cuba
Ph: 533-2233-6109 ext. 542
Fax: 533-2236-5147
Email:
dieppasub@cmg.colombus.cu

Diving World/ Horizontes
Cayo Levisa, La Palma,
Pinar del Rio
Ph: 537-866-6075
Fax: 537-833-4585

Covarrubias/ Puertosol
Villa Covarrubias
Playa Covarrubias
Puerto Padre, Las Tunas
Ph: 53-314-6230
Fax: 533-236-5305

Eagle Ray/ Cubanacan Nautica
Playa Guardalavaca, Banes
Guardalavaca, Holguin
Ph: 53-243-0316
Fax: 53-243-0185
Email: cubanacan.nautica@
          guard.gvc.cyt.cu

El Colony / Puertosol
Parque Nacional Marino Punta Frances
Carretera de la Siguanea Km 42
Isla de la Juventud
Ph: 53-619-8181
Fax: 53-619-8420
Email: gercomerc@colony.gerona.inf.cu

Faro Luna/ Cubanacan Nautica
Hotel Faro Luna, Carretera de
Pasacaballos Km. 18,

Playa Rancho Luna, Cienfuegos
Ph: 53-432-45-1340
Fax: 53-432-45-1340
Email: dcfluna@acuc.cfg.cyt.cu

Gaviota
Marina Gaviota Varadero
Peninsula de Hicacos, Varadero, Matanzas
Ph: 534-566-7755
Fax: 534-566-7756

Guajimico/ Cubamar
Villa Guajimico, Carretera de Trinidad
Km 22, Cumanayagua
Cienfuegos
Ph: 534-3-245-1204
Fax: 534-3-245-1206
Email: gjo@agua.cfg.sld.cu

Las Brujas/ Gaviota
Cayo Las Brujas
Villa Clara
Ph: 534-220-4199
Fax: 534-220-7599

Maria La Gorda/ Puertosol
La Bajada, Guanahacabibes, Sandino,
Sandino Pinar del Rio
Ph: 538-277-1306
Email: mlagorda@ip.etecsa.cu

Melia Cayo Guillermo/ Cubanacan Nautica
Hotel Melia Cayo Guillermo
Ciego de Avila
Ph: 533-330-1627
Fax: 533-330-1328
Email: gerencia@marlin.cav.cyt.cu

Playa Giron / Horizontes
Hotel Playa Giron
Peninsula de Zapata, Matanzas
Ph: 53-59-4118
Fax: 53-59-4141

Playa Sirena/ Puertosol
Playa Sirena, Cayo Largo del Sur,
Archipielago de los Canarreos
Cayo Largo
Ph: 53-454-8213
Fax: 53-454-8212
Email: gcom@psol.cls.tur.cu

Octopus/ Horizontes
Hotel Playa Larga
Villa Playa Larga
Parque Natural Montemar
Matanzas
Ph: 53-59-7294
Fax: 53-59-4141

Puerto Escondido/ Cubamar
Batey Puerto Escondido, Carretera
Panamericana Km 80,
Jibacoa, Santa Cruz Del Norte, La Habana
Ph: 537-866-2524
Fax 537-866-2523

**Puntarenas Super Club/ Cubanacan
Nautica**
Hotel Puntarenas
Carretera Kawama
Varadero, Matanzas
Ph: 534-566-8470
Fax: 534-566-7093
Email: ventas@aqwo.var.cyt.cu

Sea Lovers/ Gaviota
Playa Esmeralda, Carretera de
Guardalavaca, Banes, Holguin
Ph: 53-243-0030
Fax: 53-243-0065

Sharks' Friends/ Cubanacan Nautica
Brisas Santa Lucía, Playa Santa Lucía,
Camagüey
Ph: 533-236-5182

Fax: 533-236-5182
Email: marlin@sunnet.stl.cyt.cu or
sharksfriends@sunnet.stl.cyt.cu

Sierra Mar/ Cubanacan Nautica
Hotel Sierra Mar, Playa Sevilla Carretera
de Chivirico
Km. 60. Guama,
Santiago de Cuba
Ph: 532-262-6337
Fax: 532-268-2907

Sigua/ Cubanacan Nautica
Carretera de Baconao, Km. 40
Santiago de Cuba.
Ph: 532-263-6165
Fax: 532-268-6108
Email: root@carisol.scu.cyt.cu

Tarará/ Puertosol
Marina Tarará, Villa Blanca Km 18
Playa Tarará, La Habana del Este
Ciudad de la Habana
Ph: 537-897-1462
Fax: 537-897-1333
Email: commercial@tarara.mit.tur.cu

Whale Shark/ Puertosol
Hotel Rancho Luna, Carretera de
Pasacaballos, Km. 17
Cienfuegos
Ph: 534-3-245-1287
Fax: 534-3-245-1275
Email: mposolcfg@ip.etecsa.cu

A. Hougthon

Appendix

Private Restaurants of Havana

A Mi Manera
Calle 35 No. 1810 between 20 & 41
Miramar

Amigos
Calle L, No. 452 apto 2 between 25 & 27
Owner: Oscar Fonseca

Amor
Calle 23 No. 759 between B & C
Vedado
Ph: 833-8150
Upstairs 3 floors

Aries
Linea 456 between J & K
Ph: 832-4118
Owner: Mirta Lopez

Bellamar
Virtudes No. 169 (Near Amistad)
Centro Habana

Calle Diez ★ ★ ★
Calle 10 between 3ra & 5ta
Miramar, playa
Ph: 209-6702

Dona Blanquita
Paseo de Marti, No. 158 between Colon & Refugio
Centro Habana

Dona Julia
Koly 57 between 28 & 30
Nuevo Vedado
Owner: Julia Marinez

El Diluvio
Calle 72 between 17 & 19
Miramar
Owner : Milagros Capote
Ph: 202-1531

El Helecho
Calle 6 No 203
between Linea y 11
Vedado

El Laurel
Av. 5 No. 26002
(On the waterway at Marina Hemingway)

El Palio
Calle 24 & Ave. 1ra
Miramar
Ph: 202-9867
Owner: Antonio Enriche Lusson

El Paraiso
Calle 22 No. 3110
between 31-A & 33
Miramar

El Recanto
Calle 17 No. 957 between 8 & 10
Vedado, Ciudad de la Habana, Cuba
Ph: 830-4396
Owner: Maria Caridad Ferrera

Gringo Viejo ★ ★ ★ ★
Calle 21 No. 454 between E & F
Ph: 831-1946 or 832-6150
Owner: Omar Gonzalez

Hueco de 23
Calle 23 No. 1414 between 20 & 22
Owner: Matilde Bongo

Huron Axul ★ ★ ★ ★
Calle Humbolt No. 153 between O & P
Vedado
Owner: Juan Carlos Fernandez
(Just one block from la Rampa and only 4
blocks from Habana Libre Hotel)

La Casa ★ ★ ★ ★
Calle 30 No. 865 between 26 & 41
Nuevo Vedado
Owner: Silvia Cardoso

La Casa Colonial
Calle 11 No. 509 between D & E
Owner: Barbara Hernandez

La Casa Sarrasua
Calle 25 No. 510 apto 1 between H & I
Owner: Juan Bruno Sanchez

La Chansonnier ★ ★ ★ ★
Calle J, No 257 between 15 y Linea
Vedado
Ph: 832-1576
Owner: Silvia

La Cocina de Lilliam ★ ★ ★ ★ ★
Calle 48 No. 1311 between 13 & 15
Miramar
Ph: 209-6514

La Complaciente
Calle 15 No. 109 Apto 12 between L & M
Owner: Margarita LaForte

La Esperanza ★ ★ ★ ★ ★
Calle 16 No 105 between 1ra & 3ra
Miramar
Ph: 202-4361
Owner: Humberto

La Familia
Calle 6 No. 302 at Ave. 3
Miramar

La Fontana ★ ★ ★ ★ ★
Ave 3ra A No. 305 esq. 46
Miramar
Ph: 202-8337

La Guarida ★ ★ ★ ★ ★
Calle Concordia No 418
between Gervasio y Escobar, Habana Vieja
Ph: 862-4940

La Media Cubana
San Ignacio No. 77 A
between Orelly y Empedrado
La Habana Vieja
Ph: 867-3852

La Tasquita
Calle Jovellar No 160
Pl. Martires de 1868
Centro Habana

La Ultima Instancia
Calle D No. 557
between Calles 23 & 25
Vedado (upstairs)

Las Casona de 17
Calle 17 between M & N
Vedado

Las Delicias de Consulado
Consulado No. 309
Centro Habana

Las Tres Bs
Calle 21 between K y L
Vedado
Ph: 832-9276

Los Amigos
Calle M, No. 253 Apto 2 between 10 & 21
Owner: Elisabet Montero

Los Cactus de 33
Av 33 No. 3405
between 34 y 36
Playa

Los Helechos de Trinidad
Calle 25 No. 361
between K y L
(One block from Habana Libre Hotel)

Los Tres Mosqueteros
Calle 23 No. 607
between E & F
Vedado

Marpoly
Calle K, No. 154 between 11 & 13
Vedado
Ph: 832-2471
Owner: Polito

Mi Jardín
Ave. 5ta B, No. 517 esq. 66
Miramar
Ph: 203-4627
Owner: Edda y Daniel

Monguito
Calle L, No. 408 between 23 & 25
Vedado
Owner: Ricelda Guerrero

Nerei
Calle 19, No. 110 between L & M
Vedado
Owner: Guadalupe Herce

Restaurante Capitolio
Calle 13 No. 1159 between 16 & 18
Vedado
Ph: 833-4974
Owner: Julio

Restaurante Ma My's
Calle 16 No. 708
between 7ma & 31
Miramar, Playa
Ph: 203-6700
Owner: Ladianela

Sagitario
Virtudes No. 619 between Gervasio &
Escobar
Centro Habana

Torresson
Malecon No. 27 (Upstairs)
Centro Habana

Union Francesa de Cuba
Calle 17 esq a 6, Vedado
(across from Park John Lennon, upstairs
on third floor)
Ph: 832-4493

Vistamar ★ ★ ★ ★
Av. Primera No 2206
between 22 & 24
Miramar

Yiyo's
Calle L, No. 256
between 17 & 19
Vedado (upstairs in apartment 202)
Ph: 832-8977

Center for Marine Research, Univ. of Havana

Official Private Bed & Breakfasts of Havana

Jorge Luis Duany "CASA BLANCA"
Calle 13 No. 917 between 6 & 8, Vedado
Ph: 537-833-5697
Email: CBL917@homail.com
www.caspar.net/casa/

Jorge also can help visitors book any of the following *casa particulars*:

Lidia M. Alvares
28, No 210, between 19 & 21
2 bedrooms

Lurdes Denis Balcaner
27, No 910, Altos, between 4 & 6
2 bedrooms

Eva Torral Basova
G, No 102, APTO 7-6 between
CALZADA & 5ta
2 bedrooms

Marelys Hormia Batista
7MA, No 751, APTO 8, e/ PASEO & 2
2 bedrooms

Aurora & Nelson Benitez
Calle 15 No. 962, Apt. 5,
between 8 & 10, Vedado
Ph: 537-833-8659

Andres Spengler Borrego
19, No 1259, between 20 & 22
3 bedrooms

Norma Mendez Cruz
19, No 1301, between 22 & 24
2 bedrooms

Norma Labrada Diaz
Calle L No 314, 2nd floor,
between 19 & 21, Vedado
Ph: 537-832-9672

Martha G. Diaz
A, No 655, between 27 & 29
3 bedrooms

Raquel Mena Fernandez
CALZADA, No 711, BAJOS
between PASEO & A
2 bedrooms

Pilar Garcia Ferriol
10, No 4, between 1ra & 3ra
2 bedrooms

Santiago Hernandez Fdez
26, No 259, between 19 & 21
2 bedrooms

Alexis Perez Gomez
4, No 608, between 25 & 27
2 bedrooms

Aldo Lo Vasquez Guerra
B, No 154, between LINEA & CALZADA
2 bedrooms

Lilian Lechuga
PASEO, No 309, APTO 6-B, e/13 & 15
2 bedrooms

Dora I. Rodriguez Matilla
22, No 273, between 17 & 19
3 bedrooms

Lazara Martines
19, No 1464, between 28 & 30
2 bedrooms

Mirella Mesa Mendez
C, No 733, between 29 & Zapata
3 bedrooms

Nelson R. Moreno
C, No 659, between 27 & 29
2 bedrooms

Mario Nicaso
13, No 1330, between 22 & 24
2 bedrooms

Jorge Luis Visllazon Olmo
21, No 203, between J & K
2 bedrooms

Alicia S. Hdez Padron
LINEA, No 6, APTO 15 between N & O
2 bedrooms

Blass Perez Perez
26, No 261, between 19 & 21
3 bedrooms

Reyna Blanco Portuondo
CALZADA, No 1012, e/ 10 & 12
2 bedrooms

Sonia & Raisa
Linea & 4, No 812 (3rd floor), Vedado
Ph: 537-833-4434

Zoe & Rogelio
Linea & 4, No 812 (2 floor), Vedado
Ph: 537-833-4819

Fransisco Gonzalez Renan
4, No 512 between 21 & 23
2 bedrooms

Daniel Rivero
F, No 104 between 5ta & CALZADA
2 bedrooms

Hilda M. Perez Torres
27, No 954, between 6 and 8
2 bedrooms

Raul Carvajo Valdes
B, No 23, between 1 ra & 3ra
2 bedrooms

Marisol Vazques
19, No 1315, BAJOS between 22 y 24
2 bedrooms

Luis Garces Vazquez
19, No 356, APTO 2, between G y H
2 bedrooms

Martha Vitonte
Avenida de los Presidente, no. 301,
Vedado
Ph: 537-832-6475

Major Embassies in Havana

Argentina
Calle 36 No. 511 e/ 5ta y 7ma, Miramar,
Playa
537-204-2972, 204-2549, 204-2565
537-204-2140, 204 2110, 204-2573
ecuba@ip.etecsa.cu

Belize
Calle 5ta. Ave. A, No. 3608, e/ 36 y 36-A,
Miramar
537-204-3504
537-204-3506
belize.embassy@ip.etecsa.cu

Brazil
Lonja de Comercio. Calle Lamparilla. No.
2. 4to piso "K", Habana Vieja.
537-866-9052, 866-9080, 866-9051
537-866-2912
brasil@ceniai.inf.cu

Canada
Calle 30 No.518 esq. a 7ma., Miramar,
Playa
537-204 2516, 537-204-9772
537-204-2044, 537-204-1069
havan@dfait-maeci.gc.ca

Chile
Ave. 33 No. 1423 e/ 16 y 18. Miramar,
Playa
537-204-1222, 204-1223
537-204-1694
echilecu@cubacel.net

China
Calle 13 No. 551 e/ C y D. Vedado
537-833-3005, 833-3614
537-833-3092, 833-3614

Costa Rica
5ta. ave. No. 6604 e/ 66 y 68. Miramar,
Playa
537-204-6938
537-204-6937
crcubcon@ceniai.inf.cu

Dominican Republic
5ta. Ave. No 9202, e/ 92 y 94. Miramar,
Playa
537-204-8429, 204-8430
537-204-8431
edc@ip.etecsa.cu

Ecuador
Ave. 5ta-A No. 4407 e/ 44 y 46. Miramar,
Playa
537-204-2034; 204-2820
537-204-2868
embecuador@yahoo.com

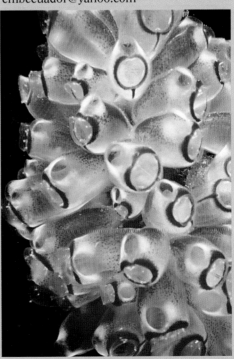

E. Macao

France
Calle 14 No. 312 e/ 3ra. y 5ta., Miramar
537-204-2132, 204-2308, 204-2080,
204-2143, 204-2792
537-204-1439
lahavane@dree.org

Germany
Calle B No.652 esq. a 13, Vedado, Plaza
537-833-2569, 537-833-2539,
537-833-3188, 537-833-2460
537-833-1586
alemania@enet.cu

Haiti
5ta. Ave. No. 6804, e/ 68 y 70, Miramar
537-204-5421, 204-5422
537-204-5423
embhaiti@enet.cu

Italy
5ta Ave No. 402, esq. a 4, Miramar
537-204-5615, 204-5618, 204-5621
537-204-5659, 204-5661
ambitcub@enet.cu

Jamaica
Calle 22, No. 503, e/ 5ta y 7ma. Miramar.
537-204-2908, 204-6959, 204-9572
537-204-2531
embjmcub@mail.infom.etecsa.cu

Mexico
Calle 12 No. 518 Esq. a 7ma. Ave.
Miramar, Playa.
537-204-7722 / 25, 204-2553, 204-2583,
204-2909
537-204-2717, 204-2294
embamexc@ip.etecsa.cu

Panama
Calle 26 No. 109 e/ 1ra. y 3ra., Miramar
537-204-1673, 204-0858
537-204-1674, 204-9011

Portugal
Ave. 7ma, No. 2207 Esq. A 24, Miramar
537-204-2871, 204-0149
embport@ip.etecsa.cu

Russia
5ta. Ave. No.6402 e/ 62 y 66, Miramar
537-204-2686, 204-1080, 204-1085
537-204-1038
embrusia@ceniai.inf.cu

Spain
Calle Cárcel No. 51 esq. a Zulueta, La
Habana Vieja
537-833-8025, 833-8026
537-833-8006
embespcu@ceniai.inf.cu

Sweden
Calle 34, No. 510, e/ 5ta y 7ma, Miramar
537-204-2831
537-204-1194
ambassaden.havana@foreign.ministry.se

Switzerland
5ta. Ave. No. 2005 e/ 20 y 22, Miramar
537-204-2611, 204-2729
537-204-1148
swissem@enet.cu

United Kingdom and Northern Ireland
Calle 34 No. 702-704 Esq. a 7ma.
Ave.Miramar.
537-204-1771
537-204-9214, 204-8104
embrit@ceniai.inf.cu

Author and father, Los Jardines de la Reina Fishing and Diving Center   D. Tipton

Manuel Mola Pedraza

Mr. Mola is a seasoned scuba diver with 24 years of experience. He was 18 years old when he ignited his passion for photography by creating a usable underwater camera by engineering a housing out of the inside tire balloon from a volleyball. He created the lens by using a dive mask to shield an old, Russian camera and successfully began taking underwater photos.

Since those early days and after acquiring a degree in physics, Manuel Mola has bequeathed his career to the waters of Cuba. His artistic eye captures the aquatic beauty he sees with his heart. He has won several international photography competitions in Cuba. His photos have been published worldwide in venues such as Sport Diver Magazine, Sub Magazine (Italy), Buceadores Magazine (Spain) and Espacio Profundidad (Mexico). He is a certified instructor of various diving organizations, Vice President of the Underwater Photography Cuba Federation, and one of only five board members in the world of the CMAS underwater commission of which Jacques Cousteau was the first president. Currently he dedicates his professional life to supporting nine diving centers in Cuba and works with well-recognized agencies to introduce Cuba's beautiful reefs to divers from around the world.

M. Mola

Donald Tipton

Mr. Tipton began his professional photographic career in 1982 and has worked in commercial and advertising photography since that time. In 1987, Tipton obtained his basic open water rating through NASDS. He continued his studies in diving by obtaining his NASDS instructors rating in 1989. Photography and videography have been an essential component of Tipton's diving. His work is a celebration of color and texture. While Mr. Tipton is a marine imagemaker, he also feels it is essential to show wildlife in their habitats. He attempts to show beaches, marshes, and intercostal waterways. He works with both black and white and color images. He also works extensively with marine mammals and other oceanic animals that are very difficult to approach. For this reason, he makes use of Drager rebreathers in most of his shoots.

His work regularly appears in magazines such as Dive, Skin Diver, Sport Diver, Fathoms, Tauchen, Mergulio, Asian Diver and others. His work appears in ads and catalogs for Drager, Aeris and other dive gear manufacturers. Mr. Tipton is represented in the world of fine art by Alan Broder at Oceans Gallery in Los Angeles. His new book *Upon the Face of the Waters* is a visual and spiritual journey through the vastness of the sea. He makes his home in Columbus, GA with his wife, Angelyn and children, Jonathan, Andrew, and Katherine.

W. Houghton

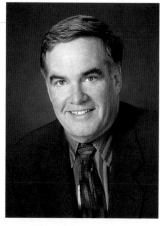

William H. Houghton

Mr. Houghton, a P.A.D.I. rescue diver, chose diving as a hobby to create an interest in a shared sport with his daughter in 1986. They have traveled extensively together. Diving was a connection that he enjoyed with his little dive buddy. He became interested in underwater photography after taking a P.A.D.I. photography class. As early as 1987 his underwater videography of the Florida Manatees appeared on the Public Broadcasting Station. Photography has been his lifelong hobby and he even owned photo-development shops before he retired at the age of 50. Since the development of the *Cuba Scuba* project, Mr. Houghton has experimented and dedicated his efforts to capturing the candid essence of Cuba on film. He currently divides his time between rural Indiana and Tampa Bay, Florida where he enjoys time with his family.

Ehidrioh Perez Acosta "Macao"

Macao was born in 1972, and certified when he was 15 years old. He played for Camagüey's champion water polo team and three years for the Cuban national team. In 1994 he earned his CMAS instructor's certificate. Just two years later, he earned his ACUC instructor's license. He speaks Spanish, English, Italian and a little German. Photography is a passionate hobby, which Macao enjoys while also observing marine life. He enjoys photographing divers in Santa Lucía to provide keepsakes of their trip. He is now the director of Scuba Cuba Sharks' Friends Diving Center. He resides in Santa Lucía with his wife Denise.

E. Macao

CHAMPION FREE DIVERS OF CUBA

For years Cuba has cultivated world champion free divers. Several have earned international recognition.

Francisco Pepin first learned to dive in Santa Lucía with Jose Dieppa. Later, he won several records. Pepin currently lives in Florida.

Another champion is Jorge Mario Garcia. He has traveled around the world for free-diving competitions. He is a former two-time world champion and now lives in Havana with his daughter.

In July of 2001, Deborah Andollo set the absolute record for men and women when she dove to 222 feet (74 meters) on a single breath. She began swimming at the age of four. Her free-diving career began in 1992 when she was working as a model for underwater photography. She dove to 120 feet (40 meters) on a single breath to everyone's surprise! Since then she has set fifteen world records in free diving. Her favorite place to train is in Isla de la Juventud. She was prestigiously honored as one of the 100 Best Athletes of the 20th Century in Cuba.

M. Mola

Deborah Andollo, world champion free-diver.

Cut these out and take them with you to show the taxi driver.

LA COCINA DE LILLIAM
Paladar

Calle 48 # 1311
e/ 13 y 15, Playa
La Habana, Cuba
Telf.: 209 6514

Horario
12:00 m - 3:00 pm
7:00 pm - 10:00 pm
Cerramos los sábados

LA FONTANA
Parrilla Criolla

Horacio Y. Reyes Lovio Bauta

Calle 3ra. A esq. 46 No. 305, Miramar,
Ciudad de La Habana, Cuba.
Tel: 202 8337, Cel: 880 1352

Abierto: 12.00m a 12:00 pm

Le Chansonnier

HÉCTOR HIGUERA MARTÍNEZ
ALQUILER Y SERVICIO GASTRONÓMICO

Calle J No 257 e/ 15 y Linea.
Vedado. Ciudad de La Habana, Cuba.
Teléf 8321576

RESTAURANT PALADAR

Amplísima bodega de vinos y más de 20 platos diferentes
en el más céntrico lugar de La Habana

Humboldt No. 153 esq. P
El Vedado. Telf.: 879 1691

Reservaciones
Aire acondicionado

La Casa
Restaurante Privado

Calle 30 No.865,
e/ 26 y 41, Nuevo Vedado,
Ciudad Habana, Cuba,

Apertura: 12:00 m.

☎ 881 7000

 **Vistamar**

Restaurant - Cocktaileria

Elegancia y privacidad

Avenida 1ra. e/22 y 24
No. 2206 - Miramar
Telf. 203-8328

Parqueo
privado